D1499403

WHAT THEY
WERE THINKING

Reflections on
Michigan Difference-Makers

⌒ A MEMOIR ⌒

First published in the United States
by MB Books, in collaboration with
Seattle Book Company

MB Books, a unit of MB Communications, LLC
2820 Hummer Lake Road
Ortonville, MI 48462
For information about this and other books by this author,
visit billhaneybooks.com.

Seattle Book Company
7300 W. Joy Road
Dexter, MI 48130

Copies of this book may be purchased at selected outlets or directly
from Seattle Book Company, 7300 W. Joy Road Dexter, MI 48130

Chapter 8 excerpts from *Blue Collar Blueprint:
How the Pistons Constructed Their Championship Formula,*
by Eli Zaret, copyright 2004, used by permission of the author

Chapter 9 excerpts from *The Anchor, Leo & Friends*,
by Berl Falbaum, copyright 1978, used by permission of the author

ISBN978-0-9845651-9-1
Cover and text design by Jacinta Calcut
Image Graphics & Design
image-gd.com

Dust jacket portrait of the author courtesy of the artist, Doug Parish

Printed in the United States of America
by Thomson-Shore

For Marcy

Life is not what one lived, but what one remembers
and how one remembers it in order to recount it.

Living to Tell the Tale
Gabriel García Márquez

Contents

Foreword

Some years ago, the *Detroit Free Press* began publishing a weekly feature designed to highlight the places, customs and eccentricities that distinguish life in Michigan from life anywhere else. Appearing under the somewhat unwieldy headline "You Haven't Lived Here Until," the column has since catalogued more than three hundred such signature experiences, ranging from feather bowling at Detroit's renowned Cadieux Café to morel mushroom hunting in Boyne City. For longtime residents, this collection is a celebration of everything that sets our state apart; for newcomers, it's an invitation, and an implicit promise: Visit enough of these places and do enough of these things, it whispers, and you will become one of us.

Nearly thirty years after leaving the *Miami Herald* to join the *Free Press*, I've checked more of those boxes than most Michigan natives; to the extent I can claim to belong anywhere, I belong here. But it's my acquaintance with thousands of fellow Michiganders, not my familiarity with the state's distinctive landscapes and tribal rites, that establish my *bona fides*.

Michiganders love their geography but, at bottom, we are social creatures not territorial ones. In most of our lives, the *who* looms larger than the *where* or the *what*. We speak reverently of hallowed spaces such as Olympia Stadium or Michigan and Trumbull, but when we close our eyes, it's the streaking figure of Gordie Howe we see, Ernie Harwell's laconic tenor that echoes in our ears.

It is the conceit of Bill Haney's memoir that what writers call a sense of place is, at its core, an affection for the sort of people who inhabit that place. Like an Elmore Leonard novel, Haney's Michigan is a place where character always trumps geography, and the story is what happens when a few unforgettable men and women collide with a particular time and place--or one another.

What They Were Thinking describes Haney's encounters with sixteen such Michiganders–thirteen men and three women, most of them no longer living–and their enduring impact on the Great Lakes State. A handful of the sixteen, including Harwell, Leonard and Jack Kevorkian, were iconic figures who continue to enjoy national and international celebrity in death; a few others—former Governor Jennifer Granholm and the late broadcast legend, J.P. McCarthy—will be instantly familiar mostly to Michiganders. But many of those recalled here are lesser-knowns with whose contributions Haney wants to acquaint us. (If you don't understand why advertising executive Ron Monchak deserves a chapter in a book that celebrates the likes of Harwell and Kevorkian, Haney would say, it's time you got to know his friend Monchak better.)

I knew a number of Haney's subjects well–or at least I thought I did, before Haney took me so much deeper into their lives. My sometimes-difficult relationship with Kevorkian, for instance, spanned more than fifteen years, and I thought my personal collection of Dr. Death stories were as bizarre as any journalist's. Then I read Haney's account of the party he threw (at a restaurant below Kevorkian's Royal Oak apartment) to celebrate the publication of a book chronicling Kevorkian's assisted-suicide crusade. Kevorkian made a cameo appearance of sorts by greeting, in a parking lot outside the restaurant, relatives and friends of his assisted suicide clients who'd been invited to Haney's party. Then the retired pathologist retreated to his apartment, where he helped yet another world-weary client end his life while Haney and his guests partied two floors below.

Two of the less-celebrated difference-makers in *What They Were Thinking* played critical roles in the defining political dramas of their time. Lieutenant Milo Radulovich, expelled from the U.S. Army he had so honorably served for the crime of associating with his own father and sister, became the poster boy for Edward R.

Murrow's exposé of Senator Joseph McCarthy's paranoiac anticommunist crusade. Carl Oglesby, an early president of Students for a Democratic Society, and Haney became friends when they worked together in Ann Arbor. They shared strong connections at the University of Michigan and kept in touch while militants who favored violence commandeered the SDS and drove Oglesby into exile. In Haney's telling, both men emerge as principled idealists who rowed against the prevailing currents of paranoia.

The timeless Harwell has deservedly earned two chapters in *What They Were Thinking*. The first reminds us that it was the devoutly patriotic sportscaster at whose behest Jose Feliciano shared his infamously idiosyncratic version of "The Star-Spangled Banner" with a national television audience during the 1968 World Series. (Harwell was aghast at the resulting public firestorm but not at the performance that triggered it, which he defended as a spontaneous expression of Feliciano's heartfelt emotion.) The second Harwell chapter, which concludes the book, recounts the premier play-by-play man's improbable year in exile and triumphant return to the team that had inexplicably banished him to premature retirement.

Haney had unparalleled access to all the principals in that memorable melodrama, and his account of Harwell's public humiliation and fan-fueled resurrection is the first plausible explanation of a hitherto inscrutable mystery.

It is a tribute to Bill Haney's own Harwellian optimism that we are left marveling not at the depths to which Michigan can sink, but the heights to which its most inspiring sons and daughters can ascend.

Brian Dickerson
July 2014

Introduction

This is a book about *why*.

Articles and books have been written about *what* the people treated in this book did, about what they created. They have been covered in print, on radio and via television. Movies have been made by them, with them or about them. One accepted an Oscar. Another was the centerpiece of a long-running stage play. Many became household names or produced something that made a permanent impression on countless lives.

These men and women moved in different circles; the arcs of their lives were so varied that few of them knew many of the others. But they had some important things in common.

All of them made an impact far beyond their occupation or their art or whatever pursuit they were principally involved in. All of them had a passion that often bordered on obsession to be the best they could possibly be at whatever they did. From the zealot for assisted suicide to the revolutionary guru of the New Left, from Ernie and J.P. to the bold automotive maverick who got the lead out of Detroit—there is something here to be learned or smiled about or wondered over.

For virtually all of them, something is known about *how* they did what they did. But to get at who they were—who they really were—you have to understand the why.

The very prominence of these people and their accomplishments may make us think we understand them and their actions quite well. Almost invariably, however, there are motives and intrigues and ethical dilemmas that never come to the public's attention. There are conspiracies and colossal blunders and grandiose schemes that have never before seen the light of day. As happens in any life, unforeseen situations become pivotal and when that happens, events are propelled down one path instead of another. Things are never the same again. One purpose of this book is to shed light on such critical moments and how these Michigan men and women were affected by and dealt with them.

No psychoanalysis here. I'm not trained for that; even if I were it would not be fitting as regards these men and women, most of whom were good friends. Cutting into them with a therapist's scalpel is much too cold and impersonal. These are vibrant, flesh and blood people. Apart from a public life of fame or celebrity or notoriety, they are very real people. I knew some of them for only a brief time, most of them for many years and very well.

I knew them all well enough to be convinced that it is better and more faithful to hear from them in their own words to the extent that can be reconstructed from hours of digital recordings, contemporary note taking and a pretty good memory. Their own words and the times we spent together permit a look behind the curtains that often shielded them from the public. Their on-the-record responses to interviewers were often necessarily carefully crafted and paint only an incomplete and imperfect picture. It is more revealing to hear what they thought when they talked at ease about their work, their actions, their aspirations and regrets. About why they made the choices they did. There is a real difference—often a great difference--between what a president of General Motors, for example, might say to a reporter for the *Wall Street Journal* and what he might remark at ease over a burger and beer in the grille room.

But why a book about *these* people?

Why not Roger Penske, Mike and Marian Ilitch, or Dan Gilbert? How about Pete Karmanos, Stevie Wonder and Mary Barra, the first female CEO of General Motors? These and others come quickly to mind as present-day high-profile people responsible for major accomplishments or bold initiatives in business, industry, education, politics, sports and entertainment. They have created jobs, renovated distressed areas of Metro Detroit, and given much-needed impetus to a painfully slow economic recovery. They have broken new ground about how our major companies live up to their responsibilities for being good corporate citizens in their communities. These well-known men and women and many others deserve to have their accomplishments recorded for posterity. But either I have scant personal knowledge of them or they have already been written about sufficiently or certainly will be, in one form or another.

The people in this book have several things in common. First, of course, they actually got something done, something that made a difference. They took risks. Some succeeded. Some failed.

Some were loved, even venerated. Just to mention the name Ernie Harwell brings a smile and warm memories. Jack Kevorkian, on the other hand, elicits a wide range of response, often quite intense. Few people will recognize the name Lt. Milo Radulovich, but how he stood up to brutal pressure in a shameful era for America had consequences that reverberate to this day.

It's a fair question to ask what I bring to these stories. What makes me think I should write about these people?

My answer is simple. For most of these stories, I was the one who was there. Often, I was the only other person there, at a moment that revealed something important or intriguing, poignant or funny as a significant event played out. Or I was privileged to be given insights that were rarely, if ever, shared with others.

I had a variety of roles and different relationships with these men and women. Sometimes, I chronicled them as a book publisher. With my colleague Ron Monchak, I published what stands as the definitive book, by Michael Betzold, on Dr. Jack Kevorkian and his assisted-suicide crusade. The same for Lt. Milo Radulovich—hardly a household name—and his fight against the smear tactics of red-baiting Senator Joseph McCarthy. That story became

an award-winning book by Michael Ranville and the centerpiece
of an Academy Award-winning motion picture. Those were stories
in which Michigan was the epicenter but the shock waves were felt
far beyond this state's borders.

Some of the others written about here were people I worked
for. A few I worked with as colleagues in business or book publishing. Some I got to know when I published books by them or
about them. Others—like Academy Award-winning filmmaker
Sue Marx—did work I admired and about which I became curious
to know more. From Marx, Elmore Leonard, Ron Monchak, Carl
Oglesby and others in these pages, we can learn what sparked their
creative genius.

Over the years I worked on this book, I discovered that people
are often unaware of the full story of momentous events—even
when they themselves are the central figures. Ernie Harwell, for
example, did not know the complex—and bungled—intrigue that
led to his firing in 1991. Nor did his many outraged fans because
Bo Schembechler took the heat for the machinations of others. Harwell's decency and humility are well known but the full story of
how and why he was cast aside is told here for the first time. I was
able to piece it together only after spending hours with all the principals involved.

Ed Cole made controversial decisions as president of General
Motors that greatly improved the quality of the air we breathe and
the performance and safety of the vehicles we drive. No less grand
were the visions he was working to realize in his post-GM career
when fate intervened. Only by chance did I miss being with him on
his final, fatal flight.

Two of Michigan's best-known characters for decades were
radio personality J.P. McCarthy and world traveler and television
host George Pierrot. Both of them had countless stories to tell and
each yearned to write a book. Posterity is the lesser for that never
happening. The story of why it didn't—and some glimpses into
their flamboyant personalities and unfulfilled dreams—is told here.

There were only a few of the people treated in these pages that I didn't know before I started work on this book. I approached them because I simply wanted to learn what made them tick, like the former governor of this state and the trio of men behind Detroit's mercurial pro basketball franchise. So I sought out Jennifer Granholm and Joe Dumars, Bill Davidson and Tom Wilson, as well as those close to them and people not in their inner circles. I got insights into the passions that drive leaders to take risks with far-reaching consequences. I discovered motivations that are more revealing than bare facts reported in the press and sound bites on television.

I had known Denise Ilitch only slightly, but enough to be impressed with her achievements. In talking with her for this book, I learned there was far more of a story to be told about the legacies she has created on several fronts and what drove her to commit so much of herself to the causes of others.

These stories are offered to reveal something about some fascinating people and to sharpen understanding of the events in which they were involved. I hope they do that. I hope they do more. I hope the reader will find interest and worth—and some humor and poignancy—here. Much of what is in the following pages has never been told, at least from the point of view of someone who was on the scene. I was fortunate to be there at key moments in the lives of these people of consequence, these Michigan people with passions that have made a lasting difference.

Bill Haney

"... Swanie says I have to shift into a new genre. 'Try crime
fiction,' he says. 'Stick with me, kiddo,
and I'll make you a millionaire'."

"Permaglo," Dutch said. "I had to see how they did it,
embalming a body. Only way I could get it right.
I'm standing there, watching, and the embalmer guy says
to an assistant, 'All right, he's hooked up. Start pumping in
the Permaglo.' It played right into my hands."

"Dialogue. Tight, smart dialogue. That's what readers want
to read and that's what I like to write."

1

BE COOL

Elmore "Dutch" Leonard Finds His Voice

"IT'S WHAT I DO."

That was the answer Beverly Leonard got when she asked her husband what if it didn't work, this decision he had just informed her of. He had this decent-paying job churning out ad copy at Campbell-Ewald, and he could write his own western novels on the side. What more could you ask? Now he was going to quit his job?

Elmore "Dutch" Leonard looked at his wife.

"Thinking back on it," he told me, "What I did, I wondered what one of my characters would say."

Dutch smiled and tapped his pencil on his mammoth wooden desk. That was where he wrote the novels that had made him, as he liked to say, after decades with a loyal but small audience for his dozens of published books, an overnight sensation.

"It's what I do," he said to his wife. "Westerns have run out. Swanie says I have to shift into a new genre. 'Try crime fiction,' he says. 'Stick with me, kiddo, and I'll make you a millionaire'."

Dutch had "had enough of writing ad copy about some engineer's love affair with the Hurst shifter," he told me. So he took the advice of legendary literary agent H. N. "Swanie" Swanson. And why shouldn't he? Dutch considered himself fortunate to be represented by the agent with an illustrious client roster that included, at one time or another, William Faulkner, Pearl Buck, John O'Hara, F. Scott Fitzgerald, Paul Gallico and Raymond Chandler, among so many others.

Dutch smiled when he told me that story, about how he laughed when Swanson said he'd make him a millionaire, a prophecy that came true many times over.

It's what I do.

And he did it masterfully. For sixty years he produced classic westerns and smoothly crafted yet gritty crime fiction novels. He fashioned characters so real and dialogue so right that an ever-growing legion of readers and moviegoers would nod and smile and wonder how he could keep doing it, year after year.

One way he managed to turn out a novel every year or so was that he finally quit writing for Hollywood. He wrote "way too many screenplays that went nowhere," he said. Finally, he refused to subject himself again to such an exercise in frustration, knowing that some producer's inflated ego would inevitably squeeze out anything that rang true.

So he focused on what he had proved many times over he could do so well. It would be novels. Maybe a short story now and again for a change of pace. That was it.

"When you finally get it right, I know it looks so damn easy," Dutch said. "And that's when you know you've nailed it. If it looks like writing, you've still got work to do. I know. I've been there. I had been writing for years, selling books, getting more readers, more good reviews, until finally I found it. Click, just like that, it was there. I found my voice."

Once Dutch Leonard found that voice, he never lost it, nor did it fade with use or age as is the fate of so many writers. There was no burnout. Never a hint of writer's block. No nothing new to say. Wherever he was, whatever he was doing, there was always a character, a line of dialogue working around in the back of his mind, waiting for the right situation to gain expression. His ear was always tuned for that just-right snippet of conversation at the next table, in the elevator, on the street. His eye was always searching for something that would define a character, like the custom-embroidered Stetson that topped off Raylan Givens. "Raylan really came alive for me once I put that hat on him," Dutch said. "Funny how it seems to take one little thing, one trait, to make a character whole."

He found some of his best lines and characters at Alcoholics Anonymous meetings. "Those are my kind of people," he said. He was open about being a recovering alcoholic. It didn't even bother him, he said, to write enticingly about how his characters appreciated their booze. He set many scenes in bars, lounges, casinos and clubs. Dutch never lost his taste for beer, even the non-alcoholic variety, so when he visited I would have his favorite Kaliber on hand.

Those subtle touches about how a character caressed his Stetson, lit a cigaret, fixed a drink, these were the accent strokes to paint a character in full in a Leonard novel. Not an ingenious plot twist. Not a subtle, intricate bit of exposition. Not a graceful, flowing narrative passage. What satisfied Dutch when he brought it off was the same thing that pleased his reader. In music it might be called "the relevant unexpected." A character responds to a situation with just the right but unpredicted one-word answer, or maybe no answer at all, just a look, a look that says what needs saying more than any word could do.

"Permaglo," Dutch said. "I had to see how they did it, embalming a body. Only way I could get it right. I'm standing there, watching, and the embalmer guy says to an assistant, 'All right, he's hooked up. Start pumping in the Permaglo.'"

Dutch smiled at the rightness of it.

"Played right into my hands. Permaglo embalming fluid. That's how they get them looking so natural, there in the coffin."

Another one, "fire in the hole." I was sitting in a chair in front of that enormous desk where he did all of his writing in longhand on lined yellow pads.

"Fire in the hole," he said. "That's what they say when the fuse has been lit on an old cannon, so everyone gets ready for the blast and kickback. The fuse sputters a few seconds, then whoomp. "

He liked the phrase so much not only did he use it in a couple of books, he also made it the title of a collection of stories in a 2001 book and the first episode of his television series, *Justified*. And amazingly, in that critically acclaimed and popular television series, he finally saw justice done to one of his books and characters.

It was a long time coming.

In the 1950s, readers who marveled over the authenticity of Leonard's westerns would never have guessed that he had never been to the West, had never held a handgun. That ended after Dutch spoke in the "Facets of Creativity" talk series I ran in the 1980s and `90s. The series showcased an illustrious roster of creative people from a broad spectrum of fields—inventors, artists, musicians, grand chefs, actors, lyricists and singers, movie producers and many writers.

Leonard appeared in the series twice, in Bloomfield Hills and Manhattan. For his first appearance, after he finished his remarks, I presented him a memento. It was a replica of an 1848 Colt Navy Dragoon, a .44-caliber pistol reminiscent of a gun he wrote about in an early western. "First one I ever had in my hands," he said, stroking that long-barreled percussion revolver. Sometimes when I visited at his house, he would take it off the shelf and fondle it.

"This gun reminds me of a whopper I made in an early book. The editor missed it too, so it's still in print in the early editions," he said. "Had a marshal and a bad guy in a standoff. At the crucial moment, I had the marshal use his thumb to slowly take off the safety on his pistol. Well, a reader pointed out that you have a safety on an automatic, but not on a revolver."

That made me wonder and so I asked, "Where did you get your knowledge about the West?"

"Everything I knew about the west I got from a magazine I subscribed to, the one with the great photographs of scenery,

Arizona Highways."

Visuals were important to Dutch—actually crucial because he often wrote of places he had never been. He once told me he wanted to do a book set in the south, deep in redneck country, he said. And while he had been born in New Orleans, in 1925, he lived there only briefly as a very young child before the family finally settled in Detroit in 1934. So he had his researcher, Gregg Sutter, travel around and take photographs of whatever he saw that might be interesting. Dutch showed me a set of pictures taken of a Ku Klux Klan rally. As he described what interested him in the photographs, he pointed to the storefronts, the streets, and the Klansmen in their white robes. But mostly he focused on the people, the faces in the crowd.

That was all he needed to kickstart his engine. He used some of those images to trigger his imagination for a couple of books, including *Tishomingo Blues.*

Other times, it wasn't the people in the photographs, it was a name he would put on the characters that these men in the photograph just had to have. Names were so important to Leonard. Often, he would start with a name, or what a character with a name like, say, Raylan Givens, had to look like. He might be triggered by what kind of hat he would wear, what beer he would drink, what kind of music he listened to. Yeah, he'd say, looking at the photograph, damn if that isn't Raylan, right there.

Often, talking on the phone about the book he was working on, Leonard would get on a roll and soon this writer who insisted he was lousy at plotting would be describing the convoluted, unpredictable web these vivid characters would find themselves tangled up in. You could almost feel that you didn't have to be there, on the other end of Dutch's line, for him to be working it out this way. It was always a treat to hear him wing it effortlessly, discovering something new for himself along the way. And then, many months or even years later, you would see those words, those characters, that so-dead-on dialogue there on the printed page of his newest novel.

There were some mean characters in those books. Readers knew that eventually they would meet a bad end. While that might be what readers were expecting and rooting for, not Dutch. He liked all of his characters, even the bad guys. Maybe even especially the bad guys. He didn't stack the deck against them as many authors do. That was in part because of his insistence on writing each scene from a single, unwavering point of view. If the scene were going to be from the point of view of a violent killer, Dutch still had to deal with that character's motivation, his back story, with what brought him to the place and situation he was in.

"Doing that, you find yourself at least understanding if not sympathetic," he said. "Most of my characters that people remember are the flawed ones. I don't really spend much time writing about good people. They're boring. I go for the off-center types. Even my so-called good guys are marked in one way or another. Some have done time. Some uphold the law, but it's more 'let's not be fanatical about it.' When a marshal, say, is faced with a situation where he wants to get the right outcome, then his own personal code trumps the letter of the law."

That sometimes caused problems for Dutch. Some readers didn't seem to understand that it was his character expressing a thought or using foul language, not him. He was just the author.

More than once at a Leonard lecture, I watched how he enjoyed reading the same letter from a long-time reader. The woman started the letter calmly describing how she had read and enjoyed all of his previous books. But as the letter went on, she became more and more infuriated by the swearing by one character in his most recent book. "There is no excuse for that kind of shitty language," she wrote. "So just see if I buy another of your dirty fucking books."

Dutch said he didn't send her a response because he didn't want to upset her further. Not only that, he wasn't quite sure what he might say. Despite being regarded as the master of the dead-on comeback, Dutch admitted that in real life he wasn't always that facile.

When I introduced him in the Facets of Creativity series in New

York, I finished with a story he had told me. He was at a ski lodge in Colorado one brilliant winter day. Dutch was a confirmed non-athlete but he enjoyed watching certain sports, such as tennis and baseball, and especially skiing. He was at the base of the slope, smoking a cigaret and watching skiers flashing down the hills. He caught sight of a graceful skier and watched as she finished her run. With one final graceful swoop, she sent up a spray of crystals, the reflected sunlight dancing off the snow and her flowing golden locks.

As I described it then in my introduction of Dutch, "She glided to a railing a few feet from Dutch, lifted one ski and began to unlace her boots. Mouth agape, Dutch stared at this beautiful creature. She turned quickly, looked directly at him and said, 'I don't know what feels better: taking off your boots or getting laid.'"

"Dutch stared at her and said..."

And at this point I handed the mic to Dutch. He looked at me, then at the audience and, with a feigned stunned expression and in his husky smoker's baritone, said a very loud, "Duh."

When the laughter died down, the master of the trenchant comeback looked at the audience, then up at the ceiling as if searching for what to say next.

"Yeah, that was maybe six years ago. I've been working on the right line to come back with. Haven't found it yet. But if I do, I'll find a way to use it in a book."

Then he looked at me and frowned.

"Unlaced? Un-*laced*? Really, Bill? I'm old, but not that old. Skiers haven't had laces on their boots for—what?—thirty-forty years?"

That day, as was typical for him, after his talk Dutch took questions from the audience. People invariably brought up questions on the points that eventually grew into Elmore Leonard's Ten Rules for Writers.

1. *Never open a book with weather.*
2. *Avoid prologues.*
3. *Never use a verb other than "said" to carry dialogue.*

4. *Never use an adverb to modify the verb "said"*
    …he admonished gravely.
5. *Keep your exclamation points under control. You are allowed*
    no more than two or three per 100,000 words of prose.
6. *Never use the words "suddenly" or "all hell broke loose."*
7. *Use regional dialect, patois, sparingly.*
8. *Avoid detailed descriptions of characters.*
9. *Don't go into great detail describing places and things.*
10. *Try to leave out the parts that readers tend to skip.*

My most important rule is one that sums up the 10.
If it sounds like writing, I rewrite it.

Sometimes there were other cautions he would offer, including one that he would mention, but clearly felt ambivalent about. It didn't make the cut for Dutch's list because, while it made sense for other writers, he had no intention of following it himself. It was, therefore, a kind of flexible rule he expressed in different ways at different times. What it amounted to was, "Don't talk away your story."

Probably good for most writers. Not for him.

Perhaps no writer talked more about his own work in progress and with more other writers than than the "Dickens of Detroit," a label affixed to him by some New York reviewer. Dutch chuckled over that descriptor, but I doubt he liked it. It's hard to imagine two more disparate writing styles than that of the lean, dialogue-heavy Leonard and the verbose Dickens, whose style was to bludgeon the reader into submission with polysyllables and poundage of word count. Dickens and Leonard both did write about their cities, that much was accurate.

Dutch happily broke the stricture about talking away your story whenever the phone rang and it was a good friend or another writer. After his second wife, Joan, died, he always answered his own phone—only once when I called did his then-wife Christine pick it up. Quickly, eagerly. Sure, he would get the usual irritating phone solicitors and strange calls from readers he had never met. If it bothered him, he never mentioned it. Although he was almost always writing or thinking about writing, he seemed never too busy to talk, especially about his in-process book.

Where the rule failed to work for Dutch was obvious. The idea behind the rule is that by talking about what you're going to write you do a couple of very bad things. You lose the spontaneity. You tell someone what you're doing and in that telling it's fresh and clear and honest. And then you sit down to write it and... well, it just isn't the same now. Now you're *re*-telling it. When you try to put down the words with pen or keystrokes, the verisimilitude is, as Ernie Harwell would say on a deep home run, "L...o...n...g gone." That's bad enough but it gets worse. And that's the second problem. Writing after you've burned off the high in the telling is just not as much fun. The thrill of discovery is gone. Now it's work.

"I used to be a solid ten pages a day," Dutch told me after a book-signing event in New York City on his promotional tour for *Rum Punch*, his thirtieth novel. "Ten pages. For years. Now I'm six pages. Not that I'm slower, less productive. What I found, I'm throwing away less than I used to, revising not so much. It's a pretty good six pages."

In those later years, Dutch became a bit harder on the Elmore Leonard of the early years. Overly so, I thought. He was particularly harsh on the way he had handled narrative and exposition in the early books. "That was before I learned I didn't have to obligate myself to get that stuff out of the way as quickly as possible so I could get on with the dialogue. Dialogue. Tight, smart dialogue. That's what readers want to read and that's what I like to write."

When he lectured to audiences comprising mainly writers, Leonard would read a passage of description of a location in his early western, *Escape from Five Shadows*. Then he would read a version of how he would write it now. He had reduced the copy to less than a quarter of the original. He was pleased with his new terse sentences; he had shorn away nearly all the descriptive prose. His new version was much like a passage from the early Hemingway of which he once was so admiring. We talked about the descriptive opener of Papa's short story, "Soldier's Home." Dutch insisted it said everything that needed to be said, not one word more:

> *Krebs went to the war from a Methodist college in Kansas. There is a picture which shows him among his fraternity brothers, all of them wearing exactly the same height and style collar. He enlisted in the Marines in 1917 and did not return to the United States until the second division returned from the Rhine in the summer of 1919.*
>
> *There is a picture which shows him on the Rhine with two German girls and another corporal. Krebs and the corporal look too big for their uniforms. The German girls are not beautiful. The Rhine does not show in the picture.*

Dutch read that passage aloud, smiled and said, "What more do you need?"

For the same reason, Dutch liked his own rewrite of *Shadows*. I told him I preferred his original and by comparison the rewritten version was so taut it was sterile. It deprived the reader of the sense of place he had told me he so admired in the fiction of George V. Higgins.

"I hear you," he said. "A matter of taste."

Dutch was as comfortable with himself, with his own literary product, as a writer can be—which can never be total. But he was also well aware of what his readers and reviewers had to say.

Early on, there weren't many reviewers to listen to—or readers, for that matter. At his first book-signing, at a small bookstore in Birmingham, Michigan, Leonard signed exactly two copies. "One of those was for the owner of the store," Dutch said. He doubled that number at the same store a year later. "I'm on a roll now," he said, "but two of those were for my son-in-law." Years later, when I had him speak in New York in the Creativity series, he did a signing that evening at Barnes & Noble. As was typical for him then, patrons were lined up out into the street.

As Dutch's popularity grew, the upper echelon of literary critics realized they could no longer ignore him or be dismissive simply because he was "just a crime fiction writer." The better literary reviewers came to acknowledge him as a fine writer despite what they regarded as a genre of lower standing. As the success of the films adapted from his books elevated his visibility, myths grew up about him, even as he publicly slammed nearly all the films based on his novels. One critic, who came belatedly to a recognition of Leonard's talents wanted to stamp himself as someone who had done his homework on this Elmore Leonard fellow. He grabbed for one cliché that exceeded his grasp. He gushed about a new Leonard novel by likening it unto the author's namesake, asserting that novelist Elmore Leonard had delivered "another high hard one, just like his namesake, the baseball pitcher Dutch Leonard."

Dutch brought that up howler frequently. He would quote that passage from the review and—after a long pause—point out that the pitcher Dutch Leonard was known for his soft, junk stuff.

Over time, reviewers and critics increasingly would latch on to some "fact" they exhumed from another reviewer's earlier article, and that would launch a whole new cycle until eventually the regurgitated myth was broadly accepted as an authenticated fact.

One such invention by a critic was that Dutch's dialogue was so authentic for a very simple reason. His thesis was that all Dutch did was stand on a street corner in a Detroit neighborhood or sit in a police cruiser with a tape recorder in his pocket and then go home and transcribe it.

That made Dutch chuckle, "Thing is, if you did that it would come out gibberish," he said. "You can't just put into print the way people—especially street people and cops—talk. They stop and start and change directions and change subjects even. What you would get is a lot of 'well... see... you know... it's like...' every few words. The trick is to know how much to leave in, how much to take out so it sounds authentic."

Dutch learned that trick early on. And perfected it. If that showed a continuing influence of Ernest Hemingway on Dutch's own style, then so be it. Once, when asked in an interview how he would characterize his own style Dutch didn't think long before saying, "My style is an absence of style."

I asked him if he had said that. "Absolutely," he said. "I've said it so many times I came to believe it myself. Because it's true."

I told him I thought it was Booth Tarkington who said, "Style is what is left over after you've told the story."

He thought about it a while, tapping his pencil on the desk. "Works for me," he said.

He also insisted he never worried about plot. It made him laugh that more than one critic lauded him as a "master of plot." To the contrary—he certainly didn't methodically outline his concept and then write to it. Instead he created some characters, put them in motion, put them in conflict, got into their minds and "let the story write itself, discovering along the way where it was going." He once said to me that he was curious to see how the manuscript he was writing was going to come out—and he had already finished three-quarters of it.

It was occasionally the same with a character. In *Gold Coast*, he wrote an early scene from the point of view of the main male character, as Leonard was at first sure it should be told. But it didn't work. So he tried another male character in the scene and told it through his eyes. Still didn't work. Then, just fooling around, he said, he took a shot at it from the viewpoint of a woman in the scene who was, until then, a minor character.

"Wham," he said. "I knew right away that nailed it. Not only did it work, she hijacked the story. From that point on, it was a different book. I couldn't wait to see where it was going to go."

He liked it that way, the thrill of discovery for himself as much as for his readers.

Another thing he liked was humor.

Dutch was mystified why there was so little humor in current novels. "If you aren't having fun writing it, the reader probably isn't having fun reading it." Dutch himself was having plenty of fun writing it. He had long since passed having to do it for any other reason. The last time I talked with him, he told me about "Blue Dreams," the book he was writing—it was to be his forty-sixth book. He sounded exactly the same as he did when I first spent time with him thirty years earlier.

We talked about something else that day, about the trip to the ballpark that never happened.

Our mutual friend, Ernie Harwell, himself a living legend as a Hall of Fame baseball play-by-play announcer, had invited us for a day with him at the ballpark, something that had become pretty much an annual event. I would pick up Dutch mid morning, then we'd collect Ernie and the three of us would spend the entire day together at Tiger Stadium. We'd arrive in time for lunch in the press dining area. Before and after lunch Ernie would lead us around the park and introduce us to the ushers, waiters, ticket takers and security people, all of whom, it seemed, Ernie knew by first name. Then he would take Dutch and me down to the field to meet the umpires, managers and players. It was fun to watch the players now positioned on the other side of the great celebrity-fan divide. Ballplayers have a lot of time on their hands and many are voracious readers, especially of current novels, and most especially of Elmore Leonard. Then we would crowd into the snug broadcast booth with Ernie, Paul Carey and Howard Stitzel and enjoy the game from the best seats in baseball.

That was how it went every time but one.

On that day, as I got ready to leave the house that morning to gather up Dutch and Ernie, the phone rang. It was Dutch.

"Bill, have you got your TV on?"

"No, why?"

"Turn it on. Any channel."

I did. I watched in disbelief. It couldn't be real.

"Dutch, what's happening?"

"A large airplane just flew into one of the twin towers at the World Trade Center. And... oh my God, one just hit the other tower. What the hell is going on?"

I had no more idea than anyone else. Dutch and I stayed on the line, staring at the television coverage, saying nothing for what seemed a very long time.

—ɯ—

AS DUTCH'S REPUTATION GREW, as more and more of his books were turned into popular movies with mega-stars, he accepted with reluctance at first, then stoicism, his steadily ascending stature. His many distinguished honors and awards attested that he was no longer simply America's most revered writer of crime fiction, he was increasingly recognized as a fine novelist regardless of genre.

So when I needed a quote by a well-known author for the dust jacket of a book I was publishing by Tim Kiska, long-time *Detroit News* reporter, I thought immediately of Dutch. But I had reservations. I didn't want to intrude on him with the kind of request I knew he got so frequently. I knew that he turned down nearly every offer to pen a foreword or provide a quote, even when considerable fees were offered. But the Kiska book did make sense, because that forthcoming book, *Detroit's Powers & Personalities*, profiled the Motor City's movers and shakers. Dutch was a Detroiter, proud of it, and placed some of his books in the city.

When I told Dutch about the Kiska book, he was upbeat, so I asked if I could impose on him to write a short blurb for the jacket. I offered to send him the galleys. "I don't need to see galleys. I've got a pretty good line on most of those folks." And then he paused. "Actually, I don't really need to do this myself, do I? You know how I write, what I'd say. Just write something for me—I'm sure it will be fine."

I was hesitant to do that and told him so—it was his name that was going to be on the back of the jacket.

"All right. If it makes you feel better, give me a look before you go on press."

The next day I sent Dutch the blurb I wrote for him for the book's jacket. I hoped he would at least appreciate the brevity:

With characters like this, who needs a plot?

"Perfect," said Dutch. "That's better than anything I would have done myself. Don't change a word."

If I had been paying attention, that would have been a loud and clear signal that Dutch was having an influence on my own writing. I thought I had invented my own credo to remind myself what was important as I wrote. I had made a sign and taped it just above the keyboard where I did my writing. Only later did I realize I may have picked up the kernel of that exhortation by osmosis from Dutch. So I told him about it. He approved. It is something he had been saying in different words and something I have increasingly passed along to writers I work with and especially to beginning writers I counsel:

Get out of the way of the story.

As busy as he was with his own work, Dutch was generous in helping other writers. He surely must have also gotten countless requests for advice from would-be writers, as well, but if he did, he never spoke of them to me. One day he asked me what I was working on. I mumbled something and he said, "If you were pitching this to a film producer and he said you had to summarize it in one sentence, what would you say?"

He gave me a minute to think.

"Okay, the title of the book is *Dealing*. In one sentence: A black wise guy named Jerome is into minor-league scams in the underbelly of Detroit, gets drawn into big time wheeling and dealing, and goes after the ultimate revenge on a CEO who caused the death of someone Jerome cared about."

"All right. Who do you see as the lead?"

I told him that Eddie Murphy was one of two or three actors I envisioned.

"Could work. I'll have a look at it if you want."

A week later, Dutch called and asked if I was open to a couple suggestions. He thought it might work better if the lead female character had a back story in which she had been doing wildcat deals in the oil patch. Hmmm. Never thought of that, but yeah, sounds promising. And about one of the characters who has to buy an unregistered handgun on the streets he said simply, "Doubtful that's the way it would go down. If you want, I'll call Gil Hill. He's the Detroit cop Eddie Murphy worked with to learn the lingo, then took him in as his partner in *Beverly Hills Cop*. He'll know how that kind of deal would have to be handled."

Indeed, Lt. Gil Hill knew. He helped with that scene and went much further. He said he loved the book and if I had a screenplay, he'd show it to Eddie Murphy. Hill was going to Los Angeles the next week to see Murphy. "It'll knock him out," Hill said, "because the male lead is just the kind of wise-talking, living-on-the-edge role he loves." But I didn't have a screenplay and sure couldn't do one in a week. So Hill took the entire book manuscript.

A few days later, Hill called me.

"I took your manuscript to Eddie," Hill says. "He took one look at that big stack of paper, says, "Shit man, don't the dude got something shorter?"

Dutch laughed when I told him what happened.

"That figures," he said. "Some of those guys are not up to reading much beyond a tight two-three page treatment with lots of white space and words of one syllable or less. Don't hold your breath waiting for something to happen. But there is one more thing I meant to mention. You spend a lot of time describing place. I'm not good at place, probably because I don't like writing place. I think I've told you before you who is the best I've read at sense of place. George V. Higgins. If you haven't, read his novel, *The Friends of Eddie Coyle.* Terrific sense of place."

Dutch found the novel and handed it to me.

"Higgins brings it off the best. Most of them overdo it and get in the way of their characters. Readers will take only so much of that, like long descriptions of the weather or scenery, then they put the book down. Probably never pick it up again. They see those big blocks of exposition, the writer showing off he's actually been to the place he's writing about or he got caught in a rainstorm once. If you don't get them to the dialogue pronto, you've lost them."

For someone who said he didn't read much modern fiction, Dutch was certainly very familiar with every writer I mentioned to him. It was similar with feature films. Dutch was contemptuous of most of what Hollywood was turning out. But what he liked, he really liked. "*The Usual Suspects,* now there's one terrific film," he said. "*Kill Bill, Fargo.* Great stuff. You can bet producers stayed the hell away from the screenwriter and the director on those. Producers, man."

At the time, Dutch was talking with a producer about casting the leads for a film adaptation of one of his books. The producer mentioned a top box office female star who said she was interested, but only if they wrote in a song for her.

"Maybe you missed something in the treatment," Dutch said "but this is not a musical. You want my recommendation? How about Teri Garr?"

"Teri Garr? She doesn't have much of a rack, does she?"

"But she can act."

The producer thought about it. "Well, there's that."

Elmore Leonard hadn't always been so cynical about Hollywood. In the late 1960s, when he was transitioning from westerns to mainstream and then crime fiction, Dutch was delighted that films were being made of his first two books that weren't westerns. "I had no idea how apt the title was of my first general fiction book," he said. "My agent was enthused about it at first. Then came the rejections from publishers—eighty-four of them. One thing was dead on—the title, *The Big Bounce*. Then we sold it to Hollywood, with Ryan O'Neal, Van Heflin, and Leigh Taylor-Young starring. Awful movie. Just awful.

"That was 1969. The next year they released *The Moonshine War*, with Alan Alda and Richard Widmark. Hard to believe, but that was just as bad. Dreadful. I finally gave up expecting anyone to ever do a decent film from one of my novels."

It got better with his later works, but for more than forty years Dutch was disgusted with nearly everything happening with the major motion picture studios. "Ever try having a conversation about a script with one of those kids? Hardly any of them older than twenty-eight. Haven't done anything, haven't lived much and now they're calling the shots on budgets the other side of $50 million."

One of Dutch's Hollywood encounters eventually found its way into a memorable scene in the most popular and successful film made to that date from a Leonard book. He was invited to lunch with a producer to formally agree on a deal already negotiated by his agent and the producer's staff.

The producer's people had set it up at Spago in Beverly Hills, where in those days if you were in the business you had to go every once in a while or the gossip columnists would think you'd been dropped from the A list. Dutch agreed to fly to Los Angeles for the meeting only because he was assured the deal was agreed and the meeting was merely for the obligatory handshake for a photo. Only problem, the producer didn't show. His emissary told Dutch he'd be there soon, once there was agreement on a couple deal points that needed some tweaking. Dutch knew all too well it was the typical Hollywood ascendence/submission gambit to whittle down the author's points. Only then would the producer show up to sign and for the grip-and-grin photo.

Dutch walked away, told his agent to take the property to another studio, and asked him to never bring him another overture from that producer. But it wasn't a total waste of time. Three years later, art imitated life as the scene was performed yet again—and in the same restaurant—this time by John Travolta in the film of Dutch's book, *Get Shorty*.

Some writers are windy about a prospective work, taking soundings, judging reactions. Many writers talk expansively about a book once they have finished it and they're making the rounds promoting it. But even though I have been publishing books since 1967, until Dutch I never knew an author who talked so freely about a work in progress.

Finally, I figured out why. I realized I didn't even have to be there, nor did any of the many other writers Dutch talked with. He wasn't looking for affirmation or any kind of a reaction from me. He was working it out, test driving his options as he talked.

One reason his writing is so easily consumed is that the reader has the sense of being a part of the conversation. That is precisely what Dutch was going after: writing that doesn't read like writing. One tool in his kit was the conversation he would have with another writer, describing where he was in a project and what his characters were doing. Sometimes a line of dialogue would emerge that set the tone for a scene. Could happen.

I doubt that the way Elmore Leonard created would work for many other writers, but it certainly served him well. As the man said:

"It's what I do."

For six decades and forty-seven novels, nobody did it better.

Ernie Harwell was leaning against a wall, tape recorder in hand, talking with an usher, nodding, smiling and saying a hearty "Hi folks" to fans who recognized him as they filed into the park. At a distance, even there outside the grandstands, you could hear the mellow sounds of the game: ash against horsehide, the crowd oooh-ing at some prodigious batting practice poke, vendors hawking hot dogs and crackerjacks.

2

TALKIN' BASEBALL

Ernie Harwell, the Voice of the Tigers—Charlie Gehringer, the Silent Second Baseman

LIKE A FEW MILLION OTHER BASEBALL FANS IN MICHIGAN and the Midwest, for years I considered Ernie Harwell a member of the family.

Just a detail that we had never met, because we had been through a lot together, ol' Ern and I. He arrived in Detroit just a year before the fabulous season when 61's were wild. In 1961 the Tigers' Stormin' Norman Cash batted .361 and the Yankees' Roger Maris broke the Babe's record—with or without an asterisk—with 61 home runs. Still the Tigers finished second to New York. But it was great in '68, as the Bengals came from behind time and again to claim their first World Series title since 1945. Good years, there were a few, but by and large too few to mention. The Tigers would do again what they'd often do, and by July, fall from contention.

Still, Ernie would help his listeners savor the rare delicious moments. In that resonant baritone, redolent of summer evenings in his native Georgia, he would recount the exploits of Mark "The Bird" Fidrych, stalking the mound at Tiger Stadium, talking to the baseball, telling it how to behave. Or Aurelio Rodriguez at the hot corner, backhanding a shot down the line with that tattered black glove and flat-lining a seed to first. Whenever Rocky Colavito or Willie Horton stepped to the plate, I would stop what I was doing and wait for that sharp crack of the bat and Ernie's call... "There goes a deep one to left field and ... that ball is l...o...n...g gone."

Ernie had been in my home or car, out with me on the boat or beach, or even riding shotgun on my tractor as I mowed fairways.

Oh yes, I knew Ernie Harwell very well indeed. Merely a detail that until 1984, I had never met him.

That changed one sunny day in May 1984.

Earlier that spring I had the Tiger fans' annual premonition. That familiar feeling that came with the late winter thaw. I had felt it every March. Why should 1984 be any different? Yes, surely this would be the year the Tigers would reclaim their rightful perch above those aggravating Indians, those pesky White Sox, and even the arrogant Yankees. I recalled that in 1950 for much of the summer the Tigers appeared to be a lock. But then along came Labor Day and the annual September swoon. That winter there was little joy in Tigerville.

The next ten years were lean ones until Ernie arrived in 1960 and quickly got the Tigers competitive again. And none too soon— the 1968 glory year would be the only interruption in a stretch of more than 30 years of frustration.

That was all about to change, the heart of the diehard fan knew, in 1984.

For Detroit Tiger fans, Hope Springs Infernal.

But this time it would be different. I was so confident that I spent the fall of 1983 and that winter delving into Tigers history. I didn't stop until I had gathered thousands of important or intriguing tidbits about the team and its players. By February of '84, I had created a calendar highlighting the great moments as well as little-known Tiger trivia over the years. But a calendar on such a subject needs more than words, it needs images to come alive, so I commissioned the incomparable artist Doug Parrish to illustrate the calendar with drawings of the stars and the characters from Tigers lore. Parrish himself had been a Tigers batboy in 1936. More than that, he was the designated buddy for teenage fireballer Bob

Feller when the Cleveland Indians came to Detroit.

The baseball publishing house Diamond Communications produced my "Detroit Tiger Fan's Calendar/1985." Such is the cycle of calendar publishing that copies must be available many months in advance and promotion should be underway late spring of the year previous to the calendar's date.

For once, the Tigers cooperated. They did it in record fashion, sprinting to a 35-5 record, the best start in major league history. I couldn't have asked for a better season to launch my Tiger Fan's calendar. Now if only they kept up the momentum into October.

So at noon on a sunny day in May 1984, I found myself heading up a ramp at Tiger Stadium, looking for the man I knew so very, very well and had never met.

He was leaning against a wall, tape recorder in hand, talking with an usher, nodding, smiling and saying a hearty "Hi folks" to fans who recognized him as they filed into the park. At a distance, even there outside the grandstands, you could hear the mellow sounds of the game: ash against horsehide, the crowd oooh-ing at some prodigious batting practice poke, vendors hawking hot dogs and crackerjacks.

"You must be Mr. Bill Haney, " he said. "I'm Ernie Harwell and I'm glad to meet you."

Well, he couldn't have been half as glad as I was, but there was no doubting his sincerity. To meet Ernie Harwell for the first time is to restore your faith in humanity and in your own gut instincts. You see in an instant that there is no such thing as Ernie Harwell's public persona. This is a man totally without artifice. No self-importance. Not a single pretension. No need to shift gears from the Harwell of the radio waves to the private Ernie. When you have met one too many media stars, sports heroes, and entertainment celebrities you see how very rare this is. Talk to Ernie Harwell for two minutes and you know that everything you always intuited about him is true.

"That's a fine-looking calendar," he said. "Let me turn this recorder on and you can tell me about it."

Never was there a more casual interview. Ernie rewound the tape and listened a few seconds to be sure it had recorded.

"Well, that takes care of our pre-game show," he said. "Have you got a few minutes to come up to the booth? Have a look at the field from the best seat in baseball. Maybe we can find a cup of coffee and talk a while."

I had been to many games at the Stadium long before the new owner Tom Monaghan changed the name from Briggs to Tiger. I had sat in the bleachers and the upper and lower grandstand decks. I had seen a few games from reserved seats down the lines along third base and first base. And on a few memorable occasions had felt quite special though out of place in the box seats next to the visitor's dugout. In the 1940s, that box had been the province of H.A. (Happy) McDonald, the man who owned the creamery where my father was a truck mechanic. Once or twice a year my father would have the use of those seats. It seemed like we could reach out and touch Tiger first-baseman Hank Greenberg, who I was sure was the tallest man in all of baseball, if not the entire world.

Nothing though, had prepared me for the view from Ernie's broadcast booth at Tiger Stadium. The field wasn't out there somewhere, it was seemingly directly below and only a few yards away. As we sat there, I thought of the games I had heard announced from Tigers broadcast booths by Ernie's predecessors, Ty Tyson, Van Patrick, Mel Ott, and the great Harry Heilmann. So many memories in that booth, that baseball field, that stadium.

Ernie took me to a little office where a pot of coffee was brewing. Before we sat down, he introduced me to his broadcast partner Paul Carey and engineer Howard Stitzel. Over the years I had sent Ernie a few notes I thought might be of interest to him and books I had published I thought he might enjoy. He had mentioned these on his broadcasts as something from "my good friend Bill Haney" in Grass Lake, Ann Arbor, Dexter, or wherever I was living in at the time. Well, when I heard him mention me on the radio, I did feel like his good friend despite the fact that we hadn't formally met. Details. When I asked him how he knew that a foul ball into the crowd was caught by a man from Ypsilanti or Caro or Clarkston, he laughed and said that was one of the most frequent questions he got.

Ernie remembered the books I had sent him and asked how I managed to be involved in book publishing while working full time as a communications agency executive. We talked about that a while and then I asked him when he was going to write a book.

"Oh, I don't suppose there would be much interest in any book I would write," he said. "My brother Richard is the writer in the family. He's done many books. He's an authority on Margaret Mitchell and her book, *Gone With The Wind*. Most of my stories are just twenty seconds or so, just long enough to tell between pitches."

I told Ernie I was sure he had a wealth of material could be mined to produce a very good book. I was sure it would be popular not only with Tigers fans but also throughout the baseball world. The longer we talked, the more convinced I was that Ernie should seriously consider doing a book.

"Ernie, the reason I get involved in publishing books is to capture for posterity stories that otherwise might be lost forever. The shape you're in you might just live forever, but let's assume that doesn't happen. It would be a real loss if you passed from this world without leaving your stories behind in a book for your fans and future generations to take pleasure in."

A week later, I answered the phone and heard that distinctive Harwell voice. Ernie wanted to know if I could come down to the ballpark; he had something he wanted to show me. He would arrange for tickets and have an usher bring me up to the broadcast booth.

"I told Miz Lulu what you said last week about me writing a book," he said. "She told me I had better listen to that Mr. Haney. So I've got a few pages here you can read. You'll probably find out how wrong you were about me writing a book."

I took the dozen typewritten pages and went to my seat where I was quickly engrossed in Ernie's draft text. He had given me about twenty-five hundred words of copy about his controversial choice of José Feliciano to sing the National Anthem before the start of the fifth World Series game on October 7, 1968.

As Ernie told it, he hadn't set out to create a controversy when he chose Feliciano. Traditionally, establishment singers like Robert Merrill, Lucy Munroe, and Gladys Gooding had sung the pregame "Star-Spangled Banner." Because Ernie had written dozens of songs—"as a song-writer, I've got a no-hitter going," he would say—general manager Jim Campbell had asked him to select the singers for the third, fourth and fifth games being played at the Stadium. For the first game, Ernie chose Margaret Whiting, popular nationally and with strong Detroit ties. Next was Marvin Gaye, a major star and a Detroiter.

For the final Series game at the Stadium, Ernie departed from this pattern. Instead of choosing a conventional, well-known singer who could be counted on for a traditional rendition, Ernie opted for a young blind Latin singer with a recent hit called "Light My Fire" but little known to the general public. Ernie hadn't known it, but the blind Feliciano had long been a fan of his, having listened to his broadcasts of Brooklyn Dodgers and New York Giants games early in Harwell's career.

The morning of the game, Ernie took Feliciano down on the field and introduced him to the Tigers stars he was anxious to meet. The singer offered up fresh-for-the-occasion lyrics to his hit song: "Come on Kaline, light the fire. Tigers got to have desire. Got to win today."

Hours later, it was game time and there in centerfield, only his seeing-eye dog by his side, stood José Feliciano with his guitar. Off to the side stood Ernie Harwell. The crowd grew quiet and listened intently to a very different, very personal interpretation of the Anthem.

Ernie was stirred by the straight-from-the-soul rendition, but as he walked beneath the stands, he sensed that some fans disliked what they had heard. Minutes later, the Tigers switchboard operator told him she had already gotten "hundreds of calls about the singer. People are really mad."

The Tigers won the "must-win" game but the victory was almost overshadowed by the outcry over the Anthem. It was a page one and prime time TV news story across the nation. The *Detroit Free Press* ran a photo with an article leading with:

> *"A blues version of 'The Star-Spangled Banner' hit an unresponsive chord in thousands of World Series fans Monday. Outraged fans called Tiger Stadium, the* Free Press, *and local TV stations to complain about the anthem sung by blind Puerto Rican singer José Feliciano at the opening of the game."*

Harwell defended Feliciano's right to "put his own feelings into a song," and took full responsibility. A CBS crew rushed to Detroit to tape a segment with Harwell for broadcast on Walter Cronkite's evening report.

As Ernie wrote in the sample pages he gave me, "The country seethed over José's performance. Editorials lambasted it, civic groups passed angry resolutions. Patients at a veteran's hospital in Phoenix, Arizona threw shoes at the TV set during the rendition of the song…"

Typical was the outburst directed at Harwell from an unidentified telephone caller: "You're a traitor! I'll bet you're a draft-dodger. You weren't in the service, were you?"

When Ernie replied he was in the Marines for four years, the man shot back, "I don't care. Anybody who'd let that long-hair hippie ruin our 'Star-Spangled Banner' has got to be a Communist."

An unauthorized recording of Feliciano's rendition went onto the charts immediately. Even though none of the major Detroit stations would play the song, it sold 45,000 copies in Detroit alone in two weeks. Overnight, the blind Puerto Rican singer was a star of the first magnitude. Meanwhile, for an announcer working for one of the most conservative professional sports franchises in the country, and reporting to a general manager sometimes character-ized as a bit to the right of Attila the Hun, Harwell's job seemed to dangle from a thread.

As I sat there in the grandstand and finished reading Ernie's draft copy of events that had played out 16 years before, I knew that my instincts and Miz Lulu's had been right. Ernie Harwell had a unique treasure trove of stories to tell. Without question a book was just what was needed to preserve them for posterity. I knew one other thing: It is a measure of the esteem in which Er-nie Harwell was held in the hearts of Tigers fans and baseball fans nationally that the firestorm lit innocently by Feliciano died down without torching Detroit's beloved announcer.

That was the first time the humble announcer from Georgia, used to commenting on the exploits of others, would find himself the focus of such intense media attention. It would not be the last.

Not until after the Tigers won the last three games in thrill-ing fashion, overcoming a 3-1 deficit to win the Series, did Harwell hear criticism from Tiger management. Tiger owner and president John Fetzer wrote Ernie, "We have had at least 2,000 complaints on the matter, and the negative position has run a ratio of at least 100-1." Ernie's own direct mail totaled 305 of which 120 wrote in support.

I set down Ernie's copy and thought, Quite a story, Mr. Har-well, and well told.

It was still half an hour before game time so I made my way back up to the broadcast booth.

"Well, I suppose you're going to tell me you made a mistake," Ernie said, "and I should stick to the microphone."

"Not exactly, Ernie. This is great stuff and I know there's a lot more where that came from."

"That's nice to hear but I don't have the slightest idea where to go from here."

I told Ernie he didn't have to worry because that would be my job. I said I would work up a list of candidate chapters and we would volley it back and forth until we had a good working outline. I wouldn't publish the book myself because my plate was already full and I knew the book would sell better nationally if it came out from a publisher already established with a list of successful baseball books. I'd make those arrangements subject to Ernie's approval. I'd personally work with him on the manuscript and coordinate it with the publisher. Ernie's job would be to work on getting the stories down over the summer so that by the end of the year we would have the text well in hand so the book could be released in spring 1985.

Over the next few months, I met with Ernie at his house in Farmington Hills and together we went through his files. He kept his stories on 3 by 5 cards, handwritten with just the bare facts. Even so, he had two file cabinets of manila folders chockfull of his notecards. His practice was to go through his files before a game and build up a stack of cards to have ready for use throughout the game. We had settled on an outline for the book, breaking it down into fifteen chapters on subjects like characters of the game, umpires, miracles, special players, bloopers and managers. I had set a simple but important objective: that any fan of Ernie's reading the book would hear his voice as they read his words. That turned out to be easy to do because Ernie was a good writer himself, as he would prove several times in coming years. His copy read quickly and easily. His interest was in simply telling his story, not trying to show off how elegant a sentence he could write or what an impressive vocabulary he had.

We called the book *Tuned to Baseball*. What better title for an announcer whose career doing major league play-by-play would eventually span fifty-five years? I gave three prominent New York publishers a shot at the book. Typical of large New York houses, all three had difficulty comprehending that very much of merit can come from that vast wasteland west of the Hudson. They all admired the book and had high regard for Ernie, of course, but any book that is not steamy, sensational or bylined by a celebrity has tough sledding on New York's publisher's row. "A fine little book, in the best sense of that term," said one publisher. "But we see only about 3,500 in sales—it's not viable for us at that level."

Such condescension came as no surprise. It was actually a welcome response because Ernie would be better served by a smaller midwestern house. Most important was to partner Ernie with a house that would treat him well, produce a good quality book, and keep it in print over the years. If that publisher had national reach, so much the better. So I brought Ernie together with my calendar publisher, Diamond Communications, well established for books and publications on America's favorite star-crossed team, the Chicago Cubs.

The Harwell book got off to a strong start with serializations, excerpts and favorable reviews in Detroit and national press. It took Tigers broadcast station WJR and the Tigers organization itself a few weeks to shift into gear behind the book, but when they did it added further momentum.

I enjoyed letting my New York publisher friends know that advance orders for the book exceeded by far their lifetime sales projections. Within a few months the hardcover edition had sold several times that amount. Next came a quality paperback edition and eventually the rights were sold to a national publisher for a mass-market paperback.

The strong sales and great critical acclaim were due to the esteem in which Ernie Harwell was held and also to his tireless efforts in promoting the book. On one Saturday morning, he set what may be a Michigan record by signing 595 copies at an Okemos bookstore. Over the years he signed thousands of copies at bookstores, fund-raisers, church and community gatherings, libraries and other venues.

At every signing, there was a very familiar sight. People who had never met Ernie but for decades thought of him as a member of the family now had the opportunity they had long hoped for. Grandparents, teenagers, businessmen in three-piece suits—they all reacted the same. They beamed as they looked their friend Ernie in the eye, shook his hand, and told him how much enjoyment he had brought into their lives. Ernie's signings always took a bit longer than most because he actually paid attention to every person for whom he inscribed his book. Ernie Harwell was tuned to much more than baseball.

Before 1985 Ernie Harwell would not have called himself a writer. But that was when he launched what would be a successful and rewarding career as a book author and newspaper columnist. However, decades earlier he had earned his income as a writer for six years before he ever drew a paycheck using his voice on radio.

In 1934, while still in high school, Harwell wrote to J.G. Taylor Spink, the editor of *The Sporting News*, then America's pre-eminent sports publication, and applied for the job as their Atlanta correspondent. "Signing my name W. Earnest Harwell made me sound older," Ernie told me. It worked and Ernie was hired. He continued writing for *The Sporting News* even after taking a role in 1936 in the sports department of the *Atlanta Constitution* and filed feature articles for the *Sporting News* for many years thereafter.

In 1940, Ernie broke into radio at WSB in Atlanta. Then, in 1946—after four years in the Marines—he became the announcer for the minor-league Atlanta Crackers. In 1948, he made it to the Big Show as play-by-play man for the Brooklyn Dodgers. After stints with the New York Giants and Baltimore Orioles, Ernie came to Detroit in 1960 and a legendary career was launched.

As we were developing the book, Ernie wondered how much of his own history should be included. I told him he should just tell his stories and not worry about that; the stories were about other people and as I knew would be the case, Ernie told them in a way that illuminated them, keeping the spotlight off himself. Early in the process, Ernie had asked if I thought he had enough material to fill a book. There was enough material that after the success of *Tuned to Baseball*, Ernie went on to write *Diamond Gems*, which I published at Momentum Books, the publishing house I founded in 1986, and a third book, *The Babe Signed My Shoe*. He then went on to write a weekly newspaper column as well as other articles. Eventually collections of his articles were published in book form, as well as a memoir when he reached age ninety.

Ernie told me often how his career was influenced by others—by broadcasters, writers and by a few baseball players he especially admired "not only because of their talent but because they handled themselves with respect for the game." When he was writing for *The Sporting News* in 1935, he followed the exploits of the most graceful and talented second baseman of all time, as well as perhaps the quietest and most gracious gentleman ever to play the game. Just mentioning the name Charlie Gehringer always brought a smile from Ernie.

Gehringer was a 21-year-old kid from Fowlerville, Michigan when he stepped into the lineup for the Tigers in 1924. Decades later Harwell and Gehringer would be good friends and Hall of Fame teammates.

Both Harwell and Gehringer had many hundreds of friends in the major league cities around the country. But because Harwell was an active announcer, he knew the current players, coaching staff, and management of all the American League teams and many in the National League cities. He kept in touch with countless former players, some of whose careers ended even before he started his. A few of them he had helped vote into Cooperstown when he was on what was then called the Veterans Committee, or better known as "the Old-Timers Committee." Harwell may have known personally more people than anyone else in baseball; perhaps there was no one he admired and respected more than the humble Hall of Fame infielder of the Detroit Tigers, Charlie Gehringer.

Gehringer's 19-year career as the premier Tiger second baseman ended in 1942, so I never saw him in action on the field. Ernie had, of course, as Gehringer was a star of the first magnitude in the

1930s, winning batting titles and being named Most Valuable Player in 1937. I remembered listening to my father and the Big Beaver old-timers sitting around the Standard Franklin wood-burning stove in Jim Adams' barbershop trying to top each other describing Gehringer's smooth fielding and his knack for getting the key hit to win a big game. Many years later I saw clips of him in grainy newsreel films that only hinted at his grace at second base.

His statistics were staggering: a lifetime batting average of .320; 2,839 hits; seven seasons with more than 200 hits; and, in 1937, batting champion at .371 en route to American League MVP. He was the star of the Tigers 1935 World Series win and a League leader several times in runs, doubles, triples, hits, and stolen bases. He led the League in fielding seven times. He played every inning of the first six All-Star games and, against the finest pitchers in the National League, Charlie's lifetime batting average was an astronomical .500.

Even more remarkable was Gehringer's humility, generosity and decency. After his playing days were over he went on to a successful business career, including serving as the general manager of the Tigers. Among his accomplishments was signing a 20-year-old phenom from Baltimore. The skinny kid, Al Kaline, followed in Charlie's footsteps, becoming the youngest batting champion in history and carving out his own brilliant 22-year Hall of Fame career.

In 1983 I was invited to lunch at Meadow Brook Hall in Rochester, Michigan; I was told that Charlie Gehringer would be my host and he had a favor to ask of me. I found that intriguing because I had never met him and wondered how he could possibly know my name. Then I noticed that also invited to the lunch was Bill Hoglund, the general manager of Pontiac Motor Division and other Pontiac or General Motors executives I had been working with. Pontiac was a client of D'Arcy MacManus Masius, the advertising agency I had recently come to as vice president. Pontiac was a supporter of Meadow Brook Hall, so apparently they were reaching out to the agency for some kind of assistance on behalf of the Hall.

Pontiac was an important client and if they wanted me to be involved somehow, I wouldn't hesitate. The chance to meet the legendary Gehringer was a bonus.

Charlie was one of the most fit 80-year-olds I had ever met. Stories of his modesty and quiet demeanor had not been exaggerated, but one look into those sharp blue eyes and a grip of his firm handshake left no doubt he had been a special athlete in his day. Lowell Eklund, director of the Hall, told me that Charlie still played a fine game of golf, even though he was doing it backwards. I asked Charlie what Lowell meant by that and he explained that when he retired from baseball, a fan gave him a new set of golf clubs. The only problem was, the clubs were right-handed and Charlie was a lefty swinger. Not wanting to embarrass the fan by exchanging the clubs, Charlie learned how to play with right-handed clubs, and he continued to play that way for the next forty years.

Pontiac did indeed want my help with a fund-raising golf event for Meadow Brook Hall to which Charlie had allowed them to put his name. We further cemented the relationship with the Detroit Tigers by adding Al Kaline's name to the event. Ernie Harwell and Paul Carey helped out by talking up the event during their baseball broadcasts. And J.P. McCarthy had me call in on his WJR morning drive-time show to talk about the upcoming ceremonies.

It was ironic—or perhaps only poetic justice—that Charlie Gehringer should put his name and expend his energies in his later years on raising funds to preserve Meadow Brook Hall. Charlie and I were having lunch one day at the Hall when he turned to me and said something surprising. "You know, I was not allowed into the upper rooms here until recently," he said.

I asked him what he meant.

"Danny Wilson and I were good friends in the 1930s," Charlie said, "and he invited me out here often to shoot pool."

Wilson was the son of Matilda Dodge Wilson, matriarch of the family, who presided regally over the Meadow Brook Hall estate. In the old days people in the area called the hundred-room mansion and sprawling acres simply the Dodge Estate because it had been built by the automotive tycoon, John Dodge, Matilda's first husband. Her son, Danny, had become friends with Gehringer who was then the hero of the Detroit Tigers World Series triumph in 1935, a league batting champion and most valuable player.

"I was just a baseball player and that was a pretty lowly station in life," Gehringer said with a smile. "So I never would have dared arrive at the grand front entrance like we all do nowadays. I would come in through the back door at the servants' entrance. Danny would meet me there and we'd go down the hall to the billiards room."

Being treated as a lower-class person didn't stand in the way of Gehringer stepping to the plate to help fifty years later when the Hall needed revenue to survive.

"Not at all," Gehringer said. "That's just the way it was in those days. The automotive pioneers were like a higher form of life. Professional athletes were way down at the bottom in the social pecking order. Didn't bother me. I had fun shooting pool with Danny. When they asked me to help out with this fund-raiser, I was glad for the chance to pay them back for those good times."

Over the next few years, we increased participation to more than four hundred in a two-day event with a sumptuous banquet as a grand finale for participants and their guests. Revenue went to support the ever-increasing operational expenses of the Hall, which had to generate its own funds to survive. It also brought both publicity and new supporters to the Hall and underwrote student athletes at Oakland University. That was nice, but for me personally the priceless benefit was an enduring friendship with the kindly Charlie Gehringer.

In 1988, I had a chance to do something special for Charlie. More than modest, he was actually bashful, and so we had to play on his conscience to get him to agree to make the celebration of his 85th birthday the theme for that year's Gehringer-Kaline Classic. We had a list of notables at the event or represented by videotaped messages. There was a taped salute from Ernie Harwell and Paul Carey, of course, and they mentioned the Gehringer tribute on that evening's baseball broadcast. Personal appearances or video messages from governors, past and present baseball commissioners, and legendary Hall of Fame players Ted Williams, Al Kaline, and George Kell. I got to play president of the United States by writing a script for a videotaped tribute that President Ronald Reagan delivered in his trademark "great communicator" style.

The most enjoyable and lasting task was a film I wrote chronicling Charlie's exploits on the field, his accomplishments as general manager of the Tigers, his success as a businessman, and his contributions to many important community causes. We showed that film, *A Standing Ovation for Greatness*, and the Reagan tribute at the fund-raiser's dinner banquet. I thought that put a fitting cap on the celebration. But then Ed Stack, president of the Baseball Hall of Fame in Cooperstown, contacted me and asked to use the film for the Hall's special tribute to Charlie at their upcoming ceremony for the induction of Willie Stargell.

I called Ernie Harwell and told him about the invitation. Ernie had been the first active announcer to be inducted into the Hall; not surprisingly, he knew just about everyone there and rattled off a list of people I should say hello to for him.

"You'll enjoy it," he said. "Wish I could be there with you, but we've got a game. In fact, I seldom get to the induction ceremonies because we almost always have a game to call." If there was a game on the schedule, Ernie Harwell would be calling the play. Harwell had missed only two games in his entire career, which eventually spanned fifty-five years behind a major league mic.

He gave me a preview of what to expect at the Hall and put me in touch with several of his friends on the staff of the Hall. So, as a 51-year-old rookie, I packed the film in my bag and made my first pilgrimage to the most holy shrine of baseball.

Cooperstown. The very name evokes the sensations of summer, of being a kid again. Shoes scuffling up dust on a gravel road as you kick an old soup can along the way to a mowed field basking in sunshine. Baselines made with a bag of lime from Beaver Feed & Grain. Rolled-up shirts or jackets for bases, an ill-cut, white-washed plank for home plate.

The sounds, too—the crack of a Louisville Slugger against an almost-official Spalding ball. Never mind that the bat had a split in it and your hands vibrated like a tuning fork. So what if the seams of the ball had long since unraveled and the cover had peeled away like a useless scab. Hammer a nail in the bat, wrap the innards of the ball in black friction tape and get on with the game.

And the smells—burning autumn leaves at World Series time. Cider and cinnamon donuts and that most delicious aroma of all, ever so much better than a whiff of apple pie or warm chocolate-chip cookies soon to be washed down by cold milk. That priceless scent you got only when you buried your face in your baseball glove, closed your eyes, inhaled the intoxicating aroma of oiled leather, and transported yourself to that magic land.

Cooperstown. Or along the way, to Ebbets Field or The Polo Grounds, parks where Ernie had worked long before Detroit. And Wrigley Field and Fenway Park. The original Yankee Stadium. Ernie had told me countless stories about these places; some of them found their way into his books

These were the shrines of summer where a million kids worshipped, the hallowed grounds where the gods of the game played on the greenest of grass. Some say those diamonds, those parks, those fields are gone, long gone to wherever it was our childhood innocence went. Were that true it would be too bad. But happily those precious memories are alive and well. They just need the right nudge to flood forth and wash over you with feelings you may not have felt for years.

And that is why there is a Cooperstown. All right if you don't have the time to go there physically, there are other ways.

I had been to Cooperstown countless times in my mind before I actually made the journey. Finally, on July 31, 1988, I drove there from Michigan expecting only to turn over the film to the president of the Hall, take the visitor's tour and, if lucky, glimpse a familiar face from a distance. That would be enough for me and I'd be on my way. But then the officials of the Hall said they wanted to show the film at the evening dinner, where Charlie was to be honored. So they said I was welcome to stay and enjoy the day.

I telephoned Ernie and told him how the day was going. Then I joined the Hall of Fame members as they gathered for the official photograph on the expansive lawn behind the Otesaga Hotel. Every year, as part of the induction ceremonies, the photographer assembled the forty or so former players on the same spot for the official photograph, with the lake and the mountains in the far background. While the photographer set up his equipment, I spotted Charlie Gehringer standing quietly with a cluster of old-timers. Charlie introduced me to the man next to him. It was Ralph Kiner, the National League's version of Detroit's Hammerin' Henry Greenberg. Kiner led his league in homers seven straight seasons.

"Listen to this guy talk hitting," Kiner said to me, nodding at the tall man showing his classic grip on an imaginary bat. "I've been listening to him every year for I don't know how long. I keep discovering how much I still have to learn about the fine art of hitting."

Kiner was talking about one of the greatest batters in history. Ted Williams was no quiet man like Charlie Gehringer. He talked and talked and talked about the subtleties of using a wooden bat to strike a round object hurtling toward him at 100 miles an hour.

As he talked, Williams clutched that invisible bat and demonstrated the swing I had seen hundreds of times at Briggs Stadium, at Fenway Park, in films or on television. One image of the Splendid Splinter stood out. He stands in the batter's box on July 20, 1958 at Fenway with two outs in the ninth inning. He is the only batter to stand between Detroit's Jim Bunning and baseball immortality with a no-hitter. Sure enough, Williams turns on a Bunning fastball and sends it rocketing to deep right field where, amazingly, Al Kaline has just enough room to catch it and preserve Bunning's 3-0 classic.

On and on Williams went, practicing that fluid swing. Arms rippling, wrists unleashing, eyes riveted to a ball he surely saw speeding toward him. For a player with an abundance of nicknames, the one that summed him up best was Teddy Ballgame.

Suddenly Williams stopped talking and looked straight at me, probably wondering who I was and what I was doing there. Fortunately, I had a question ready. I asked him if he remembered that last at-bat in the Bunning no-hitter. Silly question.

"Kid," he said. "I remember every swing I ever took. I picked up the spin as the ball left Bunning's hand, knew it was a fastball. He made a mistake on that pitch. Put it right there for me, letter high, but I caught it one inch past the trademark, otherwise it's in the seats. One inch and it's so long no-hitter."

The player next to me laughed and I recognized him as a pretty fair left-handed hitter himself. It was Stan (the Man) Musial. Next to him, the 92-year-old Bill Terry, who batted .341 lifetime, including a glittering .401 season.

Wait until I tell Ernie about this, I thought. But then, Ernie had known all of these greats for years—he was enshrined forever in the Hall with them.

Charlie took me to meet the players off to the side in another group. I recognized one as a right-handed pitcher who made a career out of beating the Tigers like a drum, with his bat as well as his arm. Bob Lemon dominated Detroit with shutout after shutout, including a no-hitter. On a rare off day when he gave up a couple of runs, he'd knock in three with his bat and Tigers announcer Harry Heilmann would remind listeners, "That Bob Lemon is one of the finest-hitting pitchers this old game has ever seen."

"Here's a left-handed pitcher I'm glad I never had to face," Charlie said. Charlie explained how Warren Spahn would run the count to 3-0, knowing the batter would take the next two pitches and that meant he had to beat the batter on only one pitch. I remembered Spahn as being one half of the expression on fans' lips in the late '40s when the Boston Braves had two dominating pitchers: "Spahn and Sain and pray for rain."

Charlie pointed out a quartet of greats looking out on the peaceful lake and wooded hills that embraced Cooperstown and made it a sanctuary. Monte Irvin. Johnny Mize. Robin Roberts. Lou Boudreau.

Next we walked over to meet three legends from the Negro Leagues whose brilliance was never to be seen in the Major Leagues. James "Cool Papa" Bell. Buck Leonard. Roy Dandridge. Each had a million stories, a million smiles, a million memories.

Someone hit me on the shoulder and said, "Hey, great day, sun's shining. Let's play two!" Ernie Banks squeezed Charlie's arm and shook my hand. I looked at those wrists, coiled like two leather thongs, knowing he could still get around on the high hard one and rip it down the third-base line.

If there hadn't been baseball, it would have to be invented if only to immortalize names like those four the photographer was shooing toward the risers for the photographs: Enos "Country" Slaughter, Pee Wee Reese, Lefty Gomez, and Roy (Campy) Campanella.

As Charlie and the others made their way to the risers for the pictures, I wondered what these men would have done with their lives all those summers if there hadn't been baseball. At that time, I knew only a few of these Hall of Famers personally—Ernie Harwell, Charlie Gehringer, Al Kaline, Hank Greenberg. If these four were typical, they all would have excelled at something else. But at that moment, a life without baseball was simply too dismal to contemplate.

I wished that Ernie had been there, but he was at the microphone calling a game, proving yet again he meant it when he said, "maybe the most notable thing about my career is that I always showed up for work."

That evening, at the dinner for Hall of Fame members only, the theme was a salute to Charlie Gehringer on his 85th birthday. The centerpiece entertainment was a showing of my film, *A Standing Ovation for Greatness*. When the film finished and the lights came up, forty-one baseball greats stood as one to honor my friend Charlie, not only for his greatness as a baseball player but also for his decency, integrity and kindness as a person.

Three days later, back in my Bloomfield Hills office, I called Ernie Harwell and told him about my pilgrimage to Cooperstown, a place he had been so many times and where his own story and where later a film I produced about him, *The Great Voice of the Grand Old Game*, would be permanently enshrined. Minutes later I got a call from the official Hall of Fame photographer. He said he knew I had taken quite a few photographs myself and wondered if I had taken any of the assembled group of players. I told him I had indeed, that I had actually shot right over his shoulder and took several of the same pictures he was taking for the official photograph.

"Have you seen your prints yet?" he asked. "How did they come out?"

I told him they were fine. In fact, I had them in front of me. I asked if there were problems with his.

"They were fine except for one thing," he said. "I took fifteen shots and wouldn't you know it, in every damn one, Ted Williams has his mouth open, looking away, talking to somebody. Every year he does that to me. What about yours? I thought I'd nailed him this time. Have you got one where Ted doesn't have his yap open?"

I told him I had two where everybody was looking right into the camera and smiling, even Williams.

"Well, you've got the official 1988 photograph then, if you don't mind me using it. Next year I'm going to sew that guy's lips shut."

That night we had dinner with the Harwells at Rocky's in Northville, their favorite seafood restaurant. When I told Ernie about Ted Williams and the Hall of Fame photograph, heads turned at the nearby tables as Ernie's laugh cascaded around the room.

"That's the Splendid Splinter, all right," Ernie said. "What Ted knows about the art of hitting would take a mighty fat volume to fill. I know I wouldn't want to have to be the one to write it."

Neither Ernie nor I knew then that writing would become his new career when he finally stepped away from the microphone. Nor could anyone have guessed the roller coaster ride this much-revered figure would embark on in less than two years. In 1990, Ernie Harwell and his legions of fans would be shocked by what was in store for him a bitter winter day in the frigid cavern of Tiger Stadium. Ernie would ask me to be there with him that momentous day, at the corner of Michigan and Trumbull, where long since he had become not only the voice and the face, but also the very soul of the Detroit Tigers.

For Ernie and his many fans, that day would be as bitter as the mid-winter weather. But as we will see in Chapter 14, what goes around, does indeed come around—as it surely did for Detroit's great voice of the grand old game.

⁓

"I just got word that Jack has done two more assists... One of them was a woman named Martie Ruwart. She's my cousin."

The event went well but we were not surprised that Kevorkian did not show up... even as we were launching Appointment With Dr. Death, the determined pathologist did indeed have another appointment. As our party was going on in the basement, just two floors above us he was providing terminal assistance to yet another client.

"Have a nice trip," Kevorkian said.

⁓

3

APPOINTMENT WITH DR. DEATH

Jack Kevorkian—
A Zealot en route to Martyrdom

ON JUNE 4, 1990, IN THE BACK OF A RUSTED 1968 VW BUS, a pathologist with a passion spoke the last words Janet Adkins would ever hear.

Adkins had barely enough control and strength for her trembling finger to start the lethal flow of potassium chloride into her veins. Dr. Jack Kevorkian had taken that into account when he cobbled together the device he dubbed the "Mercitron." He also called his invention the "Thanatron", which meant "death machine" in Greek. No matter—by whatever name his machine would deliver Adkins from pain forever and thrust Dr. Death and the issue of assisted suicide to national prominence.

"Have a nice trip," Kevorkian said.

For nearly all of her life, Adkins had been energetic, competitive and highly active. She had traveled around the world, climbed the Himalayas, and floated on hang gliders. Even as she raised three sons, she taught English and piano and played Brahms duets with her husband. In recent years, she had learned T'ai Chi and studied reincarnation.

Then, in Portland, Oregon, this vibrant woman got her devastating diagnosis. Her Alzheimer's disease was progressing rapidly;

soon her husband would have to dress and bathe her. She considered taking pills or jumping out a window but rejected those methods because of the uncertainty of success and the distress it would cause others. Soon, her mind would be fogged and she would be totally dependent on others. That was an unacceptable prospect for Janet Adkins.

Her trip to Kevorkian's van parked in a secluded Oakland County campsite had begun on November 13, 1989. On that day, Adkins' husband, Ron, read a *Newsweek* article about Kevorkian. *Newsweek* had been intrigued with Kevorkian since the day he placed classified ads in newspapers:

DEATH COUNSELING
IS SOMEONE IN YOUR FAMILY TERMINALLY ILL?
Does he or she wish to die—and with dignity?
CALL PHYSICIAN CONSULTANT

Ron Adkins then picked up the phone and took the first step in carrying out his wife's wishes.

It was not an easy sell for the Adkinses to convince Kevorkian that Janet should be the pathologist's pioneering patient. It took six months before Kevorkian was convinced she met his criteria to qualify for assisted suicide. Finally, in the last week of May 1990, Janet Adkins traveled with her best friend and her husband across the country to Michigan, to a remote campsite in Groveland Oaks, an Oakland County park. There, Janet Adkins became the first client of Jack Kevorkian's "obitiatry" practice.

Operating totally at his own expense and adamantly refusing any fee or compensation, Kevorkian had finally achieved his goal of helping end the life of a terminally ill person. He had built a lethally effective suicide machine out of thirty dollars worth of scrap parts scrounged from garage sales, flea markets, and hardware stores. He assembled his devices at the kitchen table of his Royal Oak apartment.

Kevorkian was not a practicing medical doctor—he was a pathologist, out of work, obscure, and unquestionably eccentric. And he was much, much more than that. He was an accomplished painter of surreal images in the style of Salvador Dali but with a fixation on body parts in gruesome conglomerations. These paintings toured Michigan off and on twenty years before Kevorkian became known as a crusader for medical experimentation on condemned prisoners and the medical harvesting of body parts. The grisly content and brutal religious parody in his eighteen paintings triggered controversy wherever his work was shown. Bizarrely, his irreplaceable paintings, along with his electronic organ, harpsichord, and virtually all of his personal possessions went missing in 1985 after Kevorkian's odyssey to California where he had gone to make a documentary film featuring his paintings. None of his most precious possessions have been located since he turned them over to a Long Beach, California, moving company in 1985 to ship back to Michigan.

Kevorkian had played that electronic organ with a passion for Bach, and he was just as intense when he sat at the poker table. He boasted that, given the chance, he would be far superior to Ernie Harwell as the Detroit Tigers play-by-play announcer. He was a writer of limericks and used them in a self-published diet book that he also illustrated with his own drawings.

Kevorkian told me he had been a maverick, something of a loner, from his earliest days. Born in Pontiac, Michigan, in 1928 to Armenian immigrant parents, he graduated with honors from Pontiac Central High School in 1945. He was seventeen when he enrolled at the University of Michigan Medical School, where he did his residency training in anatomical and clinical pathology.

After graduating from the University of Michigan in 1952, he asked to work nights at his job as a pathologist at Detroit Receiving Hospital because more patients died then. That meant he could pursue his study of how eyes changed at the moment life left the body. That earned him the nickname he came to embrace, Dr.

Death. "I was sort of the laughingstock of the hospital," he said. But he persisted, and wrote up his findings for the American Journal of Pathology, calling his article "The Fundus Oculi and the Determination of Death." His colleagues were also disturbed by Kevorkian's passion to aggressively promote the harvesting of body parts for transplantation.

Soon after Kevorkian embarked on his crusade for assistant suicide, and before I had met him, I discussed the idea for a book with Ron Monchak, my partner at Momentum Books, and Tom Ferguson, our managing editor. I told them there was no doubt the man was eccentric, but perhaps it took a zealot to galvanize the issue.

Monchak was intrigued. "This is worth doing," he said.

Ferguson said, "Right issue, wrong guy."

His initial lack of enthusiasm was no surprise. Ferguson was legendary for his easily triggered skeptical gland. He was the prototypical city desk editor, a guy who would be in his best element in the night editor's slot, wearing a green eyeshade and his rock-hard cynicism like badges of attainment. That was how Ferguson became known as Michigan's journalistic salvage expert, the patron saint of beleaguered publishing causes. He was the man in charge of a publication's triage room, the old pro to whom troubled owners of publishing organizations turned. He was a take-charge guy who knew how to get copy from the idea to the printed pages, a pragmatist who relished doing whatever it took to get results.

Ferguson had an unusual technique in his first interview with a prospective client or boss. His opening shot: "The publishing business is hopeless. We're living in the post-literate age. Most people don't read once they get out of school, if they ever learned while they were there. Kids don't read at all. If you were smart, you'd close this place down tomorrow and save yourself a lot of grief and money."

If the prospective employer persisted and said, no, he was going to stay in business after all and wanted Ferguson to come to work for him, Tom would tell him the way it would have to be. He was a seen-it-all, take-no-prisoners operator who knew instinctive-ly which stories were worth doing and which ones weren't worth a column inch or five seconds of his time. Of course, to someone saddled with a troubled publication, that was irresistible. Those terms agreed, Ferguson would come on board and go at it until he had used it all up and was ready for a new crisis.

All things considered, Ferguson was a rare, if not unique talent on the Detroit publishing scene. A tough businessman, a shrewd observer, and—most appealing to me—a brilliant editor who went at copy savagely with a machete or tenderly with a scalpel, as the situation and text demanded. Yet, despite his dictatorial style or perhaps even because of it, he managed to win the cooperation and more often than not the undying gratitude of the writer whose manuscript he had just pummeled into submission.

From the time we brought Ferguson in as managing editor of Momentum Books, we marveled time and again as he took twenty pages of fascinating, well-written copy and reduced it to a page and a half.

"Show me something important I left out," he would say.

We couldn't.

The motto he lived by was, "Every word has to pay its way in." No one was immune to his blue pencil—not Monchak, not me, not William Shakespeare.

We knew that if we signed up Michael Betzold—who had been covering the story for the *Detroit Free Press*—to do a Kevorkian book, there would be no better editor for it anywhere than Fergu-son.

So we sat down with Betzold to talk about the project. We agreed this book would advocate neither one way or the other; it had to be a meticulously factual work of high journalistic integ-rity that dealt with the issues even-handedly. Still, it also must be a compelling read for a general audience. It would be the most thor-ough and authoritative account of Kevorkian's progression into zealotry en route to martyrdom, a chronicle of how one fanatic illuminated the issue of assisted suicide and thrust it to the forefront of the public's consciousness.

Moreover, this would not be an authorized version, sanitized by the principal subject or anyone else. Betzold would interview Kevorkian, his attorney Geoffrey Fieger, and Kevorkian's supporters. He would talk with the doctor's religious critics, prosecuting attorneys, and government officials. He would include relevant material on euthanasia policies in other states and other countries. He would, of course, check, double-check, and recheck his facts, as would Ferguson. The book must stand entirely on its own merits and carry no endorsement from any of the parties involved.

One goal for the book: no matter how strongly prejudiced a reader was at the outset, when he finished, the book he would have a better understanding and perhaps more sympathy for the other side.

We signed Betzold to a contract. Having covered Kevorkian's suicide assists since May 1991, he got quickly into work on the book. But things soon changed. In mid-February 1993 he called to tell me that something totally unforeseen had happened.

"I started this project as a writer," he said. "But now I'm an affected party. I just got word that Jack has done two more assists." Michael paused and I wondered what was coming next. "One of them was a woman named Martie Ruwart. She's my cousin."

Michael told me he hadn't seen Martie in years and they had not been particularly close. Still, it gave him an added perspective on the issue, a sensitivity that guided him throughout the rest of the process.

Once Betzold turned in his manuscript, he and Ferguson spent countless hours volleying copy back and forth. After some final shaping and polishing, we had what we had sought months earlier—the definitive book on Dr. Jack Kevorkian and his crusade to bring assisted suicide to the forefront of America's consciousness. We titled the book exactly what it was—*Appointment with Dr. Death*.

—⁓—

BETZOLD SUGGESTED A SITE FOR THE AUTHOR'S PARTY, and we agreed that it would be convenient for those we expected to attend. Not incidentally, it was also a modest venue, which seemed somehow appropriate, given the subject matter of the book. We would use an unpretentious room in the basement of a restaurant in downtown Royal Oak called Mr. B's.

As our production manager and I unloaded boxes of books from our cars parked in the lot behind the restaurant, a van pulled up nearby and four or five people got out. They walked toward us and asked if we knew where the entrance was to Mr. B's. I told them we were going there also and they introduced themselves. These were the survivors of the suicide of someone dear to them. We had invited the widows, widowers, relatives and friends of some of Kevorkian's suicide clients.

As we were thanking them for coming, a wiry man in a cardigan sweater hurried toward us from across the parking lot. The small knot of our guests quickly surrounded Dr. Jack Kevorkian, hugged him and thanked him for helping end the suffering of someone they loved.

We had invited Jack, of course, but knowing his nature, we hadn't expected him to attend. The guests went into the restaurant. Michael Betzold arrived and joined Jack and me. We asked Kevorkian if he would be joining us.

"I'll try," he said, "But it doesn't look likely."

I asked him if he had just come to say hello to people he knew would be at the event.

"No, it's just a coincidence that I bumped into you. I was glad to see those folks, though. Some of them have kept in touch by phone or mail. It's not an easy thing." He stopped and pointed toward the building where we would soon be holding the event. "Did you know that's where I live? Same building as Mr. B's, the upstairs apartment."

That was actually the reason Betzold had suggested the location. He had previously visited Kevorkian in his modest apartment.

The event went well but we were not surprised that Kevorkian did not show up, although we didn't know why until the next morning. Then we learned that even as we were launching *Appointment With Dr. Death*, the determined pathologist did indeed have another appointment. As our party was going on in the basement, just two floors above us he was providing terminal assistance to yet another client.

From that point on, events unfolded rapidly. Kevorkian became one of the best-known names in America. Just the mention of his name was a sure-fire laugh-provoker for late-night talk show monologists and stand-up comics. Ray Charles' song "Hit the Road, Jack" got a whole new life on music tracks covering segments on Kevorkian. Commentators from one end of the medical establishment to the other wrote articles and op-ed pieces condemning Kevorkian as a heartless ghoul or praising him for elevating an ages-old issue to public prominence.

• On October 30, 1995, a group of doctors and other medical experts in Michigan announced support of Kevorkian. They proposed to create a set of guiding principles for the "merciful, dignified, medically assisted termination of life."

• On February 1, 1996, *The New England Journal of Medicine* published voluminous studies of the attitudes of physicians in Oregon and Michigan showing significant support for doctor-assisted suicide under certain conditions.

• On March 6, 1996, the U.S. Circuit Court of Appeals in San Francisco ruled that mentally competent, terminally ill adults have a constitutional right to receive aid in dying from doctors, health care workers and family members. This was the first time a federal appeals court endorsed assisted suicide.

• On March 14, 1998, Dr. Jack Kevorkian participated in his 100th assisted suicide, a 66-year-old Detroit man. Shortly afterwards, the Dutch Supreme Court released a study on euthanasia, reporting that some 10,000 requests are received in that country each year from people requesting assist in dying in one manner or another. More than 3,500 of these are granted, usually by a doctor injecting a lethal drug.

—〰—

IN 1997, I MET WITH JACK KEVORKIAN AT HIS REQUEST, a meeting arranged by the head of Wayne State University's Department of Journalism, Jack Lessenberry, who is also a highly regarded journalist and a writer for national publications. We met at the Southfield office of Geoffrey Fieger, Kevorkian's attorney. Fieger was already well known for his bombastic theatrics in court where he had won many multi-million dollar lawsuits, often for medical malpractice.

Kevorkian told me he was contemplating the prospect of being in jail and wanted to have something useful to do while he was incarcerated. What did I think, he asked, about him revising and publishing the diet book he had self-published years ago? Lessenberry had given me a copy of that book, *Slimmeriks and the Demi-Diet*, in which Kevorkian wrote of himself:

> *The author's official position*
> *Is not in the field of nutrition*
> *It wasn't his dish*
> *When at Ann Arbor, Mich.*
> *He became a postmortem physician.*

As I talked with Kevorkian in a conference room in Fieger's offices, he spent more time chasing down tangents about interesting words than we did discussing the book. He said he had virtually memorized the dictionary; that was easy enough to believe because he often interrupted his own train of thought to comment on the etymology of a word. When we finally stayed on topic for a few minutes, I told him I had two problems with his basic dietary premise. His "secret technique" was that people should simply fill their plate with whatever they pleased, but then eat only half and toss the rest away.

"I can't see that working for most people," I said. "First, many people have a thing about wasting food. Second, it would seem to take exceptional will power—which obviously most overweight people don't have in abundance—to enjoy the taste of something on their plate and then discard half of it."

Also, while I understood what he meant by the title, it would have to be changed to really work in selling the book. That in turn led to the vexing problem we would encounter in marketing the book.

"I imagine we'd get a good deal of attention, if not hoots of derision," I said, "in promoting Dr. Death's Ultimate Diet Book."

We were interrupted by Geoffrey Fieger bursting into the room.

"Where's the deal?" he demanded of me. "What's the offer you're putting on the table?"

"Geoffrey," Kevorkian said, before I could respond. "Mr. Haney and I have been having a nice conversation and now you come blundering in here. Why don't you just go back in your office and leave us alone."

A FEW MONTHS LATER, I SAW KEVORKIAN AGAIN AT A PARTY hosted by one of our Momentum Books authors, the portraitist Patricia Hill Burnett. The food, elegantly served by a fine caterer, was abundant and delicious. Kevorkian and I took our plates and moved off to a corner where we could talk quietly. Once again, the conversation bounced from baseball to his diet book, from limericks to a curious pronunciation Jack had just overheard in nearby conversation. Abruptly he stopped talking and I noticed he was looking across the room at a cluster of men enjoying the high-caloric offerings. In the center of the group was the more-than-ample figure of then-Governor John Engler. Jack shook his head and set aside his plate, on which half of the food remained.

"I rest my case," the slender pathologist said.

—⁂—

ON NOVEMBER 22, 1998, JACK KEVORKIAN—WHO HAD DEFIED many ultimatums—crossed the ultimate red line beyond which there would be no turning back. He personally administered a lethal injection to Thomas Youk, 52, who was in the final stages amyotrophic lateral sclerosis (Lou Gehrig's Disease). Because ALS weakens nerves to muscles, Youk had been unable of his own volition to trigger Kevorkian's machine.

So Kevorkian did it for him.

But Kevorkian went further. He videotaped the process, showing himself providing the lethal injection. Then, as if assisting in his own suicide, he sent the tape to CBS.

During the broadcast of the tape on CBS's *60 Minutes*, commentator Mike Wallace asked Dr. Kevorkian, "You killed him?"

"I did," Kevorkian said. "But it could be manslaughter, not murder. It doesn't bother me what you call it. I know what it is."

On the program, Youk's wife, Melody, said: "I was so grateful to know that someone would relieve him of his suffering."

The prosecuting attorneys had a different reaction.

"After viewing the edited portions of the video last night," Oakland County Prosecutor David Gorcyca said, "it appeared a homicide was committed in violation of the laws of the State of Michigan."

Kevorkian welcomed the news that he would be tried for first-degree murder. "I don't consider it murder," Kevorkian said. "I consider it the way things should be."

He had been tried four times with Geoffrey Fieger as his defense counsel. Fieger had for years represented Kevorkian without fee, winning acquittal in every case but one, and that one ended in a mistrial. But now, Kevorkian said, he would represent himself. He was determined to provoke a legal showdown on the rights of terminally ill patients to die by their own choice.

"Dr. Kevorkian has served a valuable purpose in bringing this issue to the fore in terms of the needs of suffering people," Fieger said. "But I don't think he will serve any purpose by martyring himself."

The trial was a disaster for Kevorkian. In earlier trials, Fieger, a dominating court presence with a flair for the dramatic, a skillful orator who had won tens of millions for clients in malpractice suits, had captivated and won the jury over to Kevorkian's side. This time, though, Fieger was off the case and Kevorkian proved quickly the truth of the adage that "he who defends himself in court has a fool for a client."

On April 13, 1999, Dr. Jack Kevorkian was convicted of second-degree murder and delivery of a controlled substance in the death of Thomas Youk. He was sentenced to ten to twenty-five years in prison and his appeal of the judgment was denied.

—⁂—

ON DECEMBER 14, 2005, I WROTE TWO LETTERS. I asked Michigan Governor Jennifer Granholm to show clemency to Jack Kevorkian, to allow the seriously ill man to die outside prison walls. The second letter was to Kevorkian. Following a comment by Kevorkian to me that he expected to be bored in prison if he couldn't read and exercise his mind, I offered to visit and bring him some books.

On December 16, 2005, Kevorkian's advocates and supporters appealed to the parole board and Governor Granholm for leniency. They contended that Kevorkian—ill with diabetes and Hepatitis C—was in failing health and he would likely die in prison unless clemency was granted. The board denied parole. Governor Granholm declined to overrule their recommendation.

Throughout 2006, many individuals and organizations urged the Governor to set Kevorkian free.

In February 2007, as Dr. Jack Kevorkian, prisoner #284797, remained incarcerated at Thumb Correctional Facility, Lapeer, Michigan, he said, "I expect to die in prison." His passionate supporters said if that were to come to pass, the State of Michigan would have done in cold blood what Dr. Death had himself been imprisoned for—assisting in a death.

But on June 1, 2007, after eight years of incarceration, Kevorkian walked out of prison a free man. On one side was his yet-again reinstated lawyer Geoffrey Fieger. On the other side was CBS correspondent Mike Wallace.

Upon his release, Kevorkian restated the promise he had made in his parole hearing to never again assist in a suicide. Instead he planned to live quietly on his small pension and social security while writing and giving a few speeches. By Kevorkian's own count, he had assisted more than 130 terminally ill clients to end their lives, asserting again and again, "Dying is not a crime."

One thing that did not change was Dr. Jack Kevorkian's view that humane assisted suicide must be available. "I'll work to have it legalized," he said. "But I won't break any laws doing it."

As Kevorkian's health deteriorated, he was diagnosed with liver cancer. On May 18, 2011, he was hospitalized with pneumonia and kidney problems. His condition worsened rapidly and on June 3, 2011, a week after his eighty-third birthday, he died from a thrombosis. No heroic measures or artificial attempts were made to prolong his life. His death was painless. His organs were not harvested for use by others, as he so fervently advocated. His body was buried at White Chapel Memorial Park Cemetery in Troy, Michigan.

The epitaph on his tombstone reads, "He sacrificed himself for everyone's rights."

The Catholic Church in Detroit lamented that Kevorkian had denied scores of people their right to humane deaths. Judge Thomas Jackson, who presided over Kevorkian's first murder trial in 1994, expressed sorrow at his death. He said that the 1994 case was brought under "a badly written law" aimed at Kevorkian.

As for the issue that dominated the life of Dr. Death, the subject of assisted suicide drew more media attention, public discussion and thoughtful consideration from governments and the medical establishment than ever before. What was once only talked about in hushed voices before Jack Kevorkian came on the scene became a major and volatile social issue.

Who would have predicted before Dr. Death became a household word that Al Pacino—or any top tier Hollywood actor—would star in a major film about the grisly, depressing business of assisted suicide? Yet *You Don't Know Jack* earned rave reviews from audiences, awards, critical acclaim and a healthy box office.

Jack Kevorkian remained as polarizing and controversial in death as he had been in life. To some, he would always be a fanatical ghoul with a morbid obsession about death. Advocates for the freedom of the right to die hailed him as the zealot who by sheer force of his will and passion drove the issue out of the closet and thrust it—very literally—center stage.

~~

"When I was growing up I was forever challenging the traditional roles for boys and girls. I have always advocated for a level playing field, always challenged traditional roles of women in society... it's not just bias about race or gender or social status, it can be unconscious bias on any of a multitude of factors. We miss such a potentially rich learning experience when we limit who can come to the table."

"Work is the fabric of my life," says Denise Ilitch. "I have never been and don't ever expect to be a nine-to-five person. You really don't ever punch out."

~~

4

LISTENING, LEARNING
AND LEADING

Denise Ilitch—In Quest of Excellence

THERE WAS A TIME IN HER LIFE WHEN DENISE ILITCH COULDN'T RESIST running up the stairs.

Her family had just moved into a new home, the first time the twelve-year-old had been in a home with an upstairs.

"It was a two-story house and I was going to have my own bedroom for the first time, a big moment in my young life," Ilitch recalls. "I was so mesmerized by the upstairs. That was just foreign to me because our last neighborhood had all single-floor houses. I just kept running up those stairs."

In that respect, things haven't really changed all that much for Ilitch over the years.

In a multifaceted career as businesswoman, lawyer, entrepreneur and publisher, Ilitch has seemingly never encountered a stairway she couldn't climb all the way to the top. It has been much the same in her world of community service. She works with a passion on the causes to which she is dedicated—her roles as a University of Michigan Regent, champion of many community causes in Metro Detroit, and public and private philanthropy.

To many people, Ilitch is perhaps best known from her years

as a creative and innovative executive of Little Caesars Enterprises where she rose to the position of vice president. "I started working in the pizza business when I was fourteen years old," she says, "and worked in many jobs there over the years."

Ilitch went on to work in many roles in many settings.

"Work is the fabric of my life," she says. "I have never been and don't ever expect to be a nine-to-five person. You really don't ever punch out."

Ultimately, she became president of Ilitch Holdings where she had management responsibility for its broad and deep portfolio of businesses including Little Caesars, Detroit Tigers, Detroit Red Wings, and Fox Theatre, among many others. The combined annual income for the portfolio of companies in the privately held corporation was estimated at $2.6 billion in 2013.

Ilitch received a JD degree from the University of Detroit in 1980 and is "Of Counsel" at the law firm Clark Hill, where she advises clients in the areas of business practice, corporate law, and government policy.

While at Ilitch Holdings, she was a driving force behind the establishment of side-by-side professional sports complexes in Detroit at a time when businesses and residents were leaving the city instead of returning and trying to reinvigorate it. Ilitch broke new ground with her leadership of a monumental urban-development project that upgraded and energized a moribund area of downtown Detroit and created thousands of new jobs. She spearheaded the building of Comerica Park, the new home of the Detroit Tigers, creating a unique side-by-side setting alongside Ford Field, the new venue for the Detroit Lions.

To pursue her lifelong passions for design, writing and fashion, Ilitch left the corporate world and embarked on an entrepreneurial venture. She founded Ilitch Enterprises and that structure gave her the platforms and the freedom to express her passions for communicating with a focus on style, fashion, design and the many forms of art and craft.

Ilitch has always put a high priority on communication, continually working at being a better speaker, listener and writer. It was only a natural extension then for her to become a publisher.

In 2005, Ilitch and Dennis Archer Jr., both "self-confessed magazine junkies" and avid supporters of Detroit, agreed there was an unfilled need in the Detroit metropolitan area for a certain kind of publication. Long before she had any idea she would one day launch and publish a glossy magazine, Ilitch had a flair for fashion and style. That eye for harmony and originality in design and color would be demonstrated in many of her future activities and especially prominently in a new magazine with a focus on the bright side of Metro Detroit.

"Dennis and I agreed there was a hole in the periodic print publications segment in the Metro community," Ilitch says. "It may have appeared to be a slender niche, but we considered it to be an important one. We believed that providing a publication to that readership could well have effects that would ripple outward and benefit a much larger community.

They were convinced a high quality, intelligently edited magazine could, in their words, "serve as a cultural bridge between urban and suburban life in metro Detroit."

They decided the answer was a contemporary life style magazine that provided insightful articles on important and interesting people and events—and in an upbeat way with flair. The pair established Hamilton Woodlynne Publishing and in May 2006 launched the premiere edition of *Ambassador* magazine.

The magazine was targeted to readers as their "liaison to the good life, with in-depth features, striking editorials and explorations into the latest trends in fashion, beauty, travel, business, technology, lifestyle and more.

In keeping with her personal philosophy of concentrating on the bright side, Ilitch has said, "You will never read anything negative in our magazine. It's all about uplifting Detroit and Detroiters. We're not part of the trash-and-burn genre."

The second venture in Ilitch's Enterprise portfolio can trace its origins to the days when, as a young girl, Ilitch shared a bedroom with her sister Lisa.

"All of Denise's walls were covered with fashion pictures she had cut out from magazines," says Lisa Ilitch Murray. "She was truly a 'girl-ly' girl, more a cheerleader type than tomboy. Even in those early days, she was fashion conscious, trend-setting."

Those tastes and sensibilities eventually led Denise Ilitch along a winding path and into yet another unpredicted career. When she took a beading class in Tucson, Arizona, she was at first interested in turning her own hand to creating something of beauty, something she had designed and fashioned herself. She was an enthusiast of couture fashion and already had a practiced and appreciative eye for all types of design. She hoped that through the class she would gain further insights into the aesthetics of fine jewelry. Before long, however, she found herself enthralled with the subtle and delicate details of design.

Not long after that, she launched another new venture, Denise Ilitch Designs.

"I'm a real visual person. I love design and art and fashion." Ilitch says. "Our goal for Designs is to be a catalyst, to develop and create collections of stylish, individual and timeless design. We strive for designs that not only captivate the accessory enthusiast, but also serve as a venue for other phenomenal design innovators and their works. We're always in quest of the unique and the exotic."

Another quest of Ilitch's quite apart from the worlds of business and commerce is to make the best contribution she can to securing and advancing the stature of the University of Michigan as a pre-eminent institution of higher education and research. That was her motivation for running in 2008 for a seat on the U of M Board of Regents.

"I ran for and am serving as a Regent because I am passionate about higher education," Ilitch says. "At the same time, there is a personal benefit for me and that is being exposed to powerful intellectual stimulation from some of the most brilliant minds anywhere."

In 2013, one of the top priorities for the Board of Regents was the search for a new president of the University to succeed Mary Sue Coleman on July 1, 2014. Ilitch was determined to help identify the absolute best individual to become the fourteenth president of a university founded in 1817. While that was the objective, the process itself became an educational and inspiring one for Ilitch.

"It was quite an experience to go through the entire process, to travel across the country and meet so many outstanding higher education professionals," Ilitch says. "It was reassuring to see how committed they are to higher education, how seriously they take their roles in providing academic excellence and preparing the world's future leaders."

As Ilitch listened to the panel of advisers who participated in the search process, she was struck with how important it was to draw from diverse perspectives.

"These were the rock stars of academia," Ilitch said. "Historians, doctors, social scientists. Pre-eminent scholars. Again and again we were made aware of unconscious bias. There is conscious bias, obviously, but there is also unconscious bias.

"I was always sensitive to that because when I was growing up I was forever challenging the traditional roles for boys and girls. I have always advocated for a level playing field, always challenged traditional roles of women in society.

"What I have learned at Michigan is that it's not just bias about race or gender or social status, it can be unconscious bias on any of a multitude of factors. We miss such a potentially rich learning experience when we limit who can come to the table. With people nowadays able to connect with the rest of the world by the tap of a computer key, and recognizing what the world is going to look like in the next ten to twenty years, it is such a waste of talent to limit to those who come to the table."

Fellow Regent Larry Deitch worked with Ilitch throughout the search process and commented on how collaborative the effort was. "Denise is very team-oriented and believes that a collaborative process is what brings people together and produces the best result. She likes to promote an open dialogue and encourages the expression of different viewpoints.

"She is always open to the point of view of others. But at the same time, when she makes up her mind she stands firm in her principles. She is not afraid to go against conventional wisdom, to 'speak truth to powers.' She is very, very straightforward. Not a game-player, a great colleague. And she has a good sense of humor."

Ilitch found the search experience exhilarating but sobering.

"Higher education is facing a lot of issues: access, affordability, diversity, the cost model and so many others," she says. "Because all the candidates are so qualified in background, experience and intelligence, what happens in searches is that it really falls to character, values and fit. What set Mark Schlissel apart from the other highly qualified candidates, in my opinion, was his heart.

"As a parent first and foremost, I'm confident that Dr. Schlissel will lead with our students' welfare as his top priority. He understands our mission and will work tirelessly to continue our academic and research excellence, our passionate desire for access and affordability, and a learning environment that is inclusive and promotes diversity."

Reflecting on previous eras at the University, Ilitch said, "It seems that each president has been the right person at the right time. Our new president is an M.D. and that made a difference to me. There's no questioning the importance of our health system, which is in an upheaval due to changes in the laws in the health sector. To navigate through all this we are going to need the kind of credentials and knowledge in the health sector that Dr. Schlissel brings. We have had great leadership at U of M. He just wants to take it to the next level."

As Ilitch pursues her broad spectrum of involvements, she draws on lessons learned in her childhood, from parents and teachers, from books, and as a college student.

She was born in Tampa, Florida, where her father worked for the local recreation center after a leg injury cut short his promising baseball career. The family moved to Michigan when she was an infant, then moved several times in the Detroit metropolitan area before she went off to college. Those moves were difficult at first for her as she quickly became attached to each new home, neighborhood and school. But there was an upside—she quickly made friends and adjusted to each new environment. Those experiences of quickly acclimating to new surroundings gave her confidence she could handle change and thrive in new situations.

"Since I was the oldest, I lived in all the houses as my parents moved to new places in the suburbs to accommodate their growing family," she says. "The hardest move for me was from our small ranch house in Dearborn Heights when I was twelve years old. There I had shared a room with my sister Lisa and my two brothers shared another room.

"I really did not want to leave that home to move to Birmingham, to our new home at 13 Mile Road and Evergreen. But before I knew it, I had adjusted, like I would always do after future moves. I loved all our homes, loved the neighborhoods and walked to school every day."

In her speeches and writings, Ilitch often refers back to experiences and lessons learned as a child and during her undergraduate days in Ann Arbor. In an interview for *Michigan Alumnus* magazine, a journalist asked Ilitch, "What did you learn from the U of M that you can apply today?"

She responded, "One of the things I learned was the University of Michigan provided an environment that pushed me, stretched me. It was open. All ideas could be put right out there in plain view. That culture taught me to accept and learn from all different types of people. There was no 'you're not allowed to participate because of the way you look or because you're too vocal, or because I don't like the color of your skin or because you have an accent that makes it hard for me to understand you'."

That culture of diversity and openness clearly made an indelible impression on Ilitch. In all her roles since her college days, Ilitch has striven to create an open, stimulating culture that gives everyone, as she puts it, "a seat at the table. When you exclude people for reasons having nothing to do with competence, that makes for a very narrow population of participants you have left."

As evidence of what such openness and diversity can achieve, Ilitch pointed to her work in many different settings in the Detroit community. "Studying at U of M and the atmosphere there prepared me to be able to go into a community like Detroit and listen to all points of view," she said, "to accept all perspectives and to be able to then problem-solve by having listened carefully."

Zaid Elia, who has partnered with Ilitch on many projects, says, "Denise is a phenomenal collaborator and a great communicator. The CEOs who are successful realize that in working with people the most important quality is to listen, to make them feel important, to really listen to what they're saying. That is a great strength of Denise. Often when we're working together she and I just start talking. Pretty soon ideas start percolating. One thing feeds into another, and in a while we see an opportunity that neither of us saw to begin with."

Ilitch had observed from an early age the importance of listening. " I have worked really hard at being a good listener. I give my father credit for that because he is really an excellent listener. He taught me the value of listening, that it is a key ingredient for being a great leader."

Another touchstone from Ilitch's childhood is the importance of books and of reading in whatever print medium—magazines, journals, newspapers—was near at hand.

"I am a voracious reader," she says, "but the book that influenced me the most wasn't at all scholarly or a work of great literature. It was a book I read when I was a young girl. It was called *The Clan of the Cave Bear*, by Jean Auel. There was a point in my teenage years when I really related to Ayla, the main character, a girl from a totally different culture, so different from the people she found herself living with.

"I had read many books before that and of course countless books after, but that book had such an impact on me. I was a young teenager when I read it and the story resonated with me about becoming your own person. I related to her not being accepted for who she was.

"The book posed important questions: What happens if you have success? How do you handle it? How do people respond to you and how do you handle their resentment? And then, what happens when you strike out on your own? Ayla's growth and empowerment totally empowered me at my early age.

"I didn't realize it at the time, but in looking back I can see what a profound impact that book had on me. I remember that when I turned the last page, I was mad, mad the way the others reacted to her just because she had the courage to strike out on her own, all alone.

"But then I thought, if she can do it, I can do it. She empowered herself, I can empower myself."

Perhaps part of Ilitch's receptivity to that story traces to a question her father had put to her three years early. They were seated at the dinner table, Ilitch recalls, when her father asked her, "What did you contribute to the world today?"

"I didn't have to think long," Ilitch says, before she replied, "Dad, I'm only ten years old."

She doesn't recall her father's response but she does remember that was a meaningful moment. "Somehow," she says, "something shifted at that point."

Ilitch's parents continued to ask her and her siblings questions like that well into their futures.

"My parents felt that we were capable of making a difference and therefore we were *expected* to make a difference. Every day I see how my parents have contributed to the community, how they tried to expand what giving is about. It isn't just money. There are so many ways a person can make a difference."

For each of her many involvements, Ilitch has a specific motivation. For example, she knows how important it is that business leaders not only espouse support for Detroit but also put actions behind their words. This motivated her and publishing partner Dennis Archer Jr. to move the offices of *Ambassador* magazine in late 2013 from the suburbs to the heart of the city on Congress Street in downtown.

"We talk about lifestyle and identifying trends," Ilitch said in announcing the move. "I can't think of a better place to do that right now than from Detroit. Urban areas are really exciting. Something as simple as walking outside your office and having a lot of options for entertainment. There's a synergy now in the city that one is able to do that a lot more than in the past."

With her involvement in important activities in so many communities, it follows that Ilitch is much in demand as a speaker. She accepts as many offers as she can, whether the groups are large or small, the only criterion being that the situation fits her liberal definition of being worth the audience's time and hers. Her messages are delivered with self-assurance and yet a humility often surprising in one who has accomplished so much across such a wide spectrum. Her demeanor as well as her message resonates particularly well with young business people and entrepreneurs, often especially with young women.

She talks frequently of the "3 C's, the qualities that have governed my career."

Ilitch cites the importance of confidence as the critical foundation to not only success in business but also to "so many aspects of our lives. If you don't believe in yourself, you don't give anyone else permission to believe in you."

"My dad may have been demanding a lot from a ten-year-old

kid when he asked what I had contributed to the world that day, but his question showed that he had confidence in me—and that made me realize I was capable of making a contribution."

For Ilitch, the key to growing in confidence is education. She credits her advanced education—especially her law degree—with playing a key role in her success in business and her careers.

"In addition to education in law, it taught me discipline, assertiveness, logical thinking, how to see all sides of a situation and how to think on my feet and not be intimidated when challenged. More than that, it enabled me to become self-sufficient. And make no mistake: self-sufficiency builds confidence."

Ilitch's second "C" springs naturally from that growing sense of confidence. "It's courage," she says. "Courage means facing a challenge instead of withdrawing from it. When you truly honor yourself and you act on what you think is best for you and others—that is an act of courage."

On this measure, Ilitch knows whereof she speaks. "I became a small-business person," Ilitch says.

After a long career in increasingly demanding and prominent roles in big business with Little Caesars and Ilitch Holdings, she took a big risk and pushed herself out of her comfort zone. She established Ilitch Enterprises and founded not one but two small businesses. *Ambassador* magazine, now in its eighth year, was launched at possibly the worst possible time for such a venture. Magazine publishing is fraught with danger in the best of times, and 2008 was anything but the best of times in the Detroit metropolitan area, not to mention the entire state and country.

But the venture succeeded for one very good reason, encapsulated in Ilitch's third and favorite "C".

"A 'Can Do' attitude is my favorite," Ilitch says, "because Can Do people believe that everything is possible. I love working with Can Do people because they make things happen."

Ilitch herself had earlier tapped into a substantial dose of that power of positive thinking as she played a role in turning a vision of a new ballpark for the Detroit Tigers into reality. The challenge was even greater than building the new ball field in the Fox Theatre district. On the drawing boards, Comerica Park was to be one of two side-by-side professional arenas, alongside the Detroit Lions' Ford Field. Many times during the long developmental process, the dream of a pair of professional sports stadiums in Midtown Detroit seemed in danger of ending as just that—a dream. But Ilitch and others involved in the venture persevered and the result is a tandem of crown jewels for the city of Detroit and the region that have contributed immeasurably to the revitalization of Detroit, particularly its downtown.

Throughout that process, Ilitch showed she meant what she has long preached about: the absolute necessity of being a listener who really hears and attends to what other people are saying.

In her talks to audiences, whether young college students, academics or established business professionals, Ilitch puts sincere and patient listening at the very top of her list of attributes that managers must master. She stresses how harmful it is for executives and leaders to stifle input. It is all too common to not listen with an open mind to opposing points of view, to fail to invite others to express a contrary opinion, and to inhibit others from questioning the boss.

In all her involvements, Ilitch also demonstrates the importance of mentoring. In all fields of endeavor, mentoring and the transferring of best practices are crucial. Knowledge that has been developed, advanced and refined by one generation is passed along to the next. Often it is a technique, an insight, that enables the pupil to stand on the shoulders of the teacher, to reach ever higher, to achieve more, to create something better. The result: The student is able to fashion a more dependable device or to create a finer work of art. In a business setting, that is how methods and systems are continually improved to lead to a more efficient, productive, vibrant workplace. It is not only the successes that impart valuable knowledge. Just as importantly, something crucial can be learned from a blunder the manager made, a mistake that now the intern can be on guard against and avoid.

Ilitch herself is regarded as an inspirational mentor by those who work with, for or alongside her. It probably came naturally to her. Since her earliest days, she has drawn from many role models, mentors and influential others who imbued her with the vital and indelible experience of learning from their successes, mistakes and challenges.

Her parents, of course, both at home and in her various business roles, were her first mentors. As she progressed through educational settings and in business, there have been others. But as an example of a person extremely important in her own personal development she cites someone she never met.

"Many people wondered whether Katherine Graham could be effective as the publisher of *The Washington Post*," Ilitch says. She talks about Graham's low self esteem and lack of confidence inflicted on her by an insensitive spouse. "But she trusted her instincts and eventually refused to allow negative influences to dictate how she felt about herself. This translated to her business and its remarkable success."

Graham transformed *The Post* from a decent big city daily newspaper into one of the nation's leading news sources. She became one of the most respected women in the industry.

The Graham case history, often extolled by Ilitch, serves as a classic embodiment of Ilitch's 3 C's—Confidence, Courage and a Can Do attitude.

While Ilitch herself downplays what she has accomplished, it comes as no surprise to others who have known her since her childhood.

"Denise was always her own person, always confident," says younger sister Lisa. "Being the first born, she was close to our parents. They gave her and all their kids lots of confidence that they could do anything. Denise especially had a lot of responsibility, working in many different capacities in the business."

But beyond her confidence and her competence, there are other facets of Ilitch often mentioned by those close to her—thoughtfulness, generosity and a sense of humor.

When Lisa Ilitch Murray was in high school, she was the beneficiary of a very unusual act of generosity from her sister. "I wanted to go to the prom but I didn't have a date. Denise said, 'How about if my boyfriend takes you?' And he did. How many older sisters would do that? She has always been that way, kind and generous."

In 1990 Lisa retired from the Ilitch businesses and started a family. In 2001, she was ordained as a minister. That same year she got a request from her older sister.

"How would you like to have the first wedding you officiate to be to marry me and Jim Scalici," Denise asked, then added with a laugh, "But are you sure it's legal for one sister to marry another?" Lisa assured her sister that would be perfectly permissible and legitimate and she would be delighted to do it.

"That was quite a moment for all of us when I pronounced Jim and Denise man and wife," Lisa said. "That was typical of the way Denise is always thinking about doing just the right thing, something thoughtful that will be nice for others.

"Denise is also very good to go to when you have a problem. She has the ability to negotiate difficult situations and not in a negative way, but instead to seek compromise when there are strongly divergent positions or opinions. For example, she has been concerned about women's issues for as long as I can remember. She wants to know how many women sit on your board or are in key positions in your organization and are they being promoted and compensated fairly."

Reflecting on the origins of that work ethic regardless of gender, Lisa says, "Denise and I had quite a role model growing up because my mother was working when that was nowhere near as common as it is today."

To be expected then, is the Denise Ilitch mantra: "Work is the fabric of my life."

As a true believer in the efficacy of work, she cites the words of former Prime Minister of India Indira Gandhi, "My grandfather once told me there are two kinds of people: those who do the work and those who take the credit. He told me to try to be in the first group... there is less competition there."

That Gandhi story provides two more "C's" for Ilitch to add to her roster of Confidence, Courage, and Can Do. As for Competition, she has been energized rather than afraid of it. And Credit has always been important to her—not for taking it for herself, but rather for giving it to the people she works with.

Her business partner Zaid Elia said, "She doesn't come into a situation with an agenda she is pushing. Instead, she works at any project, any problem in a collaborative manner to get the best results for the team. Whether it's on a board or in a charity group or in a business situation, Denise works as hard to make reality out of an idea whether it's her idea or someone else's."

Ilitch's husband, Jim Scalici, knows something about keeping up with a wife who maintains a busy schedule and seems to be always on the way somewhere. Scalici is, appropriately enough, a mover of a different sort. "I'm an airplane pilot and I drive motorcycles or pretty much anything with a motor. The only thing I haven't driven—yet—is a locomotive."

As for his multi-tasking wife, Scalici says, "There are many dimensions to Denise. She is a very kind and giving person. For example, she has tried every possible scenario for my eighty-year-old mother to come and live with us. And she looks out for the little guy, the underdog, the person who needs someone to stand up for them. She has a knack for knowing how to handle any situation. She has a very understanding and gentle nature, but when the situation calls for it, she knows how to be firm."

Ilitch is as enthusiastic about—and acknowledges being as fulfilled by—her less public roles as by her highly visible participations. "Family always comes first, of course, and in addition to our own immediate family, there are a lot of us in the extended family," she says. "And being involved in charitable and community activities is very fulfilling and rewarding in so many ways."

In support of her efforts to enhance educational opportunities, she established the Denise Ilitch Scholarship at Walsh College and serves as a Distinguished Visiting Business Executive at the University of Detroit Mercy School of Law. She has served on the board of the Detroit Branch of the NAACP, was a Detroit Red Wings Alternate Governor for the National Hockey League, and was a board member of Major League Baseball. She has received the B'nai B'rith International Great American Traditions Award, the Clara Barton Award from the American Red Cross, and was named 2007 Alumnus of the Year by the University of Detroit Mercy Law School. She is also a regular panelist on the CBS TV show, *Michigan Matters*.

One recurring theme in Ilitch's endeavors consistently gives her the most personal satisfaction. Because she doesn't insist on getting her own way and doesn't like being showered with personal recognition, she gets fulfillment from working with others to progress toward a shared goal and then standing alongside them to see the success of the venture.

Which is very probably why Denise Ilitch has had her hand in so many successes.

The country was then in the grip of McCarthyism, and in the shameless fashion of the time, Radulovich was being stripped of his commission for associating with his allegedly subversive father and sister. But Radulovich chose to fight these unjustified accusations.

Edward R. Murrow and Fred Friendly were keenly aware they were escorting television on its maiden voyage into the uncharted minefields of advocacy. Television, heretofore a medium to entertain, was being contemplated as a medium to influence.

~5~

STRIKING AT KINGS AND TYRANTS

Lt. Milo Radulovich—
The Victim Who Changed History, with
Edward R. Murrow and Senator Joe McCarthy

IN THE 1950S, POLITICIANS ON COMMUNIST WITCH-HUNTS often dominated the airwaves by warning there could be a Red hiding under any bed. Careers were destroyed and lives were ruined by fearmongering fanatics, none more vitriolic than Senator Joseph R. McCarthy.

Many innocents crumbled under the onslaught. In a bargain with the devil for leniency, some told witch-hunters what they wanted to hear, inventing stories to betray lifelong friends. They pointed fingers at somebody else, anybody else. But one American soldier living in Dexter, Michigan, stood up to bullying by self-anointed super-patriots in the military and Congress. When his cause was championed by a gutsy television reporter and a resolute producer, broadcast journalism in this country was changed forever.

In 1997, I published a book about that turning point in American history. Only later that year, when we celebrated the success of that book as part of the opening of our new Momentum Books offices in Troy, Michigan, did I meet the central figure in that drama of the 1950s, Lieutenant Milo Radulovich. Many authors and people who were the subjects of our previous books attended the grand opening. One surprise guest was Radulovich, then an unassuming seventy-year-old man whose refusal four decades earlier to be broken by demagoguery helped bring down a tyrant.

In 1953, Milo Radulovich was an Air Force veteran with an outstanding six-year record. A reserve officer attending the University of Michigan on the G.I. Bill, Lt. Radulovich became an innocent victim of hysteria fanned by Senator McCarthy. The book we published telling Radulovich's story as it had never been told before was *To Strike at a King: The Turning Point in the McCarthy Witch-Hunts*. The author, Michael Ranville, had approached me several years earlier about the project. My partner, Ron Monchak, was greatly intrigued and took over its development as Ranville worked on his manuscript.

Ranville had been immersed for years in the story. He was impressed with the quiet courage of Radulovich and the bravery of newscaster Edward R. Murrow and his producer, Fred Friendly, who put their careers in jeopardy to tell not only Radulovich's story but also its implications for the entire nation.

"Now, with the Milo Radulovich case before them," Ranville wrote, "Murrow and Friendly were keenly aware they were escorting television on its maiden voyage into the uncharted minefields of advocacy. Television, heretofore a medium to entertain, was being contemplated as a medium to influence."

Monchak's dust-jacket copy captured the story's essence:

In 1953, in the quiet little town of Dexter, Michigan, a shabby drama unfolded whose repercussions would soon be felt across the country and around the world. At first, it was only the career of Air Force Lieutenant Milo Radulovich that was at stake. The country was then in the grip of McCarthyism, and in the shameless fashion of the time, Radulovich was being stripped of his commission for associating with his allegedly subversive father and sister. But Radulovich chose to fight these unjustified accusations.

Years later, Milo Radulovich and I talked about that momentous day of the Murrow broadcast. He remembered as if it were yesterday that on Tuesday, October 20, 1953, at 10:30 p.m., Edward R. Murrow and Fred Friendly climbed out on a long and very shaky limb with their live *See it Now* broadcast of "The Case against Lt. Milo Radulovich, AO589839."

I told Milo that I had been aware of his case because of several personal connections. Like Milo, I once lived in Dexter, Michigan, and also had attended the University of Michigan at the same time he was there. I hadn't been in the military service but I strongly identified with servicemen because my three older brothers all served in combat in World War II, as my father had as a Marine in World War I. Perhaps more compelling was my memory of having to sign a loyalty oath as a condition of getting a secret clearance to work on classified government programs.

Milo told me about his gratitude to Murrow for restoring his good name. He was quietly proud of having played a role in closing a sordid chapter in American history. He was pleased that Mike Ranville had told his story so thoroughly and accurately. He said how much he appreciated that we had published it.

At the time Radulovich and I talked, forty-four years had elapsed since Murrow's epochal broadcast. The memory was still keen for him. He knew how fortunate it had been for him—and for the cause of justice and fairness in America—that Murrow and Friendly were looking for just such a "little picture to show the big picture," as Friendly put it, of McCarthy's campaign of guilt by association.

McCarthy's minions had whipped the country into hysteria in the early 1950s as they scavenged for any dirt—substantiated or not—that they could use to stain people in the military or the U.S. Department of State as a Communist, a sympathizer, or in any way soft on communism. In this atmosphere, the U.S. Army thought they had found a choice target in Radulovich, despite his exemplary six-year service record. McCarthy quickly seized on this chance to make an example. He would pillory this soldier with the eastern European name. McCarthy ranted that Radulovich should be severed from the reserves because he had "close associations with the wrong people."

Those "wrong" people were his father and his sister. The sister had once walked on a picket line to protest the Book Cadillac Hotel's refusal to grant accommodations to the great concert singer Paul Robeson, a black man. Robeson had long infuriated zealous anti-Communists with statements such as, "To be free—to walk the good American earth as equal citizens, to live without fear, to enjoy the fruits of our toil, to give our children every opportunity in life—that dream which we have held so long in our hearts is today the destiny that we hold in our hands."

Radulovich's father had also committed a "crime" in the eyes of his persecutors. His offense had been that he read *Slobodna Rec*. That tiny Serbian-language newspaper was published by the American Slav Congress, which had been designated as communistic by the U.S. Attorney General. A typical McCarthy tactic was to grab television exposure by holding up a sheaf of papers he claimed were secret documents; in reality what he waved about during his rant was a non-classified transcript available to anybody for two dollars. In a typical tirade, McCarthy blustered:

> *The reason why we find ourselves in a position of impotency is not because the enemy has sent men to invade our shores, but rather because of the traitorous actions of those who have had all the benefits that the wealthiest nation on earth has had to offer—the finest homes, the finest college educations, and the finest jobs in Government we can give. While I cannot take the time to name all the men in the State Department who have been named as members of a spy ring, I have here in my hand a list of 205 that were known to the Secretary of State as being members of the Communist Party and who nevertheless are still working and shaping the policy of the State Department.*

Milo told me—as he had told Ranville earlier—that his father did indeed subscribe to that Serbian-language newspaper, because that was the only source of news about what was going on in his native country. In the time of the witch-hunts, Serbia was a part of Yugoslavia and had completely broken with Moscow, the focus of McCarthy's attention.

In September 2005, the Radulovich story got further exposure. George Clooney released his Academy Award-winning film *Good Night, and Good Luck*, a powerful cinematic treatment of many of these events. Soon after the film came out, Radulovich told author Ranville that Clooney had invited him to attend the premiere and they had since become friends. Radulovich said Clooney told him that he had considered using our book title, *To Strike at a King*, as the title for his film. Milo said that because of Ranville's book and Clooney's film, the cloud cloud cast by the red-baiting Senator McCarthy—a cloud that loomed over his life for fifty years—had finally been lifted.

Few people could fully appreciate what it must have been like for Milo Radulovich to see his education and his livelihood jeopardized and his good name smeared. I told Milo I had a whiff of the anxiety that one feels under the threat of Big Brother coming down on you and the mere suspicion of guilt by association. As we talked, it occurred to me that one stark memory may have fired my desire to publish his story. He asked me to tell him more about it.

Some forty years earlier, in June 1956, I sat in a small, dimly lit room in the security office of Rocketdyne, a division of North American Aviation, in Canoga Park, California. Rocketdyne was the contractor for propulsion systems for U.S. ballistic missile programs, including the Redstone and Jupiter, and the Saturn booster engines. I had just completed an application for a summer job at Rocketdyne as a technical editor. My brother Bob worked there and had gotten me in the door for the interview. He stressed, "The rest is up to you." I had just finished my sophomore year at the University of Michigan and knew this job would be my first chance to use experience I had gained as an editor at the *Michigan Daily*, U-M's student newspaper. I knew also the job required a secret clearance and that could be helpful to me in getting another job in the space or defense industries once I graduated.

Finally, a security officer came in and sat across the table from me. He was wearing a prominent white oval badge that I soon learned signified "Top Secret" clearance. He was also wearing a granite face. He placed an imposing stack of forms before me and in a voice as cold and flat as his stare, he began to read. I would be well advised, he said, to understand the severity of this moment. An incorrect answer or a failure to disclose information completely was a serous offense. I was required to read a copy he would give me of the law and to read it very carefully in its entirety before signing. He would witness my signature, attesting that it was given voluntarily and, in his judgment, in full possession of my faculties.

First, I had to read a long list and indicate, for each named organization, whether I had ever been a member or knew anyone who had ever been a member or had ever attended or knew anyone who had ever attended a meeting of that organization. In each instance, I was to write down the full name of the person I knew to be associated with that organization. The list looked as if it would dwarf the Manhattan white pages.

It was clear that any organization with the word "social" or "labor" or "workers" was a tip-off to the FBI that here be communists. I could see it was all over for the unlucky fellow who knew anyone who knew someone else who had a friend who had once walked past a park bench on which there rested a copy of a publication of the Socialist Labor Party.

Except that I thought about that only much later. At the time black humor was far from my mind. Sitting in that interview room with a job in the balance and the threat of legal consequences, I was absolutely convinced that Big Brother already knew my dirty little secret: my father had been a union member throughout the 1930s and '40s and even served as a union steward.

I read each name, page after page after page. Here and there I would come to a name of a group I recognized and would stop and think about it. Listed there was a student organization at the University of Michigan that gave me pause. Then I remembered I had written an article mentioning it for the *Michigan Daily*. I had talked with a couple of its members and may even have attended a meeting as a reporter. So, a dilemma. Thus far, I had been able, in clear conscience, to check the "No" box beside every name. Now what? Does it make a difference that I was there only as a reporter? Can it be said that I really *know* these people when I merely talked with them for the article?

I started to check the No box. I hesitated. My mind raced through a dozen scenarios. The security officer had obviously convinced me this was a serious matter. What if, for example, the FBI had an informant planted in that organization and what if that informant had already reported my name as someone who "attended" a meeting and "met" with some members? And on and on and on.

Far-fetched? Yes, but still... I remembered that three years earlier, when I was in high school, I watched the chilling television coverage of the McCarthy hearings and heard the Senator's tirades about an insidious communist conspiracy in the U.S. State Department. I recalled that a reserve Air Force officer studying at the University of Michigan had lost his security clearance in part because a family member had been observed reading a foreign-language newspaper. Along with most people in America with access to a television set, I was riveted to those Senate hearings.

I thought about those still-vivid images as I worked through the ream of pages the security officer had given me. It was no longer just a question of getting approved for a security clearance so I could get a job for the summer. Now the stakes had been raised dramatically. I took at their word what the security officer and J. Edgar Hoover and the House Un-American Activities Committee had communicated: if it turned out that anyone I knew had been a member of a forbidden organization there would be serious consequences.

When, years later, I was telling Milo Radulovich about that episode, he asked me if I ever considered not signing the forms. I had to tell him that never occurred to me, but I did recall that my mood changed from fear to concern to anger.

I told Milo that as I turned to the last page where all the Young People's and Young Men's and Youth For Whatever Leftist Cell were listed, I thought, What's going on here. I had just seen a production by a brilliant playwright who had graduated from the University of Michigan many years earlier. Arthur Miller had set *The Crucible* in 1692, at the time of the Salem witch trials. Now, with tyrants like Senator McCarthy and with the power of the HUAC committee and the FBI and the security officer standing there watching me, how far had we come really since 1692 in Massachusetts?

The security officer saw I had laid down my pen. He sat down and picked up the sheaf of forms. He read carefully down each column. I followed his eyes as he traced the uninterrupted series of checks in the No boxes and not a single check in a Yes box. He saw not a single volunteered name of a Red or a fellow traveler. He did not seem pleased. Certainly he was not amused.

"You understand that when you sign this," he said, "you attest to its total accuracy and vouch that no pertinent information has been omitted?"

I nodded and signed and he witnessed. Within a week I was cleared to handle material classified as "Confidential." It would be several weeks before my Secret clearance came through.

In the mean time, notwithstanding the tightness of security, I was assigned to write technical manuals on the Redstone and Jupiter guided missile engines—and these documents would be classified as secret. I was told in indoctrination sessions that Rocketdyne was primarily interested in creating power plants for vehicles for exploration of space. However, this was 1956 and NASA (the

National Aeronautics and Space Administration) was not created as a Federal agency until 1958, so the company was obviously focused at that time on weapons programs for the military. The chief propulsion scientist in residence at Rocketdyne was a German national, Werner von Braun, the father of Germany's V-2 rocket, who had come to North America after Germany surrendered. Rockets could carry nuclear warheads—a fact as well known in Moscow as in Washington, D.C.—so a race with the U.S.S.R. was well underway to see who could stockpile the most intercontinental ballistic missiles. Somehow, here I was, a 19-year-old college student—an English major, at that—with a very small hand in America's highly classified missile program.

My work required getting data and instructions from engineers, preserving their factual integrity while transforming this material into the formulaic style of military parts lists, manuals and specifications. I finished my drafts, ushered them through the convoluted approval loops and turned my copy in to the typing pool. There, by something like magic, my text would be transferred onto long gray clay-coated sheets called Multilith masters that could then be loaded onto printing machines to generate multiple copies. To someone whose idea of high tech was a fresh ribbon in a Royal upright typewriter, this was heavy stuff.

A week later, I was notified by the typing pool supervisor that my pages of typewriter copy had been retyped into the proper format, proofed, and delivered to Document Control for reproduction of preliminary copies for final proof-reading. I went to Document Control and filled out a form to get a copy of my first product as a technical writer.

"I can't release a copy of this document to you," the clerk said.

I asked why.

"Because you're not cleared for it. This document is classified 'Secret' and you're only cleared for 'Confidential'."

"But my secret clearance is pending. It's supposed to come through any day now."

"Then come back when you're cleared for secret," he said.

"But how can this be?" I said. "I'm the person who wrote the document."

"I understand that," he said. "You can write it. You just can't read it."

—ⱱⱱⱱ—

YEARS LATER, WHEN WE PUBLISHED RANVILLE'S BOOK about Milo Radulovich and Edward R. Murrow, I told Ron Monchak that story. Ron, too, was a great admirer of *The Crucible*, as well as of Ralph Waldo Emerson from whence he had gotten the phrase "to strike at a king" to use as the title for Ranville's book. We talked about the super-patriotic and rabid religious paranoia that springs up from time to time throughout history. That refusal to look at things reasonably, that climate of suspicion that fosters an environment in which a Salem witch-hunt can be mounted or a McCarthy reign of terror can fester.

In 1997, I told Milo Radulovich that same story about my own little encounter with ultra-security hawks during the witch-hunting days of the mid-1950s. He looked at me, and after a long pause, he repeated what he told me when we first met, "You know, it was only after I started talking with Mike Ranville about the book that I was finally able to walk down the street without every few steps turning to look over my shoulder."

For the entire thirty years he was on the air at WJR,
J.P. McCarthy presided over the Number One-rated show.
As time went on, McCarthy's stature and influence grew
far beyond that of a typical radio personality.

The prized score for a publicist was to get his first-time
author or budding young star a sit-down on J.P.'s mid-day
Focus Show or a morning drive-time phone interview.

We had struck a serious snag. I was sure J.P.'s lawyer
wouldn't have a change of heart—it is not in the nature of
lawyers to tell their clients, "Aw, what the heck.
You only live once. Take a chance, do the book,
maybe things will work out."

～6～

"ON THE OTHER END OF MY LINE"

J.P. McCarthy
Rides the Great Lakes Radio Waves

THE GREAT VOICE OF THE GREAT LAKES WAS A GREAT LINE.

For decades, the great-voice tag was much more than just another slogan used by WJR, 760 on the AM dial. For years, WJR not only dominated the Detroit metropolitan market, it also blanketed the Midwest and beamed a signal that could be picked up throughout most of the United States. Those voices emanating from the Golden Tower of the Fisher Building in Detroit were as familiar as family to millions of listeners.

If you asked somebody what came to mind when they heard the phrase "the great voice of the Great Lakes," instead of naming the station, they might be as likely to name one of the prominent voices heard on those airwaves.

In the 1940s, '50s and '60s if you were a morning person, it was Bud Guest, as he "views the news from the sunny side of the street" or perhaps it was his sidekick, announcer Charlie Park. If you were a nighthawk, it was "your captain Jay Roberts on Night Flight 760."

From the 1950s into the '70s, if you tuned in for Tiger baseball, Lions football, and other major live sports coverage, the great voice was Van Patrick, followed by Bob Reynolds.

Beginning in 1960 and for four decades, for most listeners the great voice label was applied to Ernie Harwell. Bob Talbert told me he was frequently tempted to use that phrase when he wrote about Harwell in his widely read column for the *Detroit Free Press.* Talbert generally refrained from doing that because he knew that it would embarrass the congenitally modest Ernie. Talbert was right. Ernie would laugh and change the subject when people praised him or his voice too highly. "I'm just a tongue-tied kid from Georgia, showing up for work every day," he would say. Ernie had his own choice for the greatest voice, the man he said had "the voice of God." That was Ernie's broadcast partner Paul Carey, whose baritone can still be heard, old-timers will tell you, echoing on a warm summer evening at Michigan and Trumbull.

But if a poll had been taken of daytime listeners any time from the sixties to the nineties, the odds-on favorite to be considered *the* Great Voice of the Great Lakes would have to be Joseph Priestly McCarthy. It was just plain J.P. to millions of listeners around the Great Lakes, but off air to his friends it was Joe. He used J.P. as his professional name because of the scandalous Wisconsin Senator Joseph R. McCarthy. Senator McCarthy was in the public's eye in the early '50s when J.P. was a high school student at Detroit's De La Salle Collegiate. J.P. knew the disgraced junior senator from Wisconsin had put an enduring stain on the name "Joseph McCarthy" with his scurrilous attacks on innocent people whose only crime was that they might have known a "wrong" person.

For the entire thirty years he was on the air at WJR, J.P. McCarthy presided over the Number One-rated show. After two years as a staff announcer, McCarthy became the station's morning man in 1958, when he was 22 years old. His weekday 6:30 a.m. show from the Golden Tower of the Fisher Building began with his theme music "Have a Nice Day" and the trademark introduction, "It's first call to the Morning Music Hall and J.P. McCarthy."

In Detroit, the automotive community started the day much earlier than industries in most other cities. The morning drive-time slot on the city's most powerful station attracted a huge audience to McCarthy, including a high proportion of the top executives of the Big Three. Soon, J.P. was on a first-name basis with virtually every mover and shaker in town. He would invite them to call in when they had major news to announce or discuss. Because of his personal interest in sports, he also became the favored interview for the likes of Sparky Anderson, Joe Schmidt, Chuck Daly, and Al Kaline, and the top behind-the-scenes influentials in the sports world, as well. General managers, league officials, or sports agents broke many news stories—sometimes unintentionally—during a phone-in to J.P.

As time went on, McCarthy's stature and influence grew far beyond that of a typical radio personality. As his interests changed, so did the tastes of his listeners. When he got serious about boating, before long people who had never been on a Great Lake were listening to call-ins from the *Flying Buffalo* or some other yacht in the Detroit to Mackinac race. Each spring, he ran a contest with an ever-larger package of prizes for the person who came the closest to predicting the time when the last square inch of snow would melt from a northern Michigan ski slope. A thoroughbred racehorse was named after him—the human J.P. had much fun with J.P. McCarthy the gelding. When Joe took on the Police Athletic League's cause for sports programs for the city's youth, he enlisted his coterie of journalists and jocks and took contributions to record heights year after year.

As McCarthy indulged his insatiable appetite for something different to talk about, his interests expanded and his audience followed right along with him. After a few years, it was less music and more phone-in conversations with a range of callers that reached far beyond Detroit's local characters and celebrities. Joe's rolodex included presidents, Hollywood's top stars, Nobel Prize winners, politicians large and small, and the nation's sports hero du jour. If there was a big happening in Oakland County, you could bet that the next morning Joe would have L. Brooks Patterson, Oakland

County's chief executive, on the phone. A prominent trial would bring Attorney General Frank J. Kelly or attorney Geoffrey Fieger to the phone. Michigan governors and senators, past and present, rang his line regularly. In 1992, he flew to Washington, D.C., just so he could fly back on Air Force One with President George H.W. Bush.

McCarthy was one of Michigan's best-known figures nationally. In 1962, he was inducted into the National Radio Hall of Fame. In 1994, he was named "Marconi Personality of the Year" by the National Association of Broadcasters.

Despite—or perhaps because of—his changing format, his ratings continued strong. Eventually, *The Morning Show with J.P. McCarthy* seldom served up music—the menu featured alternating courses of casual talk, sports updates, rehashed topical news and—to spice it up—telephone chats with celebrities.

Whatever the ethnic celebration, McCarthy dove into it enthusiastically. Late each winter, he talked with denizens of Hamtramck and Metro Polish communities in quest of the perfect paczki for Polish Mardi Gras, or "Fat Tuesday." The middle of March was special for Irishman McCarthy. Every year, he seemed to start earlier hyping his upcoming annual St. Patrick's Day Bash. That show featured authentic music of the Emerald Isle by groups such as Blackthorn and interviews with any prominent person with a trace of Irish ancestry. He christened many an Italian or Swede "an Irishman for the day." So much in demand was an invitation to the Bash that people curried favor months in advance to get on the list.

During the big football weeks for Michigan and Michigan State, the focus would be on the upcoming game, with sound bites from earlier years and interviews with coaches and past stars such as Ron Kramer and Chris Spielman. Joe's own personal favorite piece of music the week of the UM-Ohio State game was Pat Suzuki's sultry version of "Hail to the Victors."

With his encyclopedic memory, insatiable appetite for stimulation, and prodigious energy, J.P. also hosted the afternoon Music Hall. For years he took only a brief break after his morning stint, then sat down at 10:45 a.m. to tape the *Focus Show,* which would run after the noon news. And nobody—in Detroit or anywhere else—did it better. The prized score for a publicist was to get his first-time author or budding young star a sit-down on J.P.'s mid-day *Focus Show* or a morning drive-time phone interview.

J.P.'s annual "Christmas Sing" and St. Patrick's Day Bashes were legendary. Fringe celebrities scrambled to get on the invitation lists and mingle with the big boys. In election years, national political candidates from everywhere along the spectrum were elbow to elbow waiting for a turn at J.P.'s mic. At the 1992 Bash, I stood between hopeful presidential candidates arch-conservative Pat Buchanan and California's Governor-from-Outer-Space Jerry Brown. Their hopes were flickering out from recent primary setbacks but we had a lively discussion of the issues while waiting for J.P. to wander over with his microphone.

In his spare time, McCarthy did narrations and voice-overs for industrial films. He became the sought-after voice for TV and radio commercials. His bank account grew along with his prominence.

By the late 1980s, J.P. McCarthy had passed icon status on the way to legend. His failed forays into television as the host of his own interview shows were his only major disappointments in media and entertainment. His inability to score good ratings on local TV undoubtedly diminished his chances when he tried out yet again for the morning anchor slot on national broadcast television.

For his evening television interview show, he booked important and engaging guests. However, his audience apparently had one problem neither they nor McCarthy could overcome. The J.P. on the TV screen just didn't look like the J.P. that listeners had in their minds as they heard his mellow, distinctive voice over the radio airwaves. It would be his appearance, Joe told me once on an airplane flight into New York, that would hurt him in his quest of a network morning anchor role in a medium that often valued cosmetics above substance.

McCarthy was a good-looking man in a conventional rather

than a glamorous film star way. He carried baggage, he acknowl-edged grimly, in more ways than one. It seemed that no amount of makeup could mask the dark circles under his eyes. So on a TV screen he looked a bit like an affable Dracula. His TV show never developed an audience remotely the size of his radio following.

I was commuting weekly to New York in those days, and one time found myself sitting next to McCarthy in the first-class section of the Republic "noon balloon" flight. I wasn't in Joe's inner circle of close friends, but I knew him well because I had put many of my authors on his show and had done a few appearances or call-ins myself. Minutes before I got on the plane, I heard J.P.'s voice on a radio in the terminal, so I was taken aback for a moment to see him on the plane. Then I connected that what I had heard was a broad-cast of the *Focus Show* he had taped two hours earlier.

Joe quizzed me about how Ernie Harwell's *Tuned to Baseball* book was selling. He asked about other books I had a hand in pub-lishing—he easily extracted titles and authors from his legendary near-photographic memory banks. Our conversation was going like one of his studio interviews, so I turned the tables and asked him where he was off to. He said he was going to Manhattan for an audition at the headquarters of Capital Cities. He was "taking one last shot," he said, for the ABC *Good Morning, America* anchor role being vacated by its first host, David Hartman.

"I really don't expect to get it," Joe said, "But if I don't take a run at it, I know I'll always kick myself. I've tried out for I don't know how many morning-show anchor slots. I think maybe Cap Cities is letting me read just as a courtesy. It's a long shot but what the hell, if I didn't go for it, I'd always wonder."

As we talked, Joe kept looking at the meal on the tray the flight attendant had placed before me. In those days, the food on air-planes was actually edible and Joe had already devoured his as he talked. Finally, he asked if I was going to eat my sandwich and dessert; I said I wasn't and passed them over to him.

"Look at me," he said. "Here I am forty pounds overweight,

haven't tasted a thing I've just eaten. Now I'm eating your lunch and there you sit, lean as a one-iron. What's the hell is the matter with me? I don't know, I'm wound tighter than a Titleist."

Here was the most familiar and arguably the most influential voice in Detroit and Michigan, a highly respected professional radio personality, and he was as keyed up as a freshly minted college graduate interviewing for his first job. As prominent as Joe was, he knew that with his track record on TV he had good reason to be apprehensive. He wasn't surprised when Charles Gibson was selected.

A few weeks after we talked on that flight to New York, Joe called me and asked if I could meet him at Bloomfield Hills Country Club, where he was a member. He didn't say what it was about and I didn't ask him.

After we sat down to lunch, he handed me two typed sheets. I don't like to read someone's copy in front of them, for the same reason I would never sit there and watch while someone read mine. If the copy is good, that's fine. More often than not, it isn't and then one is in a very awkward position. If you are too kind about a text that isn't good, you lose your credibility. Also, if you're too diplomatic you raise hopes and run the risk that the person will go away thinking there is a chance you will offer a contract or open a door to another publisher. Conversely, if you really don't like the writing, it makes it impossible to have a pleasant conversation after you have had to express—no matter how delicately—that something that a person has labored over and cares deeply about just doesn't work for you.

Joe had put me in a can't-win situation. I was about to ask him if I could take the copy home and read it where I could concentrate without fear of interruption. Joe anticipated that and assured me he was "a big enough boy to take it if you don't like it, and I mean that." I reluctantly agreed to read it right then. Just then, fortunately, a friend of his called to him from a nearby table and he excused himself to sit at that table for a few minutes while I read.

I could tell before I finished the first page that Joe's writing was as good as his voice. When he returned and asked what I thought, I was relieved to be able to tell him it was very good.

"That's nice to hear, except for one thing. Please tell me how in the hell anybody can write an entire book. Doing those two pages was like tearing a pound of flesh off myself, which I admit I could easily spare, but that's another story."

He said he knew he could write well, that he was capable of doing a good book, but doubted that he could put up with the agony it would take to do it. He paused for a moment, then said he had one other problem. He had discussed with his lawyer the idea of doing a book and his lawyer told him it would have serious financial implications.

I didn't think that Joe was referring to royalties when he mentioned financial implications because I supposed any earnings from a book would be small change to him—he was almost undoubtedly the highest-paid on-air personality in the history of Detroit. Regardless, my partner Ron Monchak and I had already talked about royalties and had what we thought was a good idea for Joe to consider. Expecting Joe might have a book in mind, we had commissioned a mockup dust jacket for the book to show Joe the way we envisioned it. The centerpiece visual on the front cover featured a very journalistic, grainy black and white photograph of J.P. McCarthy wearing his customary headphones speaking into his WJR mic. Above the photo was the title we proposed for the book, "On the Other End of My Line..." That was his trademark expression to introduce whatever celebrity was calling in for an interview. I took the dummy cover out of my briefcase and laid that before him, along with a check for $25,000 made out to the Police Athletic League, his favorite charity for which he had raised enormous funds over the years.

"My partner, Ron Monchak, and I want you to know that as soon as your book comes off press, that check will go into the P.A.L. account, along with a guaranteed share of the proceeds from every book we sell. And we expect to sell a lot of them. All that assumes you're able to produce a manuscript we're all happy with."

Joe looked at the mockup and smiled.

"Nice cover. Really nice," he said. "That visual pretty well nails it, doesn't it? And the tie-in with P.A.L., that's a great idea. But I'm not sure I could produce something I'd want to have my name on. Even if I did, you know how lawyers are. My guy is adamant that I hold up on something like this until my on-air career is over. He's afraid if I do a book with any substance—which is the only kind I'd want to do—then my future possible guests would be leery about coming on my show after the book is out. You know, out of concern that I might carve them up later on in another book. That's what I meant about it being in part a financial issue."

He had a good point. But that posed a problem for my Momentum Books company. A great part of the attraction to a publisher in doing a book authored by an on-air figure or an active newspaper columnist is that the person has a continuing presence and a built-in promotional forum. J.P. McCarthy could write the identical book a year after retiring and it would sell only a fraction of the copies the same book would move had it appeared while he was still active. I knew from expensive experience how hard it was to promote a book when the author was someone who *used to be* someone. While I didn't envision McCarthy becoming a hermit after retirement, he certainly would lose much of his visibility and his prime forum the minute he walked away from the WJR microphone for the last time.

So we had struck a serious snag. I was sure J.P.'s lawyer wouldn't have a change of heart—it is not in the nature of lawyers to tell their clients, "Aw, what the heck. You only live once. Take a chance, do the book, maybe things will work out."

When I got back to the office I updated Monchak on the brick wall the McCarthy project had run into. On my list of candidate future projects for Momentum Books, I moved the J.P. McCarthy book into the "very doubtful" column.

—m—

I CONTINUED TO SEE JOE AS I PUT GUESTS ON HIS SHOW—writers, film actors, producers, musicians, artists and others who came into town to participate in my "Facets of Creativity" talk series. Joe seemed to especially enjoy guests I brought from the music and motion picture worlds, including songwriter Jimmy Webb ("By the Time I Get to Phoenix," "Wichita Lineman," and many others); Joe Raposo ("It's Not That Easy Bein' Green," Sing, Sing a Song," and the Sesame Street music he wrote); Sheldon Harnick (lyricist of *Fiddler on the Roof* and many other Broadway musicals); and Steven Bach (production chief of United Artists studios and an author).

It was also impossible to miss seeing McCarthy at charity events. Anyone organizing a fund-raiser in Michigan had two names at the top of the most-sought-after list: Ernie Harwell as featured speaker and J.P. McCarthy as master of ceremonies. If an invitation bore either of those names as being on the program, the event was virtually assured of a strong turnout.

For many years, I helped run the Gehringer-Kaline Meadow Brook Golf Classic, a fund-raiser to support Meadow Brook Hall and student athletes at Oakland University. The affection for Charlie Gehringer and the admiration for Al Kaline brought us strong support throughout the worlds of sport and business. From baseball came greats like home-run champion and Hall-of-Famer Hank Greenberg and Elden Auker, a star submarine-ball pitcher on the Tigers' 1935 World Series Championship team, along with Charlie and Hank. One-time catcher and well-known announcer Joe Garagiola was a featured speaker. Garagiola remarked that he looked up Charlie's amazing statistics and figured out that he could have caught up to Charlie in base hits if only he had played 84 more years. Baseball Commissioner Bowie Kuhn, popular umpire and author Ron Luciano, and many others took part.

For Charlie's eighty-fifth birthday, though, we wanted to do something very special. We arranged videotaped messages from George Kell, Al Kaline, and Ernie Harwell who were covering a Tigers road game. We had letters from Ted Williams and other base-ball greats and national celebrities. We had a taped video message from baseball commissioner Peter Uerberroth. And we had pro-duced a twenty-minute film I wrote, "*A Standing Ovation for Great-ness*," that recapped Charlie's careers on the diamond, as general manager of the Tigers, and in business and community life. But we needed two more coups to make it an evening that Charlie and the more than four hundred guests would never forget. One was to se-cure J.P. McCarthy as master of ceremonies. The other was a special salute from the nation's number one baseball fan, a former baseball announcer who had gone on to other pursuits, most notably to a leading role in the West Wing of the White House.

When it came to securing the involvement of J.P. McCarthy for an event, people in Detroit knew that the intervention of J.P.'s close friend, Joe Colucci, was invaluable. So omnipresent was Colucci in the marketing circles in Detroit that a popular comment was, "It's illegal to have an event in Detroit unless Joe Colucci is there." J.P. received so many requests and invitations that he often turned to Colucci to tell him which ones he should accept. Colucci told us J.P. had agreed to emcee our evening program, but cautioned that McCarthy was going to Moscow just days before the June event to broadcast from the Reagan-Gorbachev summit conference. J.P.'s secretary told us he was due back the day of the Gehringer event. However, there was no controlling whether the flight would be on time. She said we should have a backup ready to emcee, just in case.

The other special item took more doing but one-time Chicago Cubs announcer and then-President Ronald Reagan said he was delighted to be asked. He was very familiar with Charlie Gehring-er because he had done the play-by-play for the 1935 World Series between the Tigers and the Chicago Cubs. He said he would be pleased to sign a special proclamation and do a videotaped mes-sage—provided I wrote the script. He would have the message taped in the Oval Office. I told Howard Baker, the President's Chief of Staff, we would fax him the text in which the President would express his gratitude for Charlie's contributions that enriched so many communities. The President would also salute him for the dignity he brought to the game of baseball and every other dimension of his life.

So on a pleasant June evening, everything was ready in the huge Shotwell-Gustafson Pavilion at Meadow Brook Hall for a memorable program to begin at 6 p.m.—except that at 5:30 there was still no sign of J.P. McCarthy. But Joe had a reputation for living up to his commitments and sure enough, at 5:45 he arrived, sat down beside me and asked for the script. He had been up without sleep, he said, for almost two days, but when the house lights went down and the spotlight went up, he was on top of his game. Joe breezed through the program as if he had rehearsed it a dozen times. To him, it was just another day at the office.

—⁂—

OVER THE NEXT COUPLE OF YEARS, EVERY TIME I SAW JOE at a charitable event or a golf outing, he would bring up *our* book as if it were always top of mind with him. Whenever I walked into his studio with an author for an interview on his noontime *Focus* show, before I could introduce Joe to the author, he would greet me with "Billy Boy, we have got to get started on our book."

After that happened several times, I knew that Joe's talent at procrastination combined with the pain it caused him to sit down and write, and his lawyer's concerns, made it all but certain we would never get started on *our* book.

Then one day after a round of golf at Orchard Lake Country Club, Joe saw me in the men's locker room and asked if I would meet him in the grille room for a drink.

"How well do you know Joe Falls?" he said.

"Not real well. But well enough that he called me a couple months ago and asked me to have a look at two of his manuscripts, one a novel, one non-fiction. I took him to lunch at Indianwood so he could tell me more."

"How'd that go?"

"Well, he broke a tooth on a hard roll and that made him pretty cranky at first. Then I asked him about his manuscripts and he perked up. All authors say they want you to be candid, but when you are, if they don't like what they hear, it can be awkward. But Falls all but demanded candor. I told him some concepts sound interesting but the only thing that counts is whether a guy can make it happen on paper. Without reading a sample, there was no way I could guess whether his stuff had potential. It's one thing to write a five hundred-word column and something else again to write a hundred thousand-word book.

"I told Falls that at Momentum Books we don't publish novels, but he wanted my thoughts on it anyhow, so would I please look at it and give him an opinion. The next week I did that and had to tell him that in my opinion it was hopeless. He said the other book he hadn't really started yet but he hoped I'd be interested in that one when he was done. He told me what it was about, and that one might have a chance."

"Sounds like you don't consider him a close friend, then," J.P. said.

"No, I don't. Why?"

"That second manuscript, the non-fiction one, can I ask if that had anything to do with me?"

"No, it didn't. Not at all. It's a book of profiles and anecdotes about the hundred greatest sports figures of the last hundred years in America. I don't know how good Falls's text will be but if we publish it, I'll have Doug Parrish do original drawings to illustrate it. That will liven it up visually."

Joe seemed relieved to hear that so I asked him what was going on.

"Well, Falls got me off to the side the other night at an event I was emceeing," McCarthy said. "He told me he wanted to do a book about me. You know he did one on Schembechler a while back. Bo was not thrilled with the experience. Now here is Falls telling me he's going to do a book on me either with my cooperation or without it."

I didn't like the sound of that and could understand why J.P. was concerned. He had many friends and from all walks of life. Like many entertainment people, he might have had friends and acquaintances who were on the edge of conventional society. He raised lots of money for lots of charities and it would not be unusual if some contributions came from well-heeled people who might be considered shady characters. McCarthy went on to tell me his concern that any book Falls might do would focus on whatever gossip he could dig up that might appeal to salacious appetites.

"So I wanted you to be aware, Billy," Joe said, "that I told Falls I was already committed to doing a book with you. I hope you're okay with that."

A good thing J.P. gave me that heads-up. A week later Falls called to talk about the non-fiction manuscript I had critiqued for him. I told him we would publish it at Momentum Books if he could produce the manuscript he envisioned. He was delighted and said he agreed completely with my suggestions. He would re-work the manuscript and knew he had a lot of work to do.

"By the way," Falls said, "when we had lunch at Indianwood you didn't mention you were working with J.P. McCarthy on a book. That's something I had been meaning to get going on for at least the last five years. But since you're already onto it, I'll have to cross it off my list. Guess I should have moved on it when I had the chance."

I told Falls he would have plenty enough to keep him busy with his traveling, writing columns for *The News*, and working on his book on sports greats.

The next day, I talked with my partner Ron Monchak about our chances for doing a J.P. McCarthy book in light of these developments with Joe Falls. If J.P. continued to be concerned that Falls might do a book, wouldn't that make him more inclined to produce a manuscript himself? That would improve our chances.

But if we told him that we knew Falls had given up on the project because he thought J.P. was already committed to working with me, then J.P. would relax and probably never do a book himself. Ron and I agreed it was an easy decision.

I called Joe and told him I had heard from Falls.

"Uh-oh," he said. "Am I going to like what comes next?"

"Well, I can tell you Falls left no doubt he was dropping the idea of doing a J.P. McCarthy book."

On the other end of my line, I could hear a sigh of relief.

"Thanks for that, Billy," J.P. said. "Matter of fact, just the other day I was looking at that dust jacket mockup you gave me. You and I have to get together one of these days and get started on our book. I'll give you a call."

I told Monchak that McCarthy and I had talked and that he was obviously greatly relieved.

"I'm glad for him," Ron said. "With J.P.'s visibility and all his connections, any book with his name on would sell a lot of copies. But I'll bet that's one manuscript that will never get written."

And it never was. In spring 1995, Joe was diagnosed with myelodysplastic syndrome, a very rare disorder. Although hundreds of people came forward to volunteer their bone marrow for transplant, none matched J.P.'s rare type. Like many of Joe's friends, I got rejected.

On August 16, 1995, the J.P. McCarthy version of the great voice of the Great Lakes was silenced forever.

It was the first time a local funeral in Detroit was televised live by two stations and carried live on WJR. It was officiated by a Cardinal and attended by two bishops.

"For 30 years," said national radio personality Paul Harvey, "Detroiters have gone to work smiling, listening to J.P. McCarthy on WJR. Detroit is mourning this morning."

Paul Harvey was right about that. I mourned the loss of Joe McCarthy. I mourned also for the loss of his legacy, the J.P. McCarthy stories that never made it to print.

"You don't get hired to do those stories—you just do them. Because people need to know about them."

"Everything I've gotten into has led to something else— the job as a press photographer introduced me to some people in entertainment and the arts who became subjects and friends. My political involvement in turn led me down unexpected roads... We did everybody—Rosa Parks, Stevie Wonder, Smokey Robinson, and even Berry Gordy's dad, Pops Gordy."

"Art is not my specialty," she insists. Yet she has done several films centering on art or artists, including her Academy Award documentary, Young at Heart.

7

FROM A BROWNIE TO AN OSCAR

Sue Marx—Telling Timeless Stories with Film

"HOORAY FOR MICHIGAN!" For many who watched the Oscar presentations for 1987 films, it still reverberates in memory as "the shout."

The Sue Marx cry of triumph echoed throughout the state and around the Great Lakes and was heard everywhere in the world people were tuned into the annual gala of the Academy of Motion Picture Arts and Sciences.

It was an Oscar day for Michigan and Marx was not about to let the opportunity pass. It was a time for celebration. For acknowledgment. For thanks.

But at least one grumpy person in Michigan was not pleased.

Detroit Mayor Coleman Young chastised Sue Marx for her exuberant, "Hooray for Michigan!" as she held up the Oscar she and Pamela Conn had just won for their poignant documentary film, *Young at Heart.* Political considerations, for once, at least, had nothing to do with it. Longtime Michigan filmmaker Marx indeed did, have her offices in Detroit. Her long list of Detroit-related credits proved she had a powerful affinity for the city. She set that aside because she was determined to share a special moment with a broader audience. So she took that rare opportunity in the spotlight to acknowledge the people of the state she had served for many years with a succession of outstanding films. Marx's "Hooray!" saluted

the people and organizations throughout Michigan who had supported her along the way.

Shoulda said "Hooray for Detroit," the cantankerous mayor
grumbled.

"Yeah, Mr. Mayor," said Marx, "but the words Hollywood and
Michigan each have three syllables and Detroit has only two!"

As big a rush as it was to produce a film that won nationwide
acclaim and honors from colleagues in the film industry, *Young at
Heart* was but one of hundreds of Marx's productions. As huge as
the Oscar night audience in Michigan was, it may not have been
her largest. Uncountable millions have seen or will see Marx's special films produced for targeted audiences. One of her subsequent
projects, *The Relaxation Station*, for example, became a life-changing
experience for countless thousands of children, their parents, and
their caregivers.

The two-hour DVD produced by Sue Marx Films gives children the skills they need to manage stress and anxiety, especially
kids who are facing painful or stressful medical procedures in hos-
pitals. As she has done with so many productions, Marx has wo-
ven many threads into a tapestry in which every element blends
with and embellishes the others. Majestic and yet restful wildlife
scenes, soothing music, and a gentle voice-over of guided breath-
ing exercises calm the young patients and lessen their worries. Not
surprisingly, the film has the same tension-easing effect on viewers young or old, ailing or well. The film was originally created by
Marx and her associate Allyson Rockwell for The Children's Hospital of Michigan. The DVD found an ever-expanding audience in
other settings, including schools, medical waiting rooms, and long-
term care homes for the elderly, and with special-needs children,
particularly those with autism.

Although her portfolio is as broad as it is deep, one common
element is found in all Marx's work. She is first, last and always
a storyteller. Some of her subjects are technical, some historical.
Some are political, others deeply personal. Many of her projects

grow out of her own ideas and priorities in life. Some are brought to her by clients or underwriters. Whatever the subject, she immerses herself in it until she has absorbed its essence. Again and again, colleagues mention her unrelenting determination to understand a subject's relevance to its particular audience. Before filming begins, she knows what she wants to communicate, what emotion she wants to trigger, what results she wants to achieve. Everything in the production—the camera angles, the dialogue or narration, the music, the lighting—is chosen and tweaked to achieve those ends. Some of Marx's creativity comes into play at the outset, but some is achieved only after countless hours of editing and post-production work.

"Sue has an incredible visual sense," says Chris Cook, president of Metrocom International Inc. "She has a unique talent to tell a story in images tastefully at the highest levels of quality. Her film products have a delicacy to them."

Cook is founder and president of his own film production company, based in Ann Arbor, where he has done many highly acclaimed and award-winning projects for a range of clients including the University of Michigan and Michigan State University. On his very first film project, he was awed to find that he would be writing a script for an Academy Award-winning producer. "Sue Marx has had an influence on everything I've done since that first project years ago," he says. "Every project I get involved in, I always think, 'How would Sue do this?' When she sees my work, she's generous with praise, when it's merited, but she's also not timid about asking, 'Why did you do it that way?'"

A Marx trademark is attention to detail but she is anything but methodical in attacking a project. She doesn't choose a subject, then make a detailed scene-by-scene outline, proceed to storyboards, and work through the standard progression of many film producers. She knows what interests her intellectually, what excites her emotionally, and what she considers worth pouring her energies and resources into. A project for Wayne State's Math Corps is typical.

"I heard a story about a summer camp at Wayne State called the Math Corps and it's free," Marx says. "Every summer, Steve Kahn and Leonard Boehm, two math professors at the University, get about four hundred inner-city kids coming to camp—these are seventh, eighth and ninth graders. They keep coming back every summer and some of the tenth, eleventh and twelfth graders who are learning advanced math become mentors to the younger kids. Though the program is free, the older kids who take advanced math are paid a stipend to become teaching assistants during the six weeks. It's like military basic training. There are strict and specific rules they must abide by. The kids aren't allowed to be late or miss a class or miss handing in their homework every day. But here, they are respected and, in turn, show respect to one another. When these kids first come into the camp, they're scoring in the lower 20 percentile. Six weeks later, they're scoring in the high 80s, low 90s. Later on, 90 percent of them are graduating from high school and 85 percent are going on to college."

After hearing about this camp that had been in business for more than ten years, Marx was dismayed that not many people seemed to know about it. She knew then that she had to find a way to tell this story in film.

"I had no choice," she says. "In the summer of 2006, I started raising money to do this film myself, on my own time, in my own way. At first I thought 'Let's just do a portrait of this camp, watch the kids going through this experience.' But along the way, we see something else—we see that these kids have become a family. You know, these kids go there and they're not looking just to learn math—they're looking for family. The older ones who have been through the program come back and become older brothers for the youngers. They become mentors. The professors become father figures. And there's a college assistant who was probably there fourteen years ago as a student himself and he becomes the older brother and he's mentoring the kid under him who's probably still in high school. That one in turn has become an older brother to the kid in the seventh grade who's just starting.

"I talk about the boys, but of course there are girls in the program too. But the boys really need it because so many don't have father figures in their life. So the film has taken an unexpected turn, gone in a different direction than I originally thought it would go. It's a richer story now because we have met the most amazing young men and women."

As Professor Kahn continues to say, "All kids have greatness in them and they discover their greatness at camp."

Education, politics, health, government, art, sports, nature, entertainment, a seemingly endless list—Marx has produced films on these subjects and profiled the men and women involved in them. "I don't have a specialty," she says. "Health is not my specialty." But she has produced many films on various dimensions of health and health care. A project on the heart pump sponsored by General Motors and Harper Hospital won an Emmy Award. Another honored film was *The New Normal,* a production intended to give hope to people facing a bone marrow transplant.

"Art is not my specialty," she insists. Yet she has done several films centering on art or artists, including her Academy Award documentary, *Young at Heart.*

One constant in her various personal careers as fashion model, teacher, journalistic photographer, and film producer has been collegiality. She speaks with fervor about the help she has gotten from others who were there before her. She discovered early on how much she enjoyed the relationships she developed with scriptwriters, sound technicians and cameramen. She picked up tricks of the trade from others—film directors, actors, musicians, and the behind-the-scenes crews.

"I don't like working alone," she says. "I always have somebody working with me on my films. Maybe it's because I'm not sure enough about myself or maybe it's that when I try to do something alone I second-guess myself too much. I need somebody to tell me it's done or it's okay or maybe you should go in that direction. Film is so collaborative and my crews are so responsive and want to be included in the whole process. I can't imagine how my films would come out if the rest of the people on the project didn't participate so freely."

Curiously, although Marx admits to obsessing about every detail of a production, no one who has worked with her thinks of her as a micro-manager. In talking about Marx, the words that are used most frequently are "mentor, collaborator, teacher, partner and team leader."

Char DeWolf was hired by Marx "right out of college to do whatever needed doing so I could learn from someone who was always teaching and always enthused about people who share her passion," DeWolf says. "She made me her equal and called me her co-producer and together we won eight Emmys. Sue is always sure of herself and her skills but never takes the spotlight. She is so proud to celebrate your success with you. She is also so politically aware and takes seriously a responsibility to contribute to making this a better world."

There is a common progression for those who work with Marx: interns become assistants, then co-producers and colleagues. Many protégés emerge later in her life as clients, collaborators or friendly competitors. And all of them she cherishes as friends.

Usually her own values and interests determine what projects she will take on and how she will approach them, but not infrequently she gets surprised. Sports is not her métier. The atmosphere in which she grew up exalted the aesthetic, not the athletic. But when she heard about a group of young athletes on a quest, she was hooked.

So for a film called *Watermark*, underwritten by the Ford Fund, Marx and DeWolf followed five young Detroit-area swimmers through their training, culminating in four doing well enough to try out for the Olympics. "I don't follow sports myself, but this was really a great story about much more than winning and losing," Marx says, "What it was really about was commitment. You don't get hired to do those stories—you just do them. Because people need to know about them."

"What added to the project," Marx noted, "was that one of the five swimmers was Char's son."

Many of Marx's films were born of chance encounters. Often someone she meets or something she learns while doing one film triggers an opportunity or holds the seed of an idea for a new project. Marx's entire career, in fact, is a testament to the truism that when one door closes behind you, another opens to lead into a new room full of surprises and unexpected possibilities.

"Everything I've gotten into has led to something else—the job as a press photographer introduced me to some people in entertainment and the arts who became subjects and friends. My political involvement in turn led me down unexpected roads. We stayed in Detroit so many years—before, during and after the riots of 1967. Not moving to the suburbs as nearly all my friends did in those days led to a different kind of life, different relationships, as well as fresh challenges and opportunities."

Marx traveled a circuitous route to find her home, career, and a full and good family life in Michigan. Born in New York of Russian immigrant parents, Louis and Leona Gothelf, she spent much of her childhood on the road as her father—a scenic artist—went to wherever jobs were available as a set designer with traveling theater companies. He also did commissioned portraits. Her mother was the breadwinner. She had a strong business sense and handled the family's financial matters, as well as dealing in real estate. Both parents had strongly artistic temperaments and tastes "so there was no baseball, playing cards, or anything trivial, frivolous or mindlessly fun," Marx says.

By the time Marx was a teenager, the family had settled in East Chicago, Indiana, where Marx finished high school before enrolling in Indiana University in Bloomington. There, she earned a degree in language arts, thinking she would teach English and journalism. Instead of going directly into teaching, she decided she wanted to live in Chicago, just a 25-minute train ride from home. She got a job as a writer at a Chicago advertising agency and when she told her mother she wanted to move there rather than ride a commuter train every day, her mother responded, "Nice girls don't live by themselves in a big city." So much for the Windy City.

When Marx felt she "couldn't live in East Chicago a day longer," she moved to Detroit, where she lived with a favorite aunt and uncle. She got a teaching job and shortly thereafter met and married Hank Marx, "the love of my life," she says. Marx owned a metal-refining company but was a man of many dimensions and interests, a perfect match for Sue. While teaching and raising a family, and at the urging of her husband, she began graduate work at Wayne State University, interrupting it three times for the birth of her three daughters.

"When I was at Indiana University," she says, "I thought I was just going to teach school, get married, and some day have kids. To get a permanent teaching certificate you had to have a Masters Degree, but I realized that teaching wasn't really where I was going so I got my M.A. in social psychology."

About the same time, a good friend who was a very successful model suggested that Marx might want to try it. It was a natural step for the graceful and strikingly attractive Marx to turn to modeling; it would become an activity Marx would be involved in for years, eventually including her own children being booked for jobs.

"I wasn't really, really lean or that glamorous but it was fun and I loved to watch the photographers work. George Kawamoto was one of the photographers that allowed me into the darkroom to watch. Before long I was hooked.

"I had this little Brownie camera that took fuzzy pictures of the kids, but I had fun with it so Hank bought me a twin lens reflex camera. I took a photography class and not long after that I started really shooting—even won a national photography award for one of my pictures. That gave me the nerve to set up shop as a photojournalist."

Marx partnered with the late Marj Levin and together they created many stories for various newspapers and magazines. "We did a cover story on bachelors for the *Detroit Free Press Magazine* and John Conyers was one of them. That was about the same time I got involved in Democratic Party politics. Soon, I was doing stuff for various political candidates, working with the media, shooting pictures for campaigns and political materials. I became a precinct delegate and was even elected as a member of the Democratic State Central Committee."

Before long, Marx was taking assignments from national magazines. One day she might shoot actress-comedienne Imogene Coca, the next it could be flamboyant restaurant critic Gael Greene. "It was cool," she says, "I did lots and lots of portraits and met lots and lots of people."

As happened so often for Marx, one thing led to another. She got involved in creating fund-raising events for Conyers' campaigns. That introduced her to many entertainers, jazz musicians and celebrities who were good friends of the congressman, including Harry Belafonte, Bill Cosby, Nancy Wilson and many others.

Her reputation now growing quickly and strongly, she was hired by WWJ-TV, Detroit's Channel 4. In the late 1960s, she pitched an idea to the station for a talk show with a black host. The show's concept was similar to the format used much later by hosts such as Jay Leno and David Letterman. Her concept stirred interest but stalled until a similar idea was proposed by a freelance black producer. "I think they were a little nervous about having a black producer, but they already knew me and we had already done a pilot for the show I was pitching," Marx said. "They offered us something like a hundred dollars a week and so nothing happened then. But about two years later, they came to me and said they had an idea for a show called *Profiles in Black* and wanted me to do it."

Now the timing was right. It was two years after the Detroit race riot of 1967. "The show started in 1970," Marx said. "Gil Maddox was the host and we did everything on location. I did location scouting, pre-interviews, still shots for the ads, and all scheduling.

We did everybody—Rosa Parks, Stevie Wonder, Smokey Robinson, and even Berry Gordy's dad, Pops Gordy. Steve was still living on Santa Rosa with his mom."

Over the next several years, Marx did indeed profile "just about everybody. We did big people and ordinary folks," she says. "Anybody with a story worth telling."

It was a heady but grueling exercise.

"We shot on film, double system, filming our interview subjects on Tuesdays and Thursdays on location—in their homes, their place of work, the streets. Then we would come to the station on Saturday and edit all day. On Monday we'd transfer it to tape and put the show together for airing on Tuesday at 7:30 p.m. We did hundreds of these shows, two stories in a thirty-minute show every week, showing up with all that equipment to their place of work, their home, meeting their husband or wife, kids, co-workers and friends. We caused quite a stir in the neighborhoods and around town—huge cameras, gigantic mobile vans with large cables running from the truck into people's homes."

In the mid and late '70s, the city and the station became increasingly concerned about black-white relations. The show changed in character, becoming a studio show with more emphasis on discussion of issues and less on personalities. Not incidentally, it was also much cheaper to do a studio show. The new format was more sedate, less vibrant and edgy.

"I was getting fidgety and bored at Channel 4 and knew it was time to move on," Marx says. "I had a good friend who was on the board of an arts organization and I told her 'Every year you give out awards to Michigan artists. Wouldn't it be nice to do a film portrait of one of them at work?' She said, 'Give me a proposal and I'll take it to my board.'"

Earlier, while working at Channel 4, Marx had taken several production classes at Wayne State and had done a student film which she had shown it to Jerry Trainor, the program director at Channel 56, WTVS. "It was really pathetic technically," Marx acknowledges. "But Jerry said, 'It's good! You can make films, so go do it, just make films.' And so I started writing grant proposals."

Marx's first proposal was approved and she went on to make seven more films with funding from the Arts Foundation of Michigan and Michigan Council for the Arts. Her first film featured the internationally renowned ceramicist John Glick. It promptly won several awards. Another film focused on the Attic Theatre and still another was on John Voelker, the Michigan judge whose pen name was Robert Traver. Voelker wrote the novel *Anatomy of a Murder*, later made into a classic movie by Otto Preminger, the first really major feature film shot in Michigan.

The film that brought Marx to national prominence is an example of how she often lets the story come to her once filming has begun. Marx always begins with a good feel for the tone of the film. What she doesn't always know is precisely how she will get there. For that she has learned to trust instincts born of hundreds of productions. This is precisely what happened on a project that started out to be nothing more than a small film.

Several years after the death of her mother, Marx learned that her eighty-four-year-old father was "keeping company" with Reva Shwayder, another widowed artist in her eighties whom he had met on a painting trip to England. Here were two engaging, creative souls who had so much in common to share with each other and yet so much fresh and new to bring into the other's life. Age was no barrier—it was truly a story of young love. Marx began to sense a very special story that would touch the hearts of an audience. She began the arduous task of fund-raising so that this love story could be told.

As all could see as the filming progressed, the courtship brought a new verve to the two octogenarians and, it seemed, to everyone around them. When they announced that they were planning to marry, Marx had a perfect ending—and a problem. Reva announced that she didn't want to have a camera crew in cutoffs and jeans at their beautiful garden wedding. That obstacle was overcome with a promise that the cameraman and soundman would be properly dressed. Reva relented.

There was only one right title for the documentary—*Young at Heart.* And Marx somehow managed to get the rights without fee to use George Burns's rendition of the song.

The voters in the Academy of Motion Picture Arts and Sciences were as smitten with the poignant documentary as were the audiences—Sue Marx had an Oscar to add to a shelf now crowded with statuettes, plaques and trophies.

As Marx's reputation grew, she was in great demand for work in the political arena, art and entertainment, and public service, as well as projects for a broad range of corporations, organizations and causes. One week she might be doing a political campaign film for Dennis Archer in his run for mayor of Detroit. The next, she might be on a project for the Detroit Institute of Arts or General Motors. She created spots for Michigan's sesquicentennial, Detroit's bicentennial, the Convention Bureau, and for the Super Bowl. She did a fund-raising film for Jeff Daniels and his Purple Rose Theatre Company. And the rebirth of The Fox Theatre called *Encore on Woodward*, narrated by Bob Hope. She has made ten award-winning films for the Detroit Zoo with narrations by Daniels, Tim Allen, James Earl Jones, Julie Harris, Robert Wagner, and Leigh Taylor-Young.

Typical of her long-standing priority for helping children, *Just for Kids* was an illuminating tour of Children's Hospital.

For a change of pace, she went to Colon, Michigan, for a whimsical documentary on the tiny town and its annual gathering of magicians for the *National Geographic Explorer* television series. Magic and magicians had always fascinated Marx, so she brought a great deal of experience and a keen eye to the project. The film, titled *"It's Magic!"*, featured Harry Blackstone Jr. and was broadcast on WTVS. Blackstone and his father—the original Great Blackstone, magician and illusionist—are both buried in Colon, the home of Abbott Magic, a famed producer of tricks for magicians.

Just as lengthy as her filmography is Marx's list of people she credits for teaching, counseling, nudging or cajoling her along her various career paths. No surprise then that Marx places great stock in mentoring and passing along what she has learned.

"There aren't enough people who keep the creative vitality alive and growing," says Christina Lovio-George, who owns and manages her own boutique public relations agency in Detroit. "But Sue never hesitates to give the young bucks a crack at learning from her and that's a huge contribution. My son is just one of many who has learned from Sue. He adores her and marvels over how in all her work she homes in on the very essence of her subject."

Lovio-George says Marx has a passion for doing projects that are important and insightful and doing them at the highest level of quality. Those are crucial ingredients for "someone in a real pioneering role," Lovio-George says. "There simply were no females doing the things that Sue did so very well, right at the outset. From the start, she was not only doing her own jobs, she was always working to improve the city to make it a better place, before the riot of 1967 and even more post-riot."

In 2001, Lovio-George worked with Marx on a project that began as a single public service announcement but grew into a series of ads featuring Stevie Wonder, among other entertainers and celebrities. That work was honored with an Emmy. The team of Marx and Lovio-George won a second Emmy for their productions for the Super Bowl.

But as productive as Marx has been for several decades, she says, "I'm busier now than I've ever been. Maybe that's in part because I'm my own secretary and bill-payer in contrast to the days I was on Woodbridge, next door to the Renaissance Center, or my offices in Royal Oak, where I had full-time support. I've always had great college interns who are wizards at the technical stuff I don't know much about."

While Marx is generous with her time with protégés, interns and younger colleagues, she finds that for many tasks, it is easier to do some things herself. "The older I get, the less complicated I want my life to be," she says. "And bringing someone in, showing them what they have to do, sometimes by the time I get done explaining, it's easier just to do it myself."

But Marx doesn't see herself ever becoming a lone operator. She has worked in teams virtually her entire career in film production and has come to believe that is the only way she can be truly effective. "I'm good at second-guessing. Even if I could do it all myself, I just don't want to because I don't think the product would be as good. I need to bounce ideas off others, and react to and maybe build on what they bring to the table."

Because of her extensive roster of high-quality, successful productions, Marx is in a position to turn down opportunities that don't excite her." I like what I'm doing and the pace I'm doing it at," she says.

She knows that every project she takes on will be at the cost of something else she then won't have time or resources to do. She chooses projects that interest her personally, that present a fresh challenge, and that she thinks "will be fun to do." With her long-time associate producer Allyson Rockwell, she took on a project on Alzheimer's Disease; a series of films on architecture for Cranbrook; and a promotional video for the Detroit Riverfront Conservancy.

Marx's work has made a significant contribution to a film industry in Michigan that is among the largest, most profitable, and highest quality in America. One reason for the prominence of Detroit and Michigan in film is its stature as a leading market in advertising, particularly in radio and television spots for the automobile industry and other major national advertisers. To support commercial production there is an abundance—and frequently an over-supply—of talent and resource. Film producers like Marx draw freely from this pool at advertising agencies and their service organizations, as well as freelance writers, photographers, talent agencies, and technical specialists.

In 2011, the Traverse City Film Festival honored Marx for her many major and lasting contributions to Michigan's film industry by naming her "Michigan Filmmaker of the Year."

—∿—

WITH SUCH ILLUSTRIOUS CAREER, it remains an open question whether Sue Marx is changed by what she photographs any more than the people, issues and subjects are changed by her. Almost invariably, something seems to happen in the process of her making a film. At some point, there comes a clarity, a sharpening of focus that deepens her understanding and enables her to see clearly how best to tell the story. The result is a story powerfully told on film and an indelible impression on the filmmaker that will stay with her and influence whatever comes next.

"She has this special knack for finding just the right ingredient—the perfect music or voice, whatever it takes—to make a project come to life," says Lovio-George.

It is a touch that can be seen not only in Marx's own productions but also in a generation of film producers influenced by her. Many producers, directors and writers credit Marx as the person without whom they may never have gotten into the field and certainly without whom they feel they never would have learned the techniques that have made them successful.

Chris Cook was a newspaper reporter for more than 20 years, including a stint as an investigative reporter on a team at *Newsday* that won a Pulitzer Prize for a series on heroin traffic. His Emmys include a one-hour documentary on the early history of television, much of which was created in Detroit, for WXYZ-TV, Channel 7 for its fiftieth anniversary. His award-winning documentary, "*Dying for a Drink,* examined the dangers and social ramifications of teen binge drinking.

"Before I was fortunate to meet Sue Marx, I was struggling with a career change," Cook says. "I had left the *Free Press* during the strike. I identified documentary film as an area that made sense for me but had no idea how to get into it. The UAW was doing a piece on Doug Fraser, a celebration of his life, and needed a scriptwriter to work with an Academy Award-winning film producer. Sue probably rolled her eyes when she found out she had to work with me. But the film turned out famously and Sue became my mentor in my career conversion and a collaborator in many more projects since then."

Marx has won many awards for her films, yet she seems most pleased and grateful with three outcome that have nothing to do with her own professional achievements. First, she takes great pleasure in the successes of her protégés and the ever-lengthening list of interns, assistants and colleagues who have gone on to successful careers. Second, she is delighted that she can say of the artists she photographed or profiled in film, "Every one of these artists whose lives I invaded for a short period of time became a friend."

Finally, the production that has brought her the greatest satisfaction is her family. Her late husband Hank—to whom Marx seldom refers without adding, "the love of my life"—supported her in every endeavor. It was Hank who brought her the Brownie camera that opened the door to an exciting career. Their three daughters have gone on to fulfilling professional careers—the oldest is a pediatrician, the middle is a lawyer, and the youngest is a glass artist.

Marx gave her three daughters an early introduction to two of Detroit's most prominent and beloved citizens. When they were very young, Marx took them with her to Congressman John Conyers' office in Detroit where they helped his longtime receptionist, Rosa Parks, stuff campaign literature into mailing envelopes.

Her family, her work and her many very good friends have helped keep Michigan's outstanding filmmaker Sue Marx "young at heart."

In 1974, when Bill Davidson led a group that bought
vacant land in Auburn Hills, Michigan, no one could
envision what the complex would evolve into.
Then, with entirely private funding, Davidson's group
built what would become the premier sports and
entertainment center in the United States.

No, it did not last forever. The exhilarating ascents were
punctuated by precipitous declines. But the proprietors
of the Palace pulled off amazing accomplishments that
stamped them indelibly in the record books
and in the memories of Detroit Pistons fans.

8

STORMING THE PALACE

Joe Dumars, Tom Wilson, Bill Davidson—
Layups, Leadership and Legacies

IT'S RARE WHEN IT HAPPENS ONCE. Fans of the Chicago Cubs have been simmering in a stew of impatience since 1908 for a second crown. Dedicated followers of the Detroit Lions have been biding their time with not quite the patience of Job since 1955.

Championships in professional sports are savored precisely because they are the banquet that requires the perfect ingredients, preparation, and presentation. Top honors go almost exclusively to the franchise with the whole menu: committed management, brilliant coaching and a team of players to whom individual statistics are nothing and winning is everything.

That is why it is so rare when three individuals are able to reach such heights not once, not twice, but three times, which is precisely what Bill Davidson, Tom Wilson and Joe Dumars did. Not only that, Davidson and Wilson reached the pinnacle in not one or two, but three professional sports.

No, it did not last forever. The exhilarating ascents were punctuated by precipitous declines. But the proprietors of The Palace pulled off amazing accomplishments that stamped them indelibly in the record books and in the memories of Detroit Pistons fans. In the process, they created an entirely new brand of basketball that put a capital "D" on Defense and a premium on every basket.

It began, of course, with the building of the preeminent sports and entertainment facility in Auburn Hills, Michigan, the brain-child of Bill Davidson, orchestrated into reality by Tom Wilson. The next major milestone was the savvy acquisition of talent to put on the court.

"The Palace building itself represented a leap of faith," said Wilson. In 1974, when Davidson led a group that bought vacant land in Auburn Hills, Michigan, no one could envision what the complex would evolve into. Then, with entirely private funding, Davidson's group built what would become the premier sports and entertainment center in the United States. The pioneering architec-tural design, which features multiple tiers of luxury suites, became the inspiration and model for many arenas and event venues.

As glittering as The Palace was—hosting a steady stream of world-class entertainers and performers—it would be several years before the basketball team would achieve a quality level be-fitting their new home arena.

In the early 1980s, when the Pistons were mired in mediocrity, the team's general manager, Jack McCloskey, drafted several play-ers who would become key building blocks for the woebegone franchise: Kelly Tripuka, Isiah Thomas, Dennis Rodman and a qui-et kid from Louisiana by way of McNeese State, Joe Dumars.

Dumars' success in basketball seems all the more surprising, considering that it was not his best sport in high school.

"When I was a kid growing up in Natchitoches, outside of Shreveport, we had pretty strong competition and well-organized athletic programs," Dumars said. "There were no video games, no Internet, and all the parents I knew told the kids to get out of the house and do something. I bowled and played tennis at an early age. My favorite sport was whatever the season was. Football was easily my best sport all the way through high school. Basketball was definitely third after baseball."

Given Dumars' work ethic and a hunger to have his hands on the ball and be where the action was, it is no surprise that he played catcher in baseball and running back and defensive back in football.

But in the 1980s, stockpiling talented but comparatively shorter draft selections like Dumars was not enough to make the Pistons winners. So, over the next few years, "Trader Jack" McCloskey beefed up his roster by swapping for height and heft. He dealt for Bill Laimbeer, Vinnie Johnson, James Edwards and Mark Aguirre. He also plucked additional draft picks such as John Salley who would play key roles in the coming championship years.

By 1983, Davidson had concluded that McCloskey was assembling a competitive roster but a key ingredient was missing. He needed a coach who could fully tap the team's skilled but independent personalities. It would require someone with a firm but deft touch to rein in this wild bunch and get them pulling together toward a shared goal.

Chuck Daly, the recently deposed coach of the chaotic Cleveland Cavaliers, was perhaps the only coach in the country capable of extracting maximum performances out of such volatile personalities. Daly was hired and would preside over the Pistons for nine years, a longevity seldom seen in professional basketball. He produced back-to-back championships in 1989-90 and 1990-91 and drove his team to near misses three other years. At the pinnacle of his tenure, the Detroit Pistons were arguably the League's most-feared team. When Daly and I met over lunch at Ginopolis Restaurant to talk about him authoring a book, he told me he attributed much of that success to Joe Dumars.

In Dumars' rookie year, the team was 4-15 before he became a starter. Then, with him in the starting five lineup, the team surged to a 20-4 run.

That was a sign of what was to come in a brilliant 14-year playing career. Dumars was selected to the All-Star team six times, and four times was named to the All-Defensive first team. His contributions went far beyond mere numbers, yet he recorded 16,401 points, 4,612 assists, 2,203 rebounds, and 902 steals. He was the only Piston ever to wear the jersey No. 4; it was retired in 2000. Michael Jordan called him the best defensive player he ever faced.

In a playing career jammed with high points, there was none loftier than his performance in the 1989 NBA Finals. That brilliant all-around effort not only led his team to a sweep of the heavily favored Los Angeles Lakers, it also triggered the disintegration and prompt dismantling of the west coast's glamour team.

The versatility of Dumars, his uncanny ability to be in the right place and make the right play, was crystallized in one shining moment with Game 3 on the line. Although Dumars had scored 31 points, including 17 in the third quarter, the game was still in doubt with five seconds to play when Dumars made the play that would forever define his career. As the potential game-tying shot was in the air, Dumars seemingly flew from nowhere to block it. Not only that, in the same motion, he also flicked the ball back in bounds to a teammate. That play sealed the victory.

"Defense, work ethic, peer pressure, unity," wrote Shelby Strother, *Detroit News* columnist. "These were the hammers and wrenches in the Pistons' toolbox. Has any team ever played with so much mental toughness and intensity? Can any other team that ever played in the NBA ever insist seriously that throughout the entire season they conceded nothing, contested everything—every shot, every loose ball, every rebound?"

In a surprise to no one who had seen one of the greatest performances in NBA Finals history, in a unanimous vote Dumars was named the playoff's Most Valuable Player. Once again, he was lauded for contributions far beyond his 27.3 scoring average, and 57.6 percent shooting average. Only after the game did Dumars learn that his father, Joe Dumars II, had died an hour and a half before the game.

Of the player who had just defeated his Lakers, losing coach Pat Riley said simply, "He's a guy who can do it all."

The low-key Dumars summed it up with characteristic under-statement in Eli Zaret's outstanding book, *Blue Collar Blueprint: How the Pistons Constructed Their Championship Formula.*

"We did what we had to do to win the championship... I've been out of the game four years now and still haven't really looked at any of the games or highlights of the Finals. Interestingly enough, my son is thir-teen and I often find him in his room looking at tapes of our old games. It's fascinating for him—and I've walked in the room and watched him watch it for about five minutes and it's, 'Oh yeah, I remember that.' I think some psychiatrist could probably have a field day with me. But I feel that if I go back and watch it, it's almost like it's over or something— like I've finalized it."

Whether or not Dumars has by now finalized in his own mind his playing career, the League took steps to ensure that the class and dignity with which he played the game would endure in the form of the "Joe Dumars Trophy."

Winning a pair of NBA championships may have been enough to satisfy most owners, but Davidson was determined that a for-mula successful in one arena should be transferable to another.

Davidson had a lifelong interest in sports. He was an athlete in high school and played sports while earning a Bachelor's de-gree in business administration from the University of Michigan and a juris doctorate degree from Wayne State University. He methodically built a stable of industrial businesses and as they thrived, he extended his reach into new realms—sports, events and entertainment.

When Davidson acquired the Tampa Bay Lightning of the Na-tional Hockey League in 1999, it had been called the worst franchise in pro sports by *Forbes* magazine, having lost hundreds of millions of dollars for its previous two owners while performing dismally on the ice. Davidson named Tom Wilson as president with a charge to turn the wreck around.

Detroit-born Wilson had gone to Cass Tech and Wayne State before going to Hollywood where he acted in television sit-coms before returning to Michigan and being hired by Davidson. He knew that hockey demanded a firm, bold and imaginative leader and so he promptly installed hockey savant Rick Dudley as general manager.

Dudley engineered several deals that transformed the team, trading future draft picks for players who soon became superstars. In five years, the Lightning went from the doghouse to the penthouse, claiming the Stanley Cup in 2003-04. That made Davidson the first owner in sports history to win championships in three different leagues.

When, in 2002, Davidson installed Bill Laimbeer in the head-coaching slot of the Detroit Shock, his entry in the Women's NBA, the basketball world was giddy with delight in contemplation of total disaster for the baddest Piston of the old Bad Boys. Astute observers predicted he would never be able to relate to woman players. Laimbeer proceeded to make bold roster changes. He installed a new playing strategy to fit his concept. Seemingly overnight, the Shock made history—going from worst to first, claiming the championship in 2003 and adding another crown in 2006.

Each of Davison's three sports franchises had risen from the ashes to win its league's championship. It was no coincidence that each organization was distinguished by outstanding management strength.

Still, in June of 2001, naming Dumars president of the Pistons, the crown jewel in The Palace Sports & Entertainment empire, was anything but a slam dunk.

To be sure, Dumars had been a key contributor to a ten-year reign by the Pistons as an elite team. But then he had endured the team's rapid decline and fall as the Pistons plummeted from elite status to the very basement of the league. Through the heady winning years and the disastrous days, Dumars showed the key qualities that Davidson insisted on in his top managers: integrity, vision, commitment and stability—in short, strong leadership ability.

But it is one thing to express these attributes as a player and quite another to demonstrate them in a business environment. That is especially true when one is the individual who sets the tone for the organization and must make the crucial decisions on which fortunes will rise or fall. It is particularly dicey in team sports when one wrong call can destroy a team's delicate balance and turn a potential champion into an also-ran.

"What Joe brought that was different," Wilson said, "was his understanding of people and the crucial element of team chemistry, plus a great eye for guys who aren't quite there yet but will blossom in the right setting."

Davidson also was confident that the character that Dumars had displayed for so long on the NBA courts would translate to effective leadership of a business enterprise. When the owner first raised the possibility, in the year 2000, midway through Dumars final season, Davidson seemed more certain of it than did Dumars himself.

"Bill broached the subject with me in the middle of the season," Dumars told me. "He called me into his office after practice one day and said, 'I want to talk with you about what I'd like for you to do when you finish playing. I'd like for you to take over the leadership role in this organization. I want you to run the Detroit Pistons.'"

As Dumars looked back on that conversation, he shook his head and smiled.

"I laughed and said, 'We have a game tomorrow'," Dumars recalled. "'Can I finish this first?' So we both laughed and he said, 'Of course. I'm not talking about immediately. I'm talking about after your playing career is over with.'"

Dumars thought for a while, then told Davidson he didn't think he could step into that role right after he retired as a player. He explained, "A person can't go from being a player in the locker room with teammates and friends, then he's suddenly the guy that's negotiating their contracts. There has to be some separation for me in terms of getting away from the game."

That sort of a reaction to a job many people would instantly seize is consistent with the way Dumars has always approached major decisions in his life. He was not at all hesitant about his ability to perform the duties he understood to be part of the job. After all, he had already successfully launched and managed his own business enterprises and he had majored in business management in college. Dumars was equally certain about the direction in which he would take the Pistons, should he be at the helm. But he had other concerns.

"I didn't need time to develop a vision for the operation," he told me. "I knew that already. But I did need time to study the Collective Bargaining Agreement, to study contracts, to understand the technical aspects of the role so there would be no mistakes along the way. There were technical and contractual issues and some issues with the player's union and the CBA that I wanted to have a complete grasp of. I knew that I couldn't retire one day on a Friday and walk in on a Monday and know those things."

The issues a club president or general manager must deal with are so complex that Dumars knew it was too risky to try to learn while on the job.

"That's a recipe for making mistakes for six to nine months," he said. "So instead, I'll take that time to learn, to get on the phone with the lawyers at League headquarters, pepper them with questions. I'll talk with a couple different general managers around the League, learn how they've structured their contracts. Ask a ton of questions. Do the self-education required to step into a role like this.

"It wasn't about the concept or my vision for this team; it was strictly about the technical aspects. I knew this was the right fit for me. I knew I could do this. Just as I said to him that I knew I was not a coach. That is not where my strength lies. There are three aspects you have to have to coach and I probably had one of them.

I had knowledge of the game. But you have to also have the right persona, a certain type of personality. And you have to have a passion for whatever you are going to do. I have no passion to coach and I don't have the right temperament to be a coach."

One thing Dumars did have is the perfect personality for the role Davidson was offering him. "My personality fits this particular job," he explained. "This job requires that you have tremendous discipline. It allows you to have long-term vision. It allows you to be a thinker. It affords you the opportunity to be patient, and you need patience to be successful."

But there was one more step Dumars needed to take before he would tell Davidson what he had decided.

"I went home and talked with my wife about it," he says. "She said, 'You are made for that job.' She knew it before I knew it. Once I heard that, I was ready to go."

So, stepping back and steeping himself in the technical challenges of the job is precisely what the methodical Dumars did. "Then I went to Bill Davidson and said, 'Okay, I'm ready.'"

As Dumars had done so many times on the court and so often in his life, he stepped up. He took on the daunting task of restoring the integrity of the hometown Pistons, a once-elite franchise of the National Basketball Association that had fallen into the lower depths.

Davidson and Wilson were quietly confident that this was the right move at the right time. They knew that pundits would be surprised by the announcement they had named Dumars president of basketball operations. Onlookers would not have been so startled had they looked at Davidson's track record. After making a fortune with his Guardian Industries company, a leading manufacturer of glass and building products, Davidson had shown a Midas touch developing successful properties in totally unrelated fields, beginning with the construction in 1988 of The Palace of Auburn Hills. And in Wilson, Davidson had selected the perfect prime mover in building The Palace and orchestrating the moves that turned the

Pistons and several other sports and entertainment properties into successful and valuable enterprises.

Now they had named as president of basketball operations of the Pistons a man few would have cast in such a role without more grooming. Yes, Dumars had an illustrious playing career. Granted, he had been the consummate professional on the hardwood court and an exemplary citizen off of it. In putting a person in any key position, the person's character had always been a top priority for Davidson. That may well have been what appealed most to him about Dumars. When the NBA inaugurated its Sportsmanship Award in 1995-96 for the player who most "exemplifies the ideals of sportsmanship... ethical behavior, fair play and integrity" not only was Joe Dumars the first recipient, henceforth the award would bear his name.

Still, he had no previous experience managing an organization in such a complex, dynamic field. Of all professional sports, basketball is notorious as the one in which a player's performance often doesn't live up to the talent that secured a $100-million, multi-year contract. For every peak performer like Michael Jordan, LeBron James, or Magic Johnson, there are literally dozens of one-time college phenoms sitting on the bench on their hefty contracts, banished there by a coach disgusted with lack of effort or sour character.

Throughout his playing career, Dumars was something of an aberration. To begin with, his modest demeanor was completely out of character with the volcanic, take-no-prisoners "Bad Boys" Pistons. He sublimated his individual skills to serve the higher cause of team. His versatility was uncommon in a league dominated by one-dimensional players. He played fierce defense, dished the ball off to teammates, and when the situation demanded it, he was a deadly shooter from anywhere on the floor who won many games with his scoring. Cool under pressure, he once made 63 consecutive foul shots over a span of games.

More than that, Dumars was the quintessential team player.

Because he was willing to forego individual glory for the good of the team, he was the perfect running mate for fellow guard superstar Isiah Thomas.

"There was an opportunity we had to trade Dumars for a real good big guy," Wilson told me. "In this league you always trade real good little for real good big because big guys can dominate. We came very close to doing that and then our Pistons General Manager Jack McCloskey sat down with Mr. Davidson. He vetoed the trade—and for good reason. You almost never find a guard as talented as Dumars who is willing to fit comfortably in the second chair to an Isiah. Here was Dumars—an equal talent to Isiah, just not as flashy, not as flamboyant—and he was okay with that."

So Dumars played his entire 14-year career with the Pistons, compiling championships, records and accolades. Still, the NBA management dumping grounds are heaped with storied players who stumbled over their own legends in the transition from the court to the front office, including superstars Elgin Baylor, Dave DeBusschere, Bill Russell, Willis Reed, Wes Unseld, and even His Air-ness, Michael Jordan.

Perhaps the player who had the most prolonged and publicized difficulties in the move to the management side was Dumars' teammate, Isiah Thomas. The Hall of Famer and one-time idol known as the "Baby-Faced Assassin" moved into the management ranks with the Toronto Raptors but left abruptly, embroiled in controversy. Then, as president of the New York Knicks, Thomas engineered one disastrous deal after another. The Knicks soon compiled the League's worst record and found themselves saddled with more than $100 million in payouts to non-active players and coaches. As punishment, Thomas was forced to take on the additional role of head coach of a team wallowing in the basement as a result of his failed trades and drafts.

Davidson was clearly attracted to Dumars for qualities far beyond mere basketball ability and knowledge of the game. The Pistons owner had long since displayed powerful credentials as a

judge of top management ability. In a business where most owners are mesmerized by raw talent and try to build teams around
superstars, Davidson found success doing exactly the opposite. He
built from the top down, putting in charge people in whom he dis-
cerned strong leadership qualities and the ability to judge, acquire,
meld and mold talent to fit into a concept. Davidson was old-fashioned—he wanted authentic leaders in leadership positions.

Thus, his choice of Dumars would have been predictable if
viewed against his track record with an earlier Pistons era, as well
as consistent with the way he managed his other properties. Davidson had amply demonstrated that the formula that worked so
well for him in the manufacturing business could also yield positive results in far different arenas, including sports and entertainment. It was a template he would employ again and again.

Wilson remembered how confident and determined Dumars
was from the outset. "When Joe came in he said 'I don't believe in
five-year plans. What they are is excuses. With a five-year plan, I'm
not held accountable for the first four years. If it doesn't work out,
no big deal. I'll start worrying in year five. I don't believe in that.
I've got to do it now.'"

Wilson concluded that a key to Dumars' rapid transformation
of the Pistons was that, knowingly or not, he constructed a team
with players much like himself.

"It takes a particular type of individual like Joe to say he's going to build his team with character guys," Wilson said. "He said
he was going to prove that you can win with good individuals and
teamwork. It was almost folly when he said it because everybody
in basketball knows that you win with talent. It's talent above everything and here Joe is saying there is so much more to it. Now,
it's one thing to say it, another thing to believe it, and an entirely
different thing to act on it and stick to those values. But that's exactly what Joe Dumars did."

An insight into how profoundly Dumars was affected by his
mentors was recounted by Eli Zaret in *Blue Collar Blueprint*:

According to Dumars, former Pistons general manager Jack McClos-
key, who had drafted him, made a profound impression on his life. "You
emulate what you grow up with," Dumars said. "He'd walk by you, and
the kind of things he'd say and the little challenges he'd give you — I find
myself doing the same exact thing with other players here."

Dumars recalls one particular episode that sums up what McClos-
key was all about. After Dumars had been in the league a few years, one
day McCloskey walked into practice and said, "Joe, you're leading us in
free-throw shooting, aren't you?"

Dumars said, "Yes, I am."

"You're just OK," McCloskey said, then challenged him to a free-
throw shooting competition. The 63-year-old McCloskey set the rules:
50 free throws apiece. He stepped to the line and made 48 out of 50. He
handed Dumars the ball and said, "See how good you are." Dumars
made 49 of the 50.

"I saw Jack just two weeks ago," Dumars said, "and we were talk-
ing about that same story. He told me I was lucky I made that 49. He
would have never let me live it down. I've done that with players before.
I'll say, 'Let's go shoot from free throws.' I challenge them the same way
Jack challenged me."

Dumars walked into a perfect storm in the summer of 2000. After four straight losing seasons, attendance had dropped 20 percent.
The locker room had too few team players and too many individuals mesmerized by their own statistics and focusing primarily on
their future prospects when they became free agents. Worst of all,
the classy Grant Hill, highly regarded as the franchise's shining star,
appeared determined to shine on another court.

The silky smooth, regal Hill had been college basketball's elite
player when the hapless Pistons drafted him in 1994. The sports
world was so enamored of his combination of brilliant play and
good-guy demeanor that *GQ Magazine* featured him on the cover
with the caption, "Can Grant Hill Save Sports?" For five years, Hill
had played alongside Dumars, but before Hill's long-term contract
ran out, he already had decided he had played his last game as a

Piston. Dumars reluctantly accepted that he would lose his star. The only question was would it be to free agency, in which case he would get nothing for his Palace gem, or would Dumars be able to sign and trade him and at least in return get a warm body or two or some draft picks.

Dumars gritted his teeth and made the best of a bad situation. He traded his former teammate to the Orlando Magic. Dumars did not know it at the time, but he was about to reap a windfall in unintended consequences.

At the time Hill left, he said he believed his departure would be better for the Pistons—that it would let Dumars start with a clean slate and more power. Small consolation, Dumars thought at the time. But he later came to see that Hill was right. "Grant's leaving cleared the decks for me," Dumars says. "It opened the way for me to restructure the entire organization."

The loss of Hill meant the gain of Ben Wallace and Chucky Atkins in a sign-and-trade deal. Wallace quickly became the throbbing heart of a vital new Pistons team. The move also tipped other dominoes that fell Dumars' way by opening up salary-cap space. In a sport where top talent is at a premium and career-ending injuries are common, the ability to move players around to stay under the league-imposed salary ceiling is paramount.

As would be expected of two men renowned for their graciousness, when Hill departed, there was no acrimony between him and Dumars. "In this society, athletes are role models," Hill said, "whether they deserve it or not. Joe Dumars, though, is the role model's role model and the professional's professional."

Dumars moved quickly to ship out players who no longer would fit in the system. He replaced them with sharp-shooter Richard (Rip) Hamilton and veterans Corliss Williamson, Jon Barry, and Clifford Robinson—all of whom would soon play key roles for the resurgent club.

But even as Dumars was wheeling and dealing with trades, he was keeping a sharp eye on the college ranks. Established players acquired in trades could contribute right away, but success over the long term meant making the most of selections from the annual college-draft pool. No NBA scout or executive is farsighted or fortunate enough to be able to divine only future superstars. But if too many choices bomb out, a team's stock can plummet rapidly. When Dumars chose Mehmet Okur in 2001 and Tayshaun Prince in 2002, he added talent that would pay rich dividends sooner than expected.

In June 2002, less than a week after the Pistons ended their second consecutive 50-win season, Dumars made a shocking move that showed his transformation of the Pistons extended beyond a rejiggered roster of playing talent. Convinced that he needed a coach who could withstand the intense pressure of a championship run, Dumars concluded he had to make a change. So he fired head coach Rick Carlisle. It was typical of the tough and sometimes unpopular decisions Dumars made by using his own value system as a template.

Perhaps Dumars remembered what Coach Chuck Daly, the most successful coach in the team's history, had said ten years before when he decided to leave the Pistons. It was almost verbatim what Daly said to me when we talked about him writing a book. "After a while, players get tired of hearing the same things from the coach and start tuning him out," Daly said. "When that happens, it's time for a change." Some commentators speculated perhaps there was something to the rumors that tension between Carlisle and his players was building to breaking point. Or perhaps the way Carlisle used—or didn't use—talented players that Dumars had assembled entered into it. Dumars told me simply, "We had the players we needed to contend and it was a move I had to make for this team to get to the next level."

Whatever the reason, when Dumars announced the move, he fully expected it would raise eyebrows, if not draw heated criticism for cutting loose a coach who had posted 50-plus-win seasons. "I don't know if I can sit here and justify this after all the success we've had," he said.

Even though reporters and fans were stunned by at the move, they cut Dumars slack because they knew he acted only out of a conviction that a coaching change was essential for this team to win a championship. Insiders knew that Dumars was confident he had just the man in mind who could do that.

The nomadic Larry Brown had long been considered the mad genius of basketball coaching ranks. He capriciously bounced from the college ranks to the NBA and back again as he compiled perhaps the longest *curriculum vitae* in the history of the sport. Brown had accumulated an NCAA title with Kansas, brief tours with college teams Davidson and UCLA, and tumultuous head-coaching stints with no fewer than ten NBA teams to date.

Dumars forced himself to look beyond Brown's vagabond resumé that raised red flags about stability and loyalty. What he saw was a coaching genius who could extract maximum performance from playing talent.

Some of the players newer to the Pistons' organization also needed to know the boundaries of the permissible. When one player grumbled through the press about not getting enough playing time, Dumars gave him a short course in "The Piston Way," a doctrine promulgated by Isiah Thomas during the first Pistons golden era. That meant totally subordinating individual goals to the sole cause of what was best for the team. Coming from Dumars, a former great who represented the ultimate of selflessness, the message resonated throughout the organization.

By June 2003, just two years after he took over, Dumars had completely recast and reinvigorated the franchise and propelled it to the top echelon. It shocked no one when the NBA named Dumars the Executive of the Year.

Once an outpost that free agents shunned, Detroit was now a desirable destination. "Joe Dumars told me how things had changed," Wilson said. "'When I took this job,' Joe said, 'my phone never rang unless it was some over-the-hill player who just wanted a payday and he knew we were bad and had money. Now people are calling and asking if there is any way they can be a part of this. And people who were here and are now gone are saying it's the best locker room they've ever been a part of.'"

A sports team—especially a professional sports team and perhaps most especially a professional basketball team—is always a work in progress. Players take a brutal pounding, from their opponents, from the hardwood floor itself, and from their own teammates in scrimmages as rookies try to elbow veterans aside, in more ways than one. The travel grind of more than a hundred games in dozens of cities is exhausting, even in private stretch jets. By the time they are established pros, many of these players have been bouncing around courts for twenty years. Muscles tear, joints separate, bones splinter. When one key player in the starting five is disabled, the entire chemistry of the team is disrupted. So a general manager can never rest, never feel confident he has done his part and now it's up to the coaches and players to do theirs.

But fortunately for general managers, the converse is also true and one key acquisition can do wonders, as Joe Dumars was about to prove as the 2003-04 season entered its final third in February 2004.

The strong performance of former malcontents and chronic under-achievers was a key to the Pistons' success in the regular season. It was also emblematic of the ability of Dumars to envision how a player who wilted in one environment could bloom in another. In January of that year, Rasheed Wallace (no relation to Ben) was making $17 million a year for the Portland Trailblazers. He was also making his team, basketball purists, and league officials agitated and often furious with his antics, rants and technical fouls. Although Wallace's demeanor on the court was the exact opposite of the quiet, sportsmanlike Dumars, there were important qualities in the rambunctious Wallace that mirrored the Dumars' value system.

"I knew how unselfish he was, how he was willing to sacrifice to win," Dumars said. "That's the common denominator to look for in this job."

In an eye-popping three-team swap, Dumars dealt away players and draft choices to acquire the player known as 'Sheed. And then watched as the volcanic malcontent promptly became the catalyst to lead the team to a 20-6 finish and a spot in the playoffs. Not only that, the sequence of moves cleared nearly $10 million in salary-cap space as Dumars disposed of four veterans. With the Wallace move and his handling of the Grant Hill departure, Dumars proved convincingly that his six months spent studying the intricacies of salary cap management and club financing was time well spent.

In the preliminary rounds of the NBA 2003-04 playoffs, Detroit dispatched the Milwaukee Bucks in five games, the New Jersey Nets in seven, and the Indiana Pacers in six. Every draft pick and acquisition Dumars had assembled had made essential contributions.

Ben Wallace was a situational substitute with scant prospects to develop into a first-line regular when Dumars acquired him from the Orlando Magic in the Grant Hill sign-and-trade deal. In blue-collar Detroit, Big Ben became not only the cornerstone but also the foundation of a lunch-bucket crew that prided itself on just "Goin' to work."

Chauncey Billups was regarded as a one-dimensional player, a mad bomber jump shooter, as he bounced through six clubs before landing with the Pistons where he was transformed into, of all things, a playmaker, passer and defensive standout.

Richard (Rip) Hamilton was likewise admired as a pure shooter who was a liability on defense and unable to fit into a winning system. In Detroit, his quickness and seemingly boundless energy tore holes in opposing defenses, opening up his teammates for easy shots.

Another key to the Pistons' startling success in 2004 was an "X factor," Tayshaun Prince, drafted by Dumars in 2003. The previous year, Prince had languished on the Pistons bench for half of the regular season, being used only for token minutes. Then, finally given a prime-time opportunity, he exerted himself spectacularly in the playoffs. His self-effacing manner and outstanding all-around play at both ends of the floor were reminiscent of Dumars himself.

The final ingredient on the floor, of course, was Rasheed Wallace. When Dumars acquired him and Larry Brown stirred him into the mix, the recipe was complete. Finally Dumars' concept became the reality.

"All these guys felt like they had something to prove," Dumars said of his '04 champions. "They didn't expect anything to be given to them."

Shaquille O'Neal of the deflated Los Angeles Lakers put it succinctly in words that must have warmed Dumars' heart: "They just played hard, consistently hard. They played consistently good defense and just flat-out beat us in everything."

Just as a coach can go into a game with a great strategy on paper, only to see events quickly obsolete it, so too does a club executive find that he often must improvise to cope with unexpected developments. Particularly in sports, it is the executive who is quickest on his feet who prevails. Reacting is simply too slow—possible events must be anticipated and potential scenarios and strategies must be in place to act on the moment those events transpire. Dumars' role years earlier, in 1990, as the cornerstone of a decisive defensive strategy, taught him the importance of having a scheme to counter an opponent's strength.

Back then, it was called "The Jordan Rules." In the NBA in the 1980-90 era, talent was divided into two tiers: There was Michael Jordan at the Super-Elite Level, and then there was everybody else. Coach Daly had anticipated the Chicago Bulls would try to run roughshod over his Pistons and into the NBA finals on the strength of Jordan's astronomical scoring—he had been racking up 40, 50 and more points per game. To combat that, Daly had teamed Dumars with defensive stalwart Dennis Rodman to deflate Air Jordan and force the rest of the Bulls to pick up the scoring slack.

It worked. Chicago was unable to mount an effective countermeasure and Jordan and the Bulls were vanquished. For Joe Dumars, it was lesson learned.

Later in his playing career, Dumars found himself on the receiving end of innovative defensive strategies. After Thomas, Laimbeer, Rodman and John Salley had departed from the Bad Boys team, Dumars himself and scoring star Grant Hill were often the focus of attention as the team suffered through four difficult years. More lessons learned.

"The first ten years of my career here with the Pistons were absolutely great," Dumars told me. "We were winning. The last four-five years we had some tough times. That period has had as much impact on who I am as a leader as the successful times did. I saw a lot of what not to do.

"The way you are shaped as a leader can't always be just on seeing success. You have to see what lack of leadership brings about, or you may slide into it without even realizing it. I've had the benefit of seeing it and knowing what happens after observing the type of guys who were brought into the locker room, listening to their mentality, and thinking then that I can never have this type of guy if I ever run a team."

Dumars began learning lessons about leadership long before his pro career. "Whatever leadership abilities I have had little or nothing to do with basketball," he said. "My father was a man of unwavering principle. He would say, 'You stand for what is right, regardless of consequences. Don't stand there and present yourself as something you are not. You stand up for what is right and you treat people with dignity and respect. I've been on the other side far too many times in my life. I've been in foxholes with black guys, white guys, Hispanic guys—waiting to get killed. I've cried with guys when we thought we were dead and when the firefight was over, we raised up and hugged each other and knew that we would never look at life the same again.'"

It was that lesson from his father that Joe Dumars would carry with him always.

"People are people and that is how you deal with them," he said. "You never allow groups or this segment or that segment to define you. The way you carry yourself, the way you treat people—that is what defines you. So from a very young age, bouncing a basketball was never going to define me. It was always a means to an end."

As he often did when confronting a difficult decision, Dumars harkened back to his earliest days, to something he thought his father would say. "He would ask me one enduring question," Dumars recalled. "'How are you treating your people; how do they feel about you? Make sure you take care of your people. Make sure that you are there for them.'"

Dumars had to face many difficult situations at the Pistons' helm. He fired coaches who compiled outstanding win-loss records because he was convinced the team needed new leadership to improve. He traded high draft picks, like Mateen Cleaves, whose work ethic and character he regarded highly, but who lacked certain skills to fit and succeed as a Piston. And he swallowed hard to dispose of very high draft picks, like Darko Milicic, who were supremely skilled but never displayed the desire to exploit their rich physical talent.

"To be a champion, you better be passionate about what you're doing when you step out there," he stressed. "If mediocrity is what you are striving for, then you step out there feeling, 'Hey, it's just a game.' But if being the best is what you are striving to be, you better be passionate and totally committed."

Dumars' intense conviction on this point was put to the test in May 2007 when the Pistons made an abrupt, embarrassing exit from the NBA playoffs. Heavily favored as the regular season's dominant team, the Pistons never revved up their engines and were unceremoniously swept away by the upstart Cleveland Cavaliers. That memory still rankles Dumars and probably always will. He has made no secret of his dissatisfaction with the attitude and effort of some of his players. Dumars' disappointment with lackadaisical effort in the 2006-07 playoffs was especially galling because he believed the team had an excellent opportunity to re-peat as champions.

"I saw a level of complacency with some of my guys that struck me like a hammer," he said then. "That bothered me as much as the loss—the complacency with which the loss was accepted. As I go forward, it will be a mandate with the guys who are still here that, if I see it, then I know that's your way of asking me to get you out of here."

The message got through. The Pistons came out of pre-season in 2007-08 with the appearance of a squad determined to resume a position on the top rung of the league.

—⏀—

THROUGHOUT HIS CAREERS AS PLAYER AND BUSINESS EXECUTIVE, two char-acter traits enhanced Dumars credibility: He was not talkative or demonstrative like many other players, coaches and executives so what he said carried more weight. When he did speak, he was thoughtful and candid. And his actions demonstrated that in mak-ing his decisions, he drew deeply from his own experiences.

"Dumars did a remarkable job turning the franchise around," Wilson said. "When Joe took over, he said 'We are a blue-collar town. We have a different work ethic than anybody else does. Peo-ple will respond to our group of blue-collar, hard-nosed players.'

"What he did wouldn't work as well in Los Angeles, but it was perfect for the Pistons, what this city is, who he is. Joe wanted guys who would put on the uniform with pride, would move here and live here. He wanted players who would be part of the community, go into the schools, talk with the kids, and be a positive presence in this area. I don't know if Joe realized it, but the kind of people he was talking about are people who are like him."

Psychologists ruminate over whether lessons learned in sport transfer to supremacy in the worlds of business, sports and politics. What, if anything, does competitive sport impart that makes a person more successful elsewhere? Many former athletes are convinced that excellence in sports helped them in their subsequent pursuits: Byron "Whizzer" White from football stardom to the Supreme Court; John Wayne from the gridiron to the silver screen; Bill Bradley from the Princeton hard court to the U.S. Senate; Dave Bing from glory days as a Piston to successful businessman to the impossible situation as mayor of Detroit; Mike Ilitch from a baseball career cut short by injuries to head of a worldwide pizza empire and a sports and entertainment conglomerate. Countless athletes have gravitated from games to stand out in other fields of endeavor. Again and again, as they look back on their playing days, these men and women liken the drive to excel in sport and the lessons learned from failure as well as success, to what it takes to succeed in other settings.

That certainly seemed to be the case for Dumars. What he learned as a player, he later applied as the architect of a championship team.

The Pistons' NBA champions of 2004, engineered by Dumars, had much in common with the earlier practitioners of the Pistons Way, the back-to-back champions of 1989-90. Both were cohesive, unselfish squads, with solid, balanced starting quintets bolstered by key players coming off the bench. Chuck Daly and Larry Brown were both fundamentally sound coaches who could motivate—though in distinctly different ways. Both squads had great guard tandems (Thomas-Dumars, Billups-Hamilton) who could—and did—combine for fifty-point offensive outbursts when the situation demanded. But all four of these backcourt stars who could light up the scoreboard with long-range bombs and unerring free-throw accuracy were every bit as dominant on defense. When the game was on the line, these duos smothered such superstar counterparts as Magic Johnson, Michael Jordan, Reggie Miller, Jason Kidd, and Kobe Bryant with tenacious, unrelenting defense.

Those two teams played fifteen years apart in two very dif-

ferent eras for pro basketball, but perhaps the most salient common denominator was attitudinal rather than physical. These were
teams in the fullest sense of the word, with every player not only
willing but also eager to sacrifice individual statistics and glory to
a shared commitment to winning. It is noteworthy that there was
only one person playing a key leadership role on both teams. In
1989, Pistons guard Dumars had been voted Most Valuable Player
in the NBA Championship series. In 2004, it was Pistons President
Joe Dumars who had assembled seemingly disparate pieces—cast-
off players, a wanderlust coach—to meld a championship entity.
In a five-year span, Dumars' Pistons made the Eastern Conference
Finals five times, won the conference title three times, and won an
NBA championship, setting several team and League records in
the process.

Even when the Pistons were so successful early in his career
at the helm, running an elite NBA franchise did not seem to be the
ultimate role for Joe Dumars.

"I have found over the years," Dumars told me in 2008 when
the Pistons were still a powerhouse, "that with people who become
the best in their field—in sports that means the people who become
champions—there is something that happens when you become
the best at what you do. You tend to know within yourself that you
can be successful at whatever you get into. You never limit yourself at being successful at the thing you are doing because you just
know that you can transfer that success elsewhere. I'm not saying it
always happens. It doesn't. But that conviction that I can make this
work in some other sport, some other field, that's always there."

Even when he was a player, Dumars had other interests, other
involvements. In 1996, he founded Detroit Technologies, a supplier
to automotive companies. He was majority owner as well as chief
executive officer and president for ten years before he sold off his
interest to pursue other business opportunities and focus on his
role as Pistons president. Then there is Joe Dumars Fieldhouse,
an indoor sports and entertainment facility with two locations in

metro Detroit and plans to expand to other states. Dumars was not without experience as the man in charge in other settings, but as the Pistons' fortunes began to decline, he learned yet again how much more scrutiny the head of a professional sports franchise must endure than a boss in private industry.

"In industries that are not under the public microscope," he said, "the scrutiny of their decisions doesn't extend outside the four walls of their office. But when you're in a glass box, all that you can stand on is what's right. You can't stand on popularity, or trendy, or hype. You better stand on principle, on what's right. It better be strong and substantive and capable of standing up to scrutiny. If it can't, then this is not the seat you should sit in."

Dumars smiled over the difference between his role as the man seated at the desk where the buck stops and his days as a player. He said, "Playing for fourteen years gives you great preparation for this. People know whether you've had a good day or a bad day. It's right there on TV for people to see. You don't have to go home and tell the wife 'I've had a rough day at the office.' She was there at the game—she saw it. So being under that scrutiny prepares you for this. I'm all for that scrutiny. The lack of questioning for some positions ends up being an Achilles heel for the person in that position. If you are given a free rein, if there are no checks and balances, there is nothing to stop you from making mistake after mistake. Often, the best thing for a leader is criticism, second-guessing."

Dumars told me he believed he got to a leadership role by being second-guessed, by being told he couldn't make it to the big time from rural Louisiana. "Along the way, you run into every obstacle that life has to throw at you," he said.

The way Dumars related to people on the court and in the office was powerfully influenced by his own experiences as a youngster and young adult. He invariably harkened back to his own experiences to better understand the feelings of the people who worked for him and of people with whom he was in contact.

"It's okay to have sympathy for people," he said. "But sympathy alone is not enough. It's more important to have empathy. You have to understand what people are going through, but what is more important for that person is that you empathize, that you connect with them. I've been that person on the other side, growing up, where I wished that the powers that be didn't just pat me on the head, say 'I feel bad for you,' and just keep going. When they could really understand what I was feeling, well, that made a world of difference."

It was words like that—and the attitude underlying them—that resonated from the outset with owner Davidson and CEO Wilson. They detected a familiar pattern. It was precisely the formula by which they built each entity in The Palace Sports & Entertainment empire into an elite operation.

—⚘—

DAVIDSON, WILSON AND DUMARS. Three men from different eras, different backgrounds. What they shared in common was the conviction that hard work, integrity and discipline could forge an organization that would excel in business as well as produce champions in the fields of sports.

As seriously as Dumars took his responsibility for the Pistons, he never forgot that basketball is, after all, still a game. It is a game that wouldn't exist without its fans and its sports media and its analysts. Many passionate fans and observers are dead certain they could run a pro sport franchise very well indeed, just given the opportunity. Dumars accepted that. So when he talked with me about the journey he had made from Natchitoches to The Palace of Auburn Hills, he smiled a slow, knowing smile. It was the smile of a man who has stood all alone at the free-throw line with the game on the line and the ball in his hands. It was the smile that came from Been There, Done That. He said, "You know, that's one of the great things about sports. Everybody is allowed to become the pseudo-general manager of the team."

―ɯ―

DUMARS NEEDED THAT STOICISM to deal with the aftermath of occurrences beyond his control. On March 13, 2009, at age eighty-six, Bill Davidson died. For the next three years, the Detroit NBA franchise was an enigma. It was a property Davidson had purchased from Fred Zollner for $6 million and was now estimated by *Forbes* as worth $479 million. But the threat of enormous estate-tax liability made continued ownership by Davidson's widow and heirs extremely unlikely, while a prolonged delay in tough economic times would only depreciate it further. And so the property—and the team—drifted and then stalled under a cloud of uncertainty. No one knew when and how matters would get resolved.

The Pistons were stuck in limbo, waiting to learn not only of who would own them, but perhaps even where they would play. In such an unsettled environment, Dumars hands were tied from making the kind of moves a general manager must make to field a competitive team while also building for the future. No surprise then that on the basketball court, the Pistons roller-coaster once again was in motion, plummeting from the pinnacle to the pits.

In early February 2010, Pistons owner Karen Davidson announced she was considering selling the team. On February 17, Tom Wilson resigned as president and CEO of the Pistons and Palace Sports & Entertainment. He had been with the organization for thirty-two years, nearly all in a close partnership relationship with Davidson. A week later, Wilson was named president and CEO of Olympia Entertainment, one of the many Ilitch businesses, along with the Detroit Red Wings and Detroit Tigers. He had an apparent mandate to build a new hockey arena near the Fox Theatre and Comerica Park. The mammoth complex would house the Red Wings as well as an array of entertainment facilities. The price tag was estimated at $650 million. The ultimate goal was to create the premier sports, entertainment and events venue in Michigan, if not in the entire country.

Of the three men who had built and rebooted the Pistons, only one remained as the 2010-11 season dragged to a disappointing close. Joe Dumars, so used to being in the action, to taking action, could only bide his time until ownership passed into new hands.

On April 8, 2011, Karen Davidson made an announcement that lifted the cloud that had hovered for two years over the Pistons and The Palace: "We are pleased to welcome Tom Gores as the new owner of the Detroit Pistons and Palace Sports & Entertainment. Just as my late husband, Bill Davidson, was the face of the Pistons, I am confident that Tom will bring the same energy, dedication and love to this organization. I look forward to seeing Tom follow in Bill's footsteps, and carry on his legacy."

For the next two years, the uncertainties of 2009-11 continued to take a toll on the Pistons' results on the court. The 2013-14 season began with great promise, with a playoff berth in the weak Eastern Conference seemingly almost a cinch. With the biggest unknowns eliminated, Dumars was at it again, busily assembling the pieces and making salary-cap moves to position the team to make yet-another playoff run. He parted company with Richard Hamilton and Tayshaun Prince, the last holdovers from the 2004 championship team. He solidified his core of prized draftees, including the talented Greg Monroe and Rodney Stuckey. After drafting the promising Andre Drummond, Dumars had five rookies on his roster. But he was far from done dealing. In summer 2013, he brought back Chauncey Billups as a player and a mentor for his youngsters. He inked first-round draft pick and potential all-star Josh Smith and acquired by trade the inconsistent but sometimes brilliant Bradon Jennings. One month into the 2013-14 season, after Detroit beat the defending champion Heat in Miami, observers around the NBA were projecting Dumars' overhauled and re-energized Pistons as a playoff team.

But despite more talent and a seemingly more harmonious locker room, the team just couldn't seem to jell. After his Pistons coughed up leads in one fourth quarter after another, and losing streaks grew, Dumars again made a leadership change. He fired head coach Maurice Cheeks who had replaced Lawrence Franks who had been fired ten months earlier. That made eight coaches replaced in Dumars' reign.

Reflecting on his difficult first two seasons as owner, Gores said, speaking about Detroit-area fans, "I want to give them what they thought they got with me as a new owner, and I want to deliver on that. Having grown up here, what I know about Detroit fans and Michigan fans is that they'll show up. You've just got to deserve them."

When asked about Dumars' future as president of basketball operations, Gores said he could envision the relationship continuing for the long term. But already there were rumors of strained relations between Gores and Dumars. The harmonious, everybody-on-the-same-page glory days with Davidson and Wilson had long since receded in Dumars's rear-view mirror.

Through the heady championship times and the dark days, Joe Dumars had played one key role or another in what Bill Davidson and Tom Wilson had taken decades to build in Auburn Hills. But it was a new game now. New owner. New set of issues. Now every move—or failure to take action—met with skepticism in the fan base, in part because of the revolving door that found one coach barely settled in his chair before he was ousted and yet another new savior took his place. Who was picking these guys, anyhow, fans wondered. Was it Dumars or Gores? Did they see eye-to-eye on major coaching decisions? Where, fans wondered, is the next Chuck Daly?

Not least of Dumars's problems was the growing chorus of Monday morning media experts calling for his firing, a cacophony surely not lost on owner Gores. Especially strident and persistent were the call-in sports-radio show hosts reciting the litany of Dumars's transgressions going back to the drafting of Darko Milicic and exhuming every failed decision since then.

As yet another disappointing season crawled to a conclusion

in early 2014, rumors were rampant, speculation intensified. And then solidified. Pundits said it was certain Gores would remove Dumars—that is, if Dumars didn't preempt the owner and choose to walk away before his contract ran out in June 2014. There seemed no chance Dumars would continue to play a leadership role in the quest of a return to the glory days for the Detroit Pistons.

Finally, on April 13, 2014, the speculation and rumors were brushed away by the announcement of one cold, blunt fact: Joe Dumars was out as president of basketball operations. It was his option whether to stay on as an executive advisor not connected to basketball. He would be free to take a role at another NBA organization. Or to do whatever he chose.

His days as a key factor for the Detroit Pistons were over.

Still, the man who came on the scene as the kid from Natchitoches would know one thing for sure: He had teamed with Bill Davidson and Tom Wilson and spent more than half his life making a difference at The Palace. No matter what happened in the future, the records were in the book and nothing could change that.

"To be accepted into that prestigious society," George said, waving his arms as if to embrace the grandeur of the Circumnavigators Club, "the would-be initiate must stand before the membership at the annual banquet and recount how he survived a life-threatening experience. That was a bit of a problem for me because I always tried to get as far away from danger as possible."

Dining with the host of the World Adventure Series was itself an adventure. All George Pierrot needed was good food, fine wine and an audience.

$$\sim\!\!\backsim 9 \backsim\!\!\sim$$

AROUND THE WORLD
IN EIGHTY YEARS

George Pierrot Devours Detroit

THE HOST WAS BALD, OVERWEIGHT AND HIS VOICE WAS A GRAVELLY GROWL. He admitted that his show was amateurishly produced and could be "kinda dull." But somehow author and world traveler George Pierrot became an icon and his *World Adventure Series* became America's longest-running television show.

In his travels, it seemed there was no exotic port of call George Pierrot hadn't visited, no prince, premier or president he hadn't dined with. He had written countless travel and adventure articles for magazines and newspapers. Beginning in 1933 he lectured about travel and showed films of faraway places to Depression-weary Detroiters for twenty-five cents admission at the Detroit Institute of Arts. So it was only natural that in 1948 the upstart Channel 7 would turn to him for an afternoon show that would thrill viewers with footage of far-off places. That is, if it didn't put them to sleep, as it sometimes did its own host.

The *World Adventure Series* was broadcast live, as was Pierrot's subsequent show, *George Pierrot Presents*, on Channel 7 and later on Channel 4. The show usually opened with the whimsical Pierrot barely stirring his big frame from an easy chair to introduce a guest who might be clad in khaki, jodhpurs and pith helmet, and brandishing a riding crop. The guest traveler would come equipped with a reel of film and a well-rehearsed patter about the images flickering on the screen before them in the nowhere-near-ready-for-primetime footage. As the film ran out and the lights came up, not infrequently the guest would have to nudge his snoring host awake. But Pierrot would quickly recover and, in his trademark sandpaper voice, would tell an anecdote about one of his visits to the same spot.

Pierrot had always assumed he would write a book about his travels but as he approached age eighty, he still had traveling to do, places to see, people to meet. He seemed constantly to be planning the next excursion. That is, when he wasn't shaking hands with visitors as the guest celebrity at a branch opening for his longtime sponsor Standard Federal Bank. A well-practiced procrastinator, it seemed unlikely he would ever find time to write a book. Perhaps that is why he was so enthusiastic when I mentioned to him that if he wanted to do a book, I would help him shape it and then I would publish it.

I had gotten to know Pierrot some years earlier. He had magnanimously agreed to review the manuscript for the first in a series of three Great Lakes travel guides I had commissioned George Cantor to write.

Enlisting Pierrot to critique the manuscript for the first volume of the Cantor series had been an easy sell, but had I foreseen the ordeal I would be putting him through, I never would have asked him to do it. It took Pierrot many weeks to read the material, for which he called frequently to apologize. Only later did his wife Helen tell me that George's eyesight was so bad he could make out only one word at a time; even that required that he peer through an enormous magnifying glass set up on his desk with bright lights illuminating the paper.

Pierrot never complained to me about his vision problems and simply said he was greatly enthused about the project. He offered to write a cover blurb and help promote the book. He declined the three-hundred-dollar check that was our standard reader's fee, instead saying he would permit me to take him to dinner at Joe Muer's Seafood Restaurant. Legendary for his appetite as well as his travels, George had chosen Detroit's most revered seafood restaurant. It was a menu he knew by heart. And a good thing, too, because his eyes were so bad he could no longer read it.

Dining with the host of the *World Adventure Series* was itself an adventure. All George Pierrot needed was good food, fine wine and an audience. He was already well into his account of his induction into the Circumnavigators Club when the waiter showed us to our table.

A server quickly brought a basket of breads and a Joe Muer specialty, a tray of tiny, elegant swans that had been molded from pure butter. Many of these elegant little globs went untouched by patrons not out of cholesterol concerns but because diners thought them just too delicate and dainty to actually consume. Some patrons' waistlines undoubtedly benefited from that will power reinforcement. A few, perhaps, but not George's.

"To be accepted into that prestigious society," George said, waving his arms as if to embrace the grandeur of the Circumnavigators Club, "the would-be initiate must stand before the membership at the annual banquet and recount how he survived a life-threatening experience. That was a bit of a problem for me because I always tried to get as far away from danger as possible. The other initiates had told tales of harrowing escapes from a raging water buffalo, stampeding elephants, and a pit of venomous snakes. The fellow who spoke before me told how he dangled from a tree root on the side of a cliff, just like in the cartoons.

"Well, I had experienced nothing like that. But then I recalled my first job when I was a lad out west. I grew up in Washington state, where it was common for young boys living near the coast to get menial jobs at the docks or canneries. I counted myself fortunate to get hired for work on a gut boat in Puget Sound."

With that he swept his right arm out expansively to take in the great west. George had made extravagant hand gestures several times during our meal. This time, however, my eye was drawn somehow to his left hand, which rested on the table alongside the once-full tray of butter swans. Then I saw it. With his little finger, he hooked the last of those swans into his beefy palm.

"Now a gut boat is a nothing more than a big, flat barge that is loaded with tons of scrap from salmon canneries," George said. "A huge tarp is lowered onto the heap of salmon guts and trim-mings and then the barge goes out to sea and dumps the stink-ing mess. The sharks have an orgy. Well, this was in the 1920s and even in those days the local health authorities mandated that tarps be secured to keep salmon innards from spilling into the channel or washing up on the beaches. On that day, though, someone had failed to secure the tarp at one corner, so the captain sent me out to fasten it."

At that moment, a man seated at another table heard Pier-rot's distinctive voice and came over to say hello. George shook his hand and chatted with him amiably. After the man left, George said, "I haven't the slightest idea who that fellow was. Must have met him sometime. Might even be a friend or neighbor. With these damn eyes, that kind of thing happens more and more. Anyhow, where was I?"

"On the gut boat, under orders to tie down the tarp."

"Right, the tarp. To button it down I had to walk on this narrow gunwale, maybe four inches wide and slimy from fish guts that had already spilled over the railing and into the channel. But the captain has given me an order so there I go, like a tightrope walker and of course the boat is rolling and pitching. I don't get ten feet and next thing I know I'm in the water."

Here, for the third or fourth time since we sat down, George brought his napkin to his mouth and when I glanced again at his left hand, the butter swan had disappeared. George held the nap-kin in front of his mouth as he chewed for a few seconds.

"Waiter!" he called and pointed to the butter dish. "If you please, my guest is out of butter. All right, then, where were we? Oh yes, flailing around amongst those slimy fish guts. I must have swallowed a gallon of putrid channel water before I bobbed up to the surface. Just the smell was enough to make you retch, but I could have handled that except for one thing: I didn't know how to swim. You know the cliché about the drowning man grasping at a straw. Well, for me it was grab for a handful of fish guts.

"Now, here's where my narrow escape comes in. You know what happens to the innards of salmon when they hit the water? If the stomach and bladder haven't been nicked in the cleaning process, they swell up like balloons, about as big as a football. I clutched onto one of those, then another and another, until I had half a dozen gathered into a nice little floatation device. It seemed like forever, but it was only a few minutes until a deck hand saw me, reached out with a grappling hook and pulled me in. Old-timers at the Circumnavigators Club told me that was the damnedest initiation story they ever heard."

—ᴍ—

Two weeks later, George called and said he would have it no other way but that he would show me the proper way to do Eastern Market.

"First of all," he said, "we must be there well before the shopkeepers and the cooks from the fancy Grosse Pointe mansions. By 6 a.m., the Lebanese grandmothers from Dearborn and the Jewish matrons from West Bloomfield descend like a swarm of locusts and get all the good stuff. And believe me, they know just what the good stuff is."

So one morning long before sunrise, I met up with George at the site he had designated. I was ready to learn "how to do the Market." We started by picking out fried and glazed crullers and a selection of Danish pastries from a bakery. We carried our bag of sweets several doors down to George's favorite coffee shop. "They'll brew it to order by French press," George assured me. "No other way is fit to drink."

We had mowed through a good fraction of the pastries and a second cup of coffee when the sun was lighting the east horizon.

"That will tide us over for an hour or so," George said. "If we were to stop for a real breakfast now, there would be nothing left at the stalls but the culls and leftovers."

For the next two hours, it was one cubicle or open stand after another. At every stop, the proprietor knew George Pierrot and most of them picked out for him the choicest pomegranate or starfruit, or the most pungent garlic or most pristine artichoke. There were quail's eggs to cook with Japanese udon noodles and brick parmesan cheese from a town George had often visited in Italy. At every stall and for every purchase there was a story, invariably humorous, of something that had happened to George or to someone he knew. We made several trips back to George's car to load in the bounty. Finally he was satisfied he had taught me how to do Eastern Market properly.

"George, I have two questions. First, how are you going to use all this stuff?"

"Not much of it is for Helen and me except the quail eggs, noodles, and cheese. For the rest, I've got a few deliveries to make this afternoon to friends who don't know how to pick the good stuff. Second question."

"How is it that with your eyesight you're still driving a car?"

"Well, I won't argue they've got no business letting someone in my shape have a license. I can still see straight forward, but it's pretty blurry, and not a damn thing peripherally. Haven't been able to read the gages in years. But since they're careless enough to give me a license, I'm just arrogant enough to use it. I stay off the main highways. I mostly just stick to the side streets around Indian Village and the neighborhood. Won't dispute that I'm a menace on the road."

I watched him drive away and decided he might not be as dangerous as I feared. His vision was so bad that he used more care going around the block than he probably had in all his adventures since the gut boat.

—ɯ—

A FEW YEARS LATER, I TOOK PIERROT TO THE DETROIT PRESS CLUB'S annual "Steakout," where anchormen, editors, reporters and politicians satirized, lampooned and all but harpooned each other. For decades this had been a stag gathering. The explanation for excluding the growing numbers of women in the press, in business and in government was that the humor was so raunchy it would offend their delicate sensibilities. That was quickly dispelled a few years later when women were not only allowed to attend, but also took a prominent part in the program. The ladies instantly proved they could be every bit as gross as their male counterparts.

Pierrot and the others at our table agreed there was very little original humor being offered that evening. Even worse, a state representative named John Engler somehow had been given time on the program, although partisan political speeches were strictly prohibited. This Engler fellow proceeded to drone on and on, reading from a canned and highly self-serving political speech, apparently oblivious that he had long since lost the audience. The crowd got bored, then restless. Shoes shuffled, fingers drummed on tables, lots of coughing. Finally—reconciled that this fellow just might go on forever—people started talking among themselves.

George, however, had a better solution: he seized on a couple of words Engler had used repeatedly, and then spun a limerick keyed off those words. He continued doing this throughout Engler's talk and was just getting up to speed when Bill Bonds reclaimed the microphone to no small applause. Pierrot's performance was so much more enjoyable than the program on the stage and he was such a shameless ham that he held forth for the rest of the evening. People at nearby tables wondered why we were having so much more fun than anybody else.

But garrulous George had not yet hit his stride. He continued reciting limericks long after the program was over. Someone would say "17th century French peasant" and George would spiel one off. Effeminate longshoreman... New Orleans madam... Pompous member of Britain's House of Lords... Whatever the subject, Pierrot either dredged one up from memory or created one on the spot. On and on he went, through dinner and dessert, far into after-dinner drinks and cigars.

The ballroom lights came up and we could see that nearly all of the audience had departed. Our table of eight, however, was still more than half full. The five of us who remained marveled that Pierrot had been spinning limericks for hours, responding to every challenge thrown at him. We were running out of subjects to suggest so someone challenged him for a limerick about a German count with a lisp. Damned if George didn't have one. I had no doubt that if we had asked for it in a Swahili dialect, George would have delivered, or made a convincing enough show of it. He had a limerick, it seemed, for any occasion. He had a limerick about a man who wouldn't stop telling limericks. He even had a couple that weren't X-rated.

As I drove him back to his home in Indian Village, I asked him if that had exhausted his supply. He laughed.

"A few years ago at one of those Steakout events," he said, "there was an auto company big shot who knew I had a bit of a reputation with limericks. He was determined the two of us would go head to head. One of us did a limerick, the other had to match it, either with the same culture or time frame, or at least using a couple of the key words. The room emptied out, all except our table. We slipped the waiters a hundred bucks to keep us going with drinks and coffee while they cleaned up."

"Who ran out of limericks first?" I asked.

There was Pierrot's rumbling laugh again. I knew as soon as

the words were out of my mouth it was a silly question.

"At about 1 a.m., the big shot suggested we call it a draw because both of us were probably running out of ammunition. I told him I could go on until sunup. He took out his checkbook and asked me the name of my favorite charity. 'If you do a limerick every five minutes until the sun rises,' he says, 'I've got a check here for a thousand dollars I'll make out to your favorite charity. But if you repeat one or can't come up with one in five minutes, you write a check for a thousand to my favorite charity.'"

He paused, waiting for me to ask.

"Okay, George, whose check got cashed?" Another stupid question.

"It must have been about 3 a.m., and the place was empty except for the five of us. Even the waiters had gone. All of a sudden, Mr. Big Shot picks up his check off the table and tears it up. He writes a new check and holds it out to me but of course I can't read it. He says, 'George, tell me the charity you want me to write this check to. In case you can't read it, the check is for $2,500 and that's because it comes with a stipulation: You must promise to never again tell another limerick within my earshot.'"

As with some of George's stories, if that wasn't exactly the way it happened, it should have been.

—⟁—

IN 1978, ALONG WITH QUITE A FEW OF DETROIT'S CELEBRITIES, personalities and characters, George Pierrot showed up for the launch of Berl Falbaum's book, *The Anchor, Leo & Friends.* I had edited Berl's manuscript and helped usher it into print with west coast publisher John Descutner of JDW Publications. The author's party was, appropriately, at the Anchor Bar, Detroit's legendary demilitarized zone. The bar had first opened in a basement on Fort Street and Fourth. In various reincarnations it moved to more spacious quarters as Anchor II and finally Anchor III around the corner and down the block on Lafayette. The Anchor was less about a place than it was a presence, or a state of mind, as the regulars said, so it didn't much matter where it was sited exactly as long as you could count on it being the same inside when you got there.

For Falbaum's book launch party, Pierrot got there early and parked his ample frame on a bar stool next to me. He said he knew the Anchor well, of course, and agreed it would be a fine place for his own author's party—once he got around to writing his book.

The Anchor was an everyman's bar where mayors and judges sat cheek to jowl with hard characters, where a governor might be seen chatting with a fry cook, where celebrities, newspaper editors, TV anchormen, and priests mingled with assembly line workers and firemen. Within these walls, cops, prostitutes and bookies didn't hassle each other. Leo's bar was well named— anybody could drop anchor there. It was a safe harbor where official roles and duties were left at the front door. By unspoken understandings and gentlemen's agreement everything was off the record.

That such a place existed in a major American city was perhaps not so surprising; that it thrived for so long with unwritten codes that were honored by all, that was unusual.

As Falbaum wrote in his golden nugget of a book:

> *The Anchor is different. It has no caste system. Governors sit alongside printers. Mayors argue politics with reporters, while pressmen, gamblers, priests, secretaries, mailmen and others add to the camaraderie that is part of the Anchor's magnetism.*
>
> *The Anchor is run by a man called Leo whose last name is known by few and misspelled by most. For the record, Leo is LeVon Derderian Sr., a 59-year-old Armenian who has made his living running a 'sleazy, dumpy, seedy' bar in downtown Detroit.* Free Press *columnist Jim Fitzgerald called it 'one of downtown Detroit's more delightfully crummy saloons.'*

Pierrot said he remembered Falbaum's byline from his days as a *Detroit News* reporter. He asked if he had written other books.

I told him Berl was well qualified to write the definitive book on Leo and his bar, having spent many hours there "doing research" when he was a reporter for *The News* and that he knew many of the Anchor regulars.

Politicians frequenting the Anchor included Michigan Governor John Swainson, Lt. Governor John Brickley and Detroit Mayor Jerry Cavanaugh, who would bring such guests as New York Mayor Robert Wagner. A few clergymen were regulars, none more so than Monsignor Clement Kern of the Most Holy Trinity Church, a long-time beneficiary of a collection basket that had a permanent and prominent place on the bar at the Anchor.

They were there to celebrate something they shared in common: the sanctuary afforded by the Anchor, the camaraderie of its denizens, and most of all the Damon Runyanesque character who was the catalyst and the magnet: Leo Derderian.

George Pierrot might not have been a regular of the Anchor Bar but he was certainly in his element there. But then, George was in his element wherever he was.

He asked me to tell him more about Leo so I bought yet another copy of Falbaum's book from the stacks on the counter and read him a few paragraphs. In his book, Falbaum described Leo as having been born of Turkish parents and named after a thirteenth century Armenian king. Derderian described himself as:

> .... an American who grew up in the Depression with gambling all around him... I wrote numbers at the age of 13 or 14 which I reinvested in the same game—never winning anything to speak of... I played the crooked dice game... I worked at the Ford Motor Company and indulged myself with all the parts of gambling, in matching coins for paychecks, and also being a runner for the horses for the bosses of the plant to better myself by doing less work... Unfortunately, a war broke out in the attack of Pearl Harbor and I, as a pure American, enlisted in the U.S. Marines to defend my country as a good citizen...served in the Pacific in the defense of my nation... I was a union organizer for the UAW because

of the bad situation in the shops of my country...

Paraphrasing what I had learned from Falbaum and Leo himself, I told George that somehow out of all of this emerged a man who brought together the most disparate elements of Detroit "society." Leo's beneficiaries were the needy and the homeless, the underfunded causes and charitable organizations. He was a benefactor of the Most Holy Trinity Church and of the Jewish Center. He was a meal ticket for the next hungry guy who wandered in without a cent in his pocket. The Anchor was Detroit's answer to the United Nations: Greeks, Irish, blacks, Jews, Armenians. During the Detroit Riot of 1967, the Anchor became the international pressroom for reporters from England, Australia, Japan, Germany, and from around United States. Writers from New York wrote that "journalism could never survive without places like the Anchor."

According to Falbaum, the Random House book *Where to Eat in America,* called the Anchor, "an almost sleazy bar" that served the best hamburgers in Detroit. Leo was as delighted by the "almost sleazy" as he was with the accolade for his burgers.

George squinted at the cover of the book, trying to see if he could recognize anyone in the montage of caricatures. He named a couple and got them right. Then he paused and tapped a beefy finger on one. It was Doc Greene.

Of all the characters who made the Anchor almost a second home, none was more identified with the place than the redoubtable columnist, book author and raconteur Doc Greene. Falbaum's book cleared up the mini-mystery of how and why the nationally prominent Greene lost his job at *The News*. Greene had tried to set himself up on the side as the orchestrater and promoter of a heavyweight title bout between Cassius Clay (soon to become Muhammad Ali) and Joe Frazier. *The News* dismissed Greene, asserting he had created an unacceptable conflict of interest. Doc, on the contrary, told friends that he had under-estimated the strongly negative feelings that the very conservative *News* management held for the outspoken draft-evader Clay who famously said, "No Viet Cong ever called me a nigger."

Now George Pierrot, looking around at the interesting characters gathered for the Falbaum book premiere, was getting an idea. He turned to me and said, "We've got to get going on my book. We could stage the best damn book-launching party ever."

He then asked me write down names of those we would invite. He started with his close friend Lowell Thomas, whose signature drawn-out signoff from his evening radio news broadcast was one of the best-known expressions in America, "So long... until tomorrow." Then, as fast as I could write, he ticked off names of movie stars and Nobel prize-winning authors, politicians and athletes. Friends and colleagues would come to Detroit from every continent. George growled, "We'll have heads of state mingle with safari guides. Be good for both of them. There'll be chairmen of boards chatting up Tibetan sherpas. They won't understand a word the other says, but the sherpas will nod gravely."

I didn't tell George we could have only a couple hundred people. That would be just a fraction of the thousands he had met, befriended and kept in touch with in his travels to all of the continents, across all the oceans, in his almost eighty years on the planet.

"What should we title the book?" he asked.

I had already thought about it. "How about 'Around the World in Eighty Years'?"

—m—

OVER THE NEXT TWO YEARS, GEORGE HAD A SUCCESSION of health problems and yet tried to maintain a busy schedule. He would call me periodically and report he was now "digging in and at last making a little headway on the manuscript."

One evening, I just happened to be going over a partial list of candidate subjects we might include in George's "Around the World..." book when I heard the news that earlier that day George

Pierrot had died.

I waited until things quieted for his widow, Helen, and then called her.

"Yes," she said. "George really had been enjoying the prospect of finally doing his own book. I'll go through his materials when I'm up to it. I don't know how far along he got."

For a time, we both hoped that George's notes and files would give her enough to work with so she could produce a manuscript capturing at least some of his countless stories—and perhaps a few limericks—for posterity. She knew from countless letters that many people said their lives were changed by the adventures they were exposed to on George's televised shows and lectures. Many said the *World Adventure Series* whetted their appetite to see exotic places and that they owed each trip and every trek to him. There would be many readers out there for Pierrot's story, told in his own words.

A few weeks later, Helen called to tell me it was hopeless.

"Only George could do justice to George," she said. "Hardly any of his great yarns ever made it onto paper. He had all those stories in that great memory of his and he took them with him when he left. But I do wish there was some way we could preserve his last words. The last thing he said was just so much like him."

Helen told me that on the morning of the last day on this globe for Detroit's incomparable world traveler, she awoke feeling very ill herself. She asked George to call for an ambulance and he did. But before the ambulance got there, George himself was stricken. He lay on the couch, in and out of consciousness.

When the ambulance arrived, the two emergency medical technicians wheeled a gurney through the front door. Because the phone call had said it was a woman they were to pick up, the EMTs started to help Helen onto it. She waved them off, insisting that her husband was in worse shape, so they must tend to him first.

The two technicians had great difficulty getting the very corpulent George onto the gurney. The jostling brought him fully conscious for a moment and as they wheeled him out the front door, he looked up and saw what was happening.

"One of you boys better drive," George said. "I don't think I feel up to it."

He told his engineers to start over and design an engine
that was compact and powerful. "One more thing," he
said. "Make it lightweight." Neither Cole nor anyone else
could have guessed then that a half-century later GM
would build the 100-millionth descendant of the engine
for which he had been the driving force.

Ed Cole shifted priority away from raw power and
mandated that GM engines be set up for fuel economy
and invested considerable resources to make it happen.
At the same time he set a goal that GM become the
world leader in safety research and safety engineering.
He poured resources into engineering for tighter
environmental constraints, shaping GM for a future
he knew would be realized only many years
after his tenure there was over.

~~10~~

THE MAN WHO GOT THE LEAD OUT OF DETROIT

Ed Cole's Corvettes, Corvairs and Catalytic Converters

THEY CALLED HIM "THE GENERAL, THE GEORGE PATTON OF THE AUTO IN-DUSTRY."

It would have been just as fitting to call General George Patton the "Ed Cole of the Army." Throughout their long and storied careers, both men combined toughness and willingness to take bold risks with creative genius and charismatic leadership.

Ed Cole was the kind of dashing, can-do figure that made Detroit the unquestioned car capital of the world in the middle of the twentieth century. He was delighted to be called a "car guy," but was much more than that. He was also a highly innovative engineer, a savvy businessman, an adept marketer, and a strong, confidence-inspiring leader of his organization. He was, at the same time, a pragmatic realist and an idealistic visionary. In more ways than one, Ed Cole got the lead out of Detroit and injected a whole lot of pizzazz and high tech.

Cole compiled a lengthy list of major accomplishments in his forty-seven years at General Motors. He made one of his most lasting and far-reaching contributions in 1972 when, as president of

GM, he mandated that by 1975 all GM cars would be equipped with catalytic converters. Soon, the waves generated by that bold thrust cascaded throughout the industry. The reduction in lead and other toxic emissions produced incalculable benefits for the environment and public health. In 1974-76, he pioneered air safety bags on ten thousand GM cars. If Cole had been at the helm as Mary Barra's immediate predecessor in the previous decade, would Barra have had to deal with the ignition-switch catastrophe that gestated for ten years before she inherited it in early 2014? Not likely, judging from the emphasis he put on safety.

Another revolutionary decision Cole gambled on was to bring out a car that represented a radical departure for the industry and his Chevrolet division—and to present the innovative vehicle in a fiberglass body.

Long before Cole ascended to the presidency of General Motors, he was focused on the nuts and bolts of automobiles. He headed the team that developed the V8 engine for the 1949 Cadillac—that led to his promotion in 1952 to chief engineer of Chevrolet Division. There again, he had responsibility for developing a V8 engine, this one a small-block version to replace Chevy's "Stovebolt Six." Cole had left no doubt how much he hated the small-displacement V8 that was in development at Chevrolet when he got there. He told his engineers to start over and design an engine that was compact and powerful.

"One more thing," he said. "Make it lightweight."

Neither Cole nor anyone else could have guessed then that a "half-century later" GM would build the 100-millionth descendant of the engine for which he had been the driving force.

Even as Cole ascended GM's management ranks, he compiled a lengthy list of important advancements for trucks and cars. Although he kept an active hand in designing and engineering, almost from the moment he became chief engineer of Chevrolet in 1952, Cole had an uncanny perception of what would catch the consumer's eye. Just as important, he knew exactly what would jolt a driver's pulse to racing. When he became general manager at Chevrolet in 1956, he quickly made his mark as a champion of muscle cars, reflecting his own personality in his taste in automobiles. He was a dynamic, big picture, articulate maverick and many of the cars he championed showed it.

Because he trusted his own instincts and took bold risks as Chevrolet's leader, he changed the automotive industry landscape in Detroit. Two of his pet projects were at opposite ends of the driving spectrum: the high-performance Corvette and the sporty compact, rear-engine, air-cooled Corvair. Wildly dissimilar in appearance and performance, the two vehicles had one important quality in common: Ed Cole's credo that Chevrolet cars had to "kick hell out of the status quo."

Cole had a tall stature not only in Detroit, and not just on the automotive scene. At a time when the domestic car business was supremely dominant, the management hierarchies of the Big Three were genuine national celebrities. The litany of Cole's accomplishments put him on the cover of *Time* magazine's issue of October 5, 1959.

I was very aware of what Ed Cole had accomplished at GM, even though I was far removed from the car business by the time he and I met in 1976. I was then publishing scholarly books at the University of Michigan Press, but I knew Cole had carved out a special place in Detroit automotive history before his retirement in 1974. That was why I had contacted him in connection with a book I was developing at the Press.

We had already secured strong endorsements for the book from distinguished academics in the fields of business management and organizational behavior. Those positive recommendations would help in gaining approval from the Press's executive committee. But we needed an endorsement from a prominent business leader. Some authoritative, positive words from this tough, straight-talking, well-respected business executive would make the book attractive to the business community where a reading of it and the application of its findings could do the most good.

Immediately after retiring from GM, Cole had set up his own company in Bloomfield Hills. He answered the phone himself on the first ring. The reports of his gruffness were not exaggerated and I sensed he was giving me thirty seconds to make my case. "We're considering publishing a book on management styles," I said. "The manuscript is finished and academicians have already sprinkled holy water on it. But I need a frank opinion from someone in the real world who has managed people— someone like you. The book is based on solid social science research into organizational behavior. Some of that research was done at GM plants that were under your direction."

Cole immediately broke in to tell me he recalled giving approval for a GM plant to be used in that study. He thought for a few seconds, then said he remembered reading a report on the findings. For a moment I wondered if that hurt the chances of his agreeing to read the manuscript because some of the findings hadn't reflected favorably on management ranks at that plant.

"Tell me more about this book," he said. "Who wrote it?"

I told him the book would be titled, *System IV: Management of the Human Resource*. The book, written by Dr. David Bowers, focused on important new insights in organizational behavior and particularly the work of Dr. Rensis Likert, a distinguished scholar on how organizations function. The core of the book was an analysis of different managerial styles and how they influence organizational effectiveness.

In that first phone conversation, I could tell that Cole's reputation as a no-bones-about-it boss was well deserved. Of all the auto executives in Detroit, none was more blunt. That had worked both ways for him in his flamboyant career. Reporters took good care of him because he was that rare trifecta among knowledgeable top executives: accessible, quotable and sometimes prone to talk before he thought. That got him coverage in the press and it also occasionally got him crosswise with his GM colleagues as well as his competitors at Ford and Chrysler. Cole also found himself in the gossip columns too often, sometimes because of his second wife, Dolly. Typical was the time Dolly got out of a New York taxicab and left a large handbag behind. The story hit newspapers and TV shows around the country because an honest New York cabbie returned to the Coles a handbag stuffed with cash and diamonds.

Cole said he remembered well the research done at the GM plant.

"I wasn't too happy with some of those results," Cole said. "So I looked into it further myself and damned if they weren't dead on. I ordered some changes as a result of that study. Sure, send the manuscript over and I'll have a look."

A month went by with no word from Cole. We were on the calendar to propose the book to the Press's executive committee, something I didn't want to do without a positive recommendation from a business leader. I called Cole and apologized if it appeared I was rushing him but would he be able to look at the manuscript soon so we could include his assessment in our recommendation to the committee.

"Hell, I read that the day it arrived."

I asked if he had any thoughts about it.

"I don't know that I could say anything that might be helpful. In my opinion that book should be read by every manager in industry."

I told him that would do just fine. I'd like his permission to put those exact words on the cover, right above his name.

A few weeks later, I sent Cole a note thanking him. I told him the Press committee had given the green light. The book was now in the editing process and we would send him copies when it came off the presses. His quote would be on the front cover. That didn't seem to make much of an impression on him. He changed the subject right away and told me he was glad I called for another reason. He said he was thinking of writing a book and wanted to know if I would be interested in working with him.

Cole had moved into office space made available to him by one of GM's agencies, Bloomfield Hills-based D'Arcy MacManus & Masius (DM&M). The agency's office was one of the most recognizable buildings in Bloomfield Hills, perched on a little rise just northwest of the intersection of Woodward Avenue and Long Lake Road. I drove by that site hundreds of times in my high school days in my 1948 Chevy coupe. It was on a route well known to countless kids in souped-up Pontiacs and shackled Mercuries, cruising through every drive-in restaurant on Woodward Avenue from the Totem Pole in Royal Oak north to Ted's Trailer at Square Lake Road.

I learned later that DM&M had been the first agency to move out of Detroit to the suburbs. The toney suburb of Bloomfield Hills was the high-rent district but the agency had its rationale. Many GM executives lived in the Birmingham-Bloomfield area and the agency would be a convenient place for them to have early morning or late afternoon meetings. Any opportunity to be hospitable to the client should be exploited. And, it was no coincidence that it would also put them within minutes of more than half a dozen private golf clubs, especially Bloomfield Hills Country Club, less than a quarter mile away. What better place to conclude a discussion about a new advertising campaign than at the 19th hole?

Fifty years earlier, Theodore MacManus, a founder of the predecessor agency called MacManus, John & Adams, was convinced—despite his detestation of golf—that linking that sport with business made great sense for an advertising agency and its automotive clients. So he ordered the construction of a small and very exclusive golf course—later named Stoneycroft Golf Club—on his property at Opdyke and Woodward. Setting aside his personal dislike of the game, MacManus wanted a very private course. He ordained that it be used solely to entertain his clients, especially GM.

Soon MacManus's agency colleagues talked him into buying a set of clubs for himself, just to give it a try so he could personally entertain his clients, especially General Motors top executives. He played just one 9-hole round. He walked off the last green and strode directly to a very sturdy oak tree. There, "enjoying each swing far more than I had all day in this damned foolish game," he said, he proceeded to break every club in his bag across the trunk of the oak. He stepped back to admire his handiwork and loudly proclaimed, "I shall never play this ridiculous game again." And he never did.

Now, four decades later, Ed Cole, the retired president of Mac-Manus's dominant client occupied a nearly vacant wing of the sprawling agency complex built mostly on revenue from its work for GM. It was simply good sense and good business for DM&M to host distinguished GM alum Ed Cole with free rent. After all, DM&M was the only advertising agency handling two major car divisions, GM's Pontiac and Cadillac. The agency had also created the mythical "Mr. Goodwrench," for the GM Parts Division. In a close and long-standing relationship uncommon in the volatile automotive advertising segment, MacManus's successor agencies had been serving GM since 1913.

When I visited Cole to hear about his prospective book, he sat alone in a long, narrow and almost empty office with a partial view of the intersection of Woodward Avenue and Long Lake Roads and not much else. He was barely fifteen miles due north of his old headquarters office at GM, but for him it was the other side of the moon.

He apologized for the sparseness of the cavernous room, then said, "What the hell does an engineer need a lot of fancy furniture for anyhow." The walls were bare and the furniture consisted entirely of his desk and chair, a small file cabinet, and one visitor's chair in a room that could easily accommodate six people, a couple of secretaries and their furnishings. On his desk were a telephone, a single tablet of paper, a fountain pen holder and four authentic scale models of vehicles.

As we talked, he picked up one or another of the models and looked at it with curiosity as he described it to me. Two of the models were airplanes, one of which I recognized as a Lockheed C-130

"Super Hercules" cargo plane. That airplane was familiar to me—Ed was surprised to hear—because I had written technical manuals about it in 1959 when I worked at Lockheed in Marietta, Georgia. The Super Herc was a very large airplane, but it looked as tiny as a Piper Cub alongside another airplane model that Cole picked up. He smiled as he admired that model. He described it as a super-gigantic cargo plane he hoped to see flying one day. Prominently lettered on the fuselage was International Husky, Inc., which I soon learned was one of his companies.

"But for that ever to happen, I'd have to put together enough buyers to justify getting it manufactured," he said. "And even then it would need about $2.5 billion from the federal government. Over time, they'd earn that back because it would cut transportation costs by two-thirds, to about three cents a ton/mile. If it's ever built, it would be three times the size of a Boeing 747 and have many times the carrying capacity of the largest airplanes now in the air."

He paused and looked at the model wistfully. "You could transport seventy-five cars in that baby," he said. "If I can ever get it off the ground."

The other two objects were a yellow Checker taxicab and a Corvette Sting Ray. The Corvette, which he did not invent but personally godfathered to life with Zora Arkus-Duntov, would forever remind him, he said, of some of the most exciting days of his career. As for the Checker cab, it was a challenge he had taken on to make that familiar nameplate successful once again. He intended to produce an updated version of the bulky yellow taxi, an icon that immediately told movie viewers the picture they were watching was set in midtown Manhattan.

"We've got a little joint venture in the works between Checker and Volkswagen," he said. "I'll be chairman and CEO at Checker, working with David Markin, the founder and president. I'll be number one at number five."

I looked at him, puzzled.

"Most people don't know that Checker, small as it is, is America's fifth largest carmaker. Anyhow, people want and deserve a hell of a lot better vehicle than they're getting. We're working on something that will do the job and resuscitate Checker in the process. We've got a couple prototypes we're putting together now. We call 'em 'CheckeRabbits'."

Hearing the candidate new name for the updated Checker model reminded me of a story about a decision Cole had made on the naming of a new Chevrolet model. A small fortune had been spent in researching names and testing them on focus groups, panels of consumers. There were ten names being considered. The name that tested worst for the new sedan was "Vega." People commented that it made them think of something to do with people who didn't eat meat, a jungle disease, or a female body part. On favorability, it was dead last on the list. Cole looked at the results, tossed them aside and said, "The hell with it. Call it Vega."

I asked Cole about the story. He said it was true and "not the only mistake I ever made and damn sure not the biggest one either."

Ed Cole was a man of many talents—selecting good names for vehicles was not one of them.

Everything I had heard or read about Detroit's most outspoken, self-assured car guy was borne out in person. He could be terse and impatient one moment and sentimental or mischievous the next. It was easy to see how he had been the driving force behind such disparate vehicles as the Corvette Sting Ray and the stodgy Corvair. Although he had stepped down from the high-powered corporate world of the Big Three, his "retirement" was going to be anything but traditional and sedate.

We went to the nearby Fox & Hounds restaurant for lunch where Ed continued to talk about his early GM days—they sounded as if they were the most exciting and fulfilling in his career. With his new ventures, he was well on his way to rekindling that same sense of urgency from his pioneering GM days.

"I wasn't too happy when I ran up against GM's mandatory retirement age wall," he said. "I said the hell with that, I'm only sixty-five and here I'm out of the transportation business for good? Jesus, how much golf can a guy play? Now I'm into these new ventures and having more fun than I've had in years. Working fourteen hours a day and no time for things like golf."

Over lunch, Cole explained further what he had in mind with the colossal aircraft and the moribund Checker cab company. He knew he was rolling the dice against long odds. Few expected he would succeed with either venture. That seemed to sharpen his appetite all the more. Skepticism of "those so-called experts," as he called them, bothered him not a whit. He believed in his projects and that was all he needed.

Ed Cole had plenty of experience doing the unexpected and tackling the controversial. Sometimes, his initial efforts seemed to falter—as they had with the early iterations of the Corvette—but his staying power was remarkable and usually he prevailed. He cited as an example the pundits who said, "It would never happen, the conservative Chevrolet division giving birth in less than a year to the spectacular, fiberglass body Corvette."

He talked about how ironic it was that in the capstone years of his GM tenure he presided over a totally different kind of high performance. He admitted that his career had taken some strange turns. Born in Marne, Michigan, in 1909 on a dairy farm, Cole was determined to become an automotive engineer. He enrolled in General Motors Institute only to have to drop out for financial reasons in 1933. He felt fortunate to land a job as a lab assistant, rising through the ranks to eventually co-head the team that developed the 1949 Cadillac V8. He ran a GM plant in Cleveland, then in 1952 was named Chevrolet's chief engineer and later its general manager.

"We got a lot done those ten years at Chevrolet," he said. So much did Cole accomplish that he was named a GM executive vice president in 1965 and president in 1967. In those roles, he shifted priority away from raw power and mandated that GM engines be set up for fuel economy and invested considerable resources to make it happen.

At the same time, he set a goal that GM become the world leader in safety research and safety engineering. He poured resources into engineering for tighter environmental constraints, shaping GM for a future he knew would be realized only many years after his tenure there was over.

Cole talked about Peter Drucker's *Concept of the Corporation*, which he insisted was the most insightful and definitive book about General Motors. "That book did a lot to position GM at the top of economic institutions in the world," Cole said. He nodded his head as he thought about it. "But, my God, that book came out in 1946. Wouldn't you think it's about time for another book that gives a look into the way it is in today's real world of GM?"

When the check came, I reached for it and told Ed that since he waived our three-hundred-dollar reading fee, it was the least I could do.

"I don't know what they pay managing editors at university presses these days, but GM took pretty good care of me, so I'll handle this," he said. "Besides, if we do this book together, you'll get your turn. Speaking of which, let's see what your schedule is like so we can keep up the momentum on this, see whether or not I really ought to write a book."

Cole and I met twice more over the next few months and talked several times by phone. He said his projects were keeping him from focusing on the book as much as he wanted to. No surprise there.

—〰—

IT WAS NOT UNTIL APRIL 1977 THAT WE MET AGAIN. I had news for Ed. I told him I was leaving U-M Press in a few weeks to return to Bendix as director of corporate communications. I assured him that would make no difference in our working together on his book and that I would enjoy doing that. I told him if he decided to proceed he would undoubtedly want a major New York publisher and with his reputation, he could feel confident of getting one. He accepted my suggestions that I would discuss the project with my agent who would take soundings with acquisitions editors at the right New York houses when we were further along.

Ed wanted to meet again soon so we agreed on a date in early May that looked good for both us. He suggested we go to Kalamazoo where I could meet his partner David Markin and have a look at the new Checker concept car.

"I'll have a driver so we can talk in the back seat all the way there," he said. Then he paused. "On second thought," he said, "I've got my plane at the Pontiac Airport. If we fly there, we've got more time in Kalamazoo."

On May 1, the day before our planned trip to Kalamazoo, I had unexpected schedule conflicts. I called Ed and said I regretted the change of plans. Could we reschedule?

"Don't worry about it," he said. "Call me when your schedule loosens up and we'll set a new time. There'll be plenty of opportunities."

But there would be no more opportunities. And there would never be an Ed Cole story told in his own words.

Early in the morning of May 2, at Pontiac Airport, Ed climbed into the cockpit of his British-built twin-engine "Beagle." He had told me more than once how he loved flying his own plane again after GM restrictions had prohibited him from piloting any aircraft for so many years.

Months later, Federal Aeronautics Administration inspectors concluded that Ed Cole, a seasoned pilot, flew into heavy rain and zero visibility near Mendon, twenty miles outside Kalamazoo. People on the ground reported that the airplane engines cut out, restarted, and then quit again. The FAA opinion was that Cole mistrusted the readings on his instruments and developed vertigo.

Whatever the cause, the man whose courage, energy and genius amped up the heartbeat of America to a thundering roar, crashed his beloved Beagle into a plowed field and died instantly. His life ended about fifty miles from the town where he had been born 68 years before.

But the innovations Ed Cole spurred—from Corvettes to catalytic converters to safety engineering—lived on, changing the automotive world and the driving experience, and contributing to a cleaner environment.

She was a visionary looking toward a far horizon,
trying to lay the groundwork for a state
with a diversified and healthy economy.
But there was a problem...

Michigan's roller-coaster economy had been through
many lofty climbs and even steeper plummets.
Against this backdrop, the free fall that confronted
Granholm was among the most precipitous ever.
No surprise that her bold and innovative proposals to
truly diversify the economy ran into some hard realities.

~11~

STEERING THE SHIP OF STATE
ON STORMY SEAS

Jennifer Granholm's Blueprint
for a Diversified, Dynamic Michigan

COMING FROM GOVERNOR RICK SNYDER in a State of the State address, these words would trigger thunderous applause from his Republican legislature:

> *"We have laid the foundation for a new Michigan economy. We put in place the most aggressive economic development program to diversify Michigan's economy that has resulted in more than $57 billion in private investment, nearly 4,000 economic development projects, and the creation or retention of 653,000 jobs."*

See, conservatives would say, these are the kinds of results achieved by a governor who really is a leader on diversification.

One problem: those words didn't come from Governor Snyder. Those are the words of Snyder's predecessor, Jennifer Granholm, as she neared the end of her second term, in 2010.

Granholm went on to say, "And while our work is far from finished, it's time to pass the torch to Governor-elect Snyder who shares my commitment to diversifying Michigan's economy and creating jobs."

So, Rick Snyder did not invent the concept of diversification for Michigan's economy. Nor did Jennifer Granholm.

She just did more to advance it than any Michigan governor in modern history and to lay down the foundation on which her successors could build.

For decades in Michigan, anyone following the money back to its original source would learn that the lineage of virtually every paycheck could be traced to the same forebears. Some portion of nearly every family's income derived from the sales of new cars rolling off Detroit assembly lines. If a Ford Mustang, a Dodge Caravan, or an Olds Cutlass became the next hot seller, stamping machine operators and maintenance men in River Rouge or Hamtramck or Flint bought boats, snowmobiles, maybe even a new cottage up north. New decks were built on tri-levels in Livonia. Sales spiked for new carpets and pizzas in Troy, fudge on Mackinac Island, new braces for the kids in Macomb County, and reservations at the hairdresser or the golf course in Bloomfield Hills. Throughout the state, restaurants, gas stations, dry cleaners and grocery stores and their employees thrived.

Conversely, if a plant closed, it meant not just rainy days for those dislocated workers—a tsunami burst through the entire region, and even communities hundreds of miles away were hit with the waves.

Tourism and agriculture were not insignificant, but personal economic barometers rose or fell with the changing weather in the car business.

Throughout the twentieth century, Michigan's governors had to craft budgets and shape economic plans keyed off an inescapable reality: The state's economic well-being depended almost entirely on the health of Detroit's Big Three. No surprise then, that a long succession of Michigan's governors, beginning with Frank Murphy in the late 1930s, made only halting steps toward diversification, and with results that were, at best, meager. Read the campaign rhetoric, the inaugural addresses, and the State of the State addresses of governors and the familiar refrain is sounded: support the dominance of the auto industry while taking the state's economy in new directions. Take a double dose of the automotive status quo, a teaspoon of diversification and call me in the morning.

But the sun never rose on a diversified Michigan. The momentum faded even as the lofty words were uttered and it was soon business at the same old stand.

Until Granholm, the state's forty-seventh governor.

Maybe it had something to do with her Swedish lineage—an economic smorgasbord being infinitely more appetizing than repeated servings of the same dish. Michigan's first female governor, an import from Canada already, was actually serious about diversification.

She was also ahead of her time on a subject that was well past its time. Moreover, she was dealing with a state legislature that was not about to be tasered into the twentieth century, let alone the twenty-first.

They dug in their heels on diversification in full awareness of the historical fact that again and again the state was staggered by a stiff uppercut every time the national economy took a jab. More than any other state, Michigan did not move in lockstep with the rest of the nation. In difficult times, Michigan plummeted sooner and deeper into the abyss and when conditions improved nationally, the state was slower crawling out of it.

In the first years of the twenty-first century, the decline continued, then steepened in 2005 and 2006. The bubble burst on high-risk and sub-prime mortgages in 2007 and balloon payments came due on adjustable mortgages. Business loans, bankruptcies, defaults and outright abandonments of homes skyrocketed in Michigan. Sales of domestic cars plummeted again.

Michigan's roller-coaster economy had been through many lofty climbs and even steeper plummets. Against this backdrop, the free fall that confronted Granholm was among the most precipitous ever. No surprise that her bold and innovative proposals to truly diversify the economy ran into some hard realities. One obstacle was resistance in the legislature to any initiatives with an element of risk. Some legislators seemed to be holding out for a return to the good old days when Detroit was the unquestioned automotive capital of the world with a pipeline of revenues flowing smoothly into Lansing. Rather than embrace Granholm's gamble on diversification, the legislature continued to insist that the best way to offset shrinking tax revenues was simple: further draconian cuts in education, welfare and services.

In 2003, when Granholm became the state's first woman governor, seldom had a state been in such dire straits as Michigan with its ailing automobile manufacturers coughing up market share and hemorrhaging red ink by the billions.

"When I first took office, we were starting to see signs that the auto industry was challenged and that we had a budget crisis," Granholm says, "but the depth and severity wasn't fully brought to bear until 2003-4."

Granholm's prescription for this sickly state economy, however, would be radically different from her predecessors. That was because she presided over a state unquestionably on the brink.

She was keenly aware that when an industry that dominates a state's economy goes into a slump, politicians seldom speak without using their new favorite word: "diversification." The cliché du jour becomes: "Let's not put all our eggs in one basket." When the crisis eases and the cash-cow industry returns to robust health, diversification plans are quietly tucked away and politicians pat themselves on the back for their steadfastness in "going back to our roots."

In that respect, Granholm knew there was nothing original in her playing the diversification card. But there was a difference this time—the passion and tenacity of the politician. Granholm preached to all who would listen and many who would not that diversification was the best—if not the only—way to transform the state's economy for good.

She was a visionary looking toward a far horizon, trying to lay the groundwork for a state with a diversified and healthy economy. But there was a problem. She was governing at a time when the legislature and a great many of its citizens were staring at alarming shortfalls in income with scant prospect for improvement in the short term.

Long before being elected to state office, the Canadian-born Granholm had steeped herself in Michigan's history. She knew that perhaps no other state has enjoyed such brief exhilarating peaks before careening into such long and deep gut-wrenching valleys. For almost a hundred years, Michigan's fortunes have been yoked to the horseless carriage. Automotive companies, their legions of suppliers, their unions, and their corporate chieftains have dominated the landscape and the economy. Traditionally, Michigan's governors and legislatures have been submissive enablers—their motto: "What's good for the automobile industry is good for Michigan."

Some politicians spring-boarded to elective office directly from a top position in the car business. In 1962, George Romney segued effortlessly from the helm of American Motors to the governor's office. Since the 1920s, it was a seldom-challenged assumption that alternative modes of transportation posed dangers to Michigan's economy. Threats were seen in virtually all other modes of conveyance, but most especially mass transit. In more recent times, the automobile companies—generally headed by conservative Republicans—forged a powerfully effective alliance with Democratic congressman John Dingell, champion of the United Auto Workers. Together, this corporate and union tandem fought strenuously against a strong Clean Air Act, tougher fuel standards, alternative energy sources, and any substantial investment by government in industries unrelated to the automotive business.

So it was nothing new for Michigan governors to give merely lip service to diversification. What was new was Granholm's determination to make it happen.

"I have a tremendous team of economic advisers who said we

have to do a number of things," Granholm said. "And we have set those things in motion. One is diversify the economy, but everybody has been saying that for twenty years. The real question is, 'How do you do it?' What are the specific strategies that will actually have an impact on the economy in light of the fact that it is so private-sector driven in so many ways?"

To the Republican Legislature, that sounded like risky business.

From her background, Granholm would have been predicted to be anything but a risk-taker. The dominant traits in her home environment in her early years were not boldness, innovation and risk-taking but rather the more conservative values of determination, persistence and caution.

Granholm was born in 1959 in Vancouver, British Columbia, to Victor Ivar Granholm and Shirley Alfreda (Dowden). Her father, a banking consultant, was "the single most powerful influence and mentor in my life," Granholm says. "My dad is the person I put at the top of the list. He is a stoic Swede. I never heard him utter a swear word or raise his voice. His whole being and character were focused on integrity and hard work."

Granholm calls herself a "fiscal hawk" and that strain of fiscal conservatism may be traced to her early childhood and her father. "When my dad was three years old, his mother was widowed," she says. "They lived in a one-room dirt-floor cottage in the backwoods of British Columbia with no running water. They were dirt poor."

Victor Granholm's parents had emigrated from Sweden and Norway. When his father died prematurely, his mother, who didn't speak English, was left with three kids. "My dad had to work in a sawmill to provide food for the family," Granholm says. "He comes from the most humble of backgrounds and has always been humble. He has been a tremendous role model for me in terms of character. If I could be half the person that he is, I would consider myself very successful. He is a totally heroic soul."

Even after Victor became a successful banking consultant, he continued the habits of his early days. "He did not keep banker's hours at all," Granholm says. "He was up at 4 a.m. and out of the house by 5."

In 1962, when Granholm was three years old, the family moved to the United States, settling in the San Francisco Bay area. In 1977, the blonde, photogenic Jennifer moved to Los Angeles, thinking she would become an actress. Even though Granholm's parents prefer to live a simple, community-based family life, according to Granholm, her mother always told her, "You can be anything you want."

Granholm took her mother at her word and headed for Hollywood. But her career plans were detoured by something that may have first seemed a predictable diversion but soon became a passion—politics. When John Anderson ran as an independent candidate for president in 1978, the then 18-year-old college student Granholm worked on his campaign. Eager to vote in American elections, she applied for U.S. citizenship.

Granholm enrolled in the University of California in Berkeley, funding her education with student loans and a variety of jobs en route to becoming the first person in her family to graduate from college. After earning a bachelor's degree in political science, Granholm enrolled in Harvard Law School where she served as editor-in-chief of the Harvard Civil Rights/Civil Liberties Law Review. Apartheid was still being practiced in South Africa and Granholm's political focus was on boycotts of companies doing business with that country.

In the spring of 1985, when Granholm was on her way back to Harvard from spring break, she was killing time at the Newark Airport, waiting for a connection on People Express, the ultra-economy airline popular with students and others on tight budgets. She overheard a conversation between a teaching assistant and a freshman student, neither of whom she knew, but that didn't stop her from making a comment to the teaching assistant, Daniel Mulhern.

"The next thing I knew," Mulhern says, "Jennifer and I started talking and ended up sitting next to each other on the plane. When we arrived at the airport in Boston we decided to share a cab to campus. I lived about a mile and a half from the station and Jennifer lived about a half mile away, on campus."

Mulhern didn't know it at the time, but he was about to get a firm introduction to personality qualities of Granholm frequently remarked upon by others: determination, pride and self-reliance.

"She had a huge suitcase and a big backpack completely stuffed with books and other things," Mulhern recalls. "I just had a small backpack with not much in it so I said, 'Let me carry your bag' and she said very emphatically, 'No, no no.' So we walked back, me asking every block or so if I could carry her bag and with that incredible pride she kept saying no. She lugged it all the way, that big old hard-shell suitcase."

Mulhern speculates that the character traits that Jennifer appears to have inherited from her father have already been passed on to the next generation. "Our oldest daughter Kathryn was the same way from the moment she was born. Lying there on the table just minutes old she was pushing everyone away. My first encounter with my two Alpha-women was with their fierce pride, of 'I'm going to do it myself my own way.'"

Granholm's school workload and involvement in many causes posed a hurdle for Mulhern to overcome early in their relationship. "I pursued her doggedly," he says, "but she was always demonstrating, protesting. Finally I wore her down and we had a dinner date. Even then, she cross-examined me, wanting to know how many kids I wanted to have, what I intended to do in the future. We were both interested in changing the world."

Granholm and Mulhern met on April 1, 1985, and within a few weeks knew that they would get married. One day, Jennifer said to Mulhern, "Don't think that you're getting off without a formal proposal of marriage."

On July 16 that year, Mulhern surprised her with that formal proposal—it was in the dining room of New York's Plaza Hotel, where Granholm was expecting to meet a client. They were married less than a year later, on May 23, 1986, and took their honeymoon in Ireland. They also took each other's names to become Jennifer Mulhern Granholm and Daniel Granholm Mulhern.

In 1987, she earned her JD degree from Harvard. After moving to Michigan, she began her law career as a law clerk for Judge Damon Keith of the U.S. Circuit Court of Appeals in Detroit. She was admitted to the Michigan Bar, the U.S. District Court (eastern district) of Michigan, and the U.S. Court of Appeals for the Sixth Circuit that year while Mulhern spent the next two years as executive assistant for Wayne County. In 1988, Granholm served as a field coordinator for the presidential campaign of Michael Dukakis.

"She worked eighty to eight-five hours a week on that campaign," says Mulhern. "Her work ethic is astounding."

Granholm joined the U.S. Department of Justice in 1990 as a prosecutor in Detroit, where she achieved a ninety-eight percent conviction rate. In 1994, she was appointed Corporation Counsel for Wayne County, where she oversaw a staff of seventy-five and a budget of $9.5 million. Ed McNamara, Wayne County Chief Executive, was a close observer of both Granholm and Mulhern. David Katz, chief of staff in that office, tells how McNamara once gestured toward Granholm and Mulhern and said, "The only question is which one of them will one day become governor of Michigan."

Even in her early days in Michigan, Granholm consumed volumes of information about the state, providing her with a broad and deep understanding that would guide her in the future.

By 1996, Granholm had fleshed out her résumé with practical experience in municipal, real estate, and criminal law. These credentials qualified her perfectly for her next role: general counsel for the Wayne County Stadium Authority.

At that time, Granholm was pregnant with Jack, their third child, and was taken aback by a suggestion made to her by David Katz. "We were talking at a party and I asked her what she had in mind for her future," Katz said. "I reminded her that Frank Kelly was retiring and the party needed a strong candidate for Attorney General."

Katz recalls that Granholm seemed incredulous, commenting that with two children and a third on the way she wouldn't seem to make a very good candidate.

"How could I possibly do that," Katz remembers her saying.

Katz replied, "If it's okay for men, why wouldn't it be okay for you?"

Katz says that it took no great perceptiveness to see that Granholm would make a terrific candidate and he is sure he was not the only one to make that suggestion. "She had it all," he says. "Brains, talent, great communication skills. And she had the other ingredients: You could see that she was comfortable in her own skin and voters would recognize her authenticity. And then, of course, there was her charisma."

So in 1998, the politically unknown Granholm made her first foray into electoral politics. She went on the Democratic ticket as candidate for the office of attorney general. When she won, she became the only Democrat in a Republican administration.

By March of 2001, Granholm had established herself as a budding political star. Her style, passion and incisive intelligence seemed to appeal to liberals, moderates and even some conservatives. Soon, she had forged strong bonds with a deep and broad constituency.

Some observers attribute Granholm's comparatively rapid success in her first foray into politics to her ability to cherry pick some of the best minds as counselors. She has sought out—and even demanded, some say—the most unvarnished input from a bevy of economists, political gurus, communications specialists and other professionals. Less well known but of immeasurable value has been her knack for drawing out from average citizens the subtleties and nuances to which a politician must be sensitive in order to be successful.

One such counselor was Jerome Marks, who became a special adviser to the Governor. Marks started as a volunteer in the Granholm campaign for the Democratic nomination in 2001 and soon became Granholm's regular driver. Together they traversed the state and in the course of their travels, Marks became invaluable as Granholm's eyes and ears into the thinking of average citizens.

While the governor was speaking to an audience, Marks would use the opportunity to sound out people working on the event. "I was talking with the janitors and the cooks and the wait staff and the security guards," Marks said. "I would listen to what was on their minds, and I'd ask what they would ask the governor about or tell her if they had a chance. Then I'd bring her around to talk with them, one on one."

To Marks' mind, Granholm was the rare politician who truly meant it when she said she wanted candor, criticism and whatever suggestions someone cared to share with her.

"She was great at just listening to people," Marks said, "and it was easy for her because it's obvious she genuinely cares about them, about what's going on in their lives. So when the opposition was hitting at her about leadership, we were searching for one word to define what she was all about. We came up with 'committed.' Then I suggested she go further: confidence, conviction and courage. That night she was in an important debate and afterwards I got an email from her that said, 'Thanks. I used the Three C's. Worked great.'"

Taking note of her ambitious to-do list, supporters and critics alike describe Granholm as "visionary." However, her detractors often used it pejoratively, complaining that she spent too much time (and too large a fraction of the state's budget) on the long-term at the cost of real and present problems. Her supporters consider her taking of the long view to be among her most positive traits.

"She was a visionary long before she became governor," attorney Dale Jurcisin said. Jurcisin has known Granholm since she moved to Michigan; he worked with her and spouse Mulhern in

Wayne County politics and was active in Granholm's first campaign for governor, where he co-chaired the committee that wrote Granholm's policy papers. "Years before she became governor, she was learning about what would underpin her 21st Century Job Fund plan," Jurcisin says. "What she was implementing, in terms of redirecting the state economy, were concepts she was developing long ago and tapping into advisors for counsel. She did what others in the past have only talked about.

"She has more than just innate brainpower," Jurcisin says, "She has the ability to take in, learn, know and use information and data. There isn't anything that doesn't interest her. She is a human sponge for knowledge."

Jurcisin marveled, as have many others, on Granholm's ability to organize material and crystallize the issues.

"She divided policy into nine areas," Jurcisin says, "and had maybe fifteen experts in each area. She would meet with these groups, listen carefully, and almost immediately fire incisive questions. Her style was to explore all options, to be sure that nothing was overlooked."

When she entered the 2002 gubernatorial race, she had a difficult challenge. Despite her allegiance to her party, she was politically savvy enough to realize that any true and lasting progress in a narrowly divided state depended on bridging party politics. There had been a steady erosion in trust and cooperation between the two parties after the days of Republican Governor William Milliken. Granholm knew that the challenges the state faced could never be surmounted with a stalemated government.

"She is a master at making allies and friends," David Katz says.

After meeting Granholm for the first time, political allies and foes alike often comment with surprise that she is "a regular sort of person." They mention how personable and engaging she is, extremely bright and informed on any subject, and yet sincerely interested in hearing from other people, in relating to them as a person and not a political figure.

Economist Peter Eckstein wrote position papers for Granholm; he speculated that some of her effectiveness comes from "a looseness of style, a directness and maybe a little bit of goofiness in the best sense, a playfulness that you don't often see in politicians."

As evidence, Eckstein says he is generally characterized by others as a stodgy, mild-mannered economist, yet is amused that Granholm has said of him, "Peter Eckstein is a real rock star."

"I can't imagine Sander Levin or anyone else calling me a rock star," Eckstein says.

Dale Jurcisin has observed that Granholm carried out in actions her conviction that collegial arguments bring out the best solutions. Rather than avoid confrontations with political opponents, she actively sought them out.

"People sometimes mistake her friendliness for weakness," Jurcisin says. "Maybe she would be better off sometimes if she were more hard-nosed, but that's just not her style. She truly believes it is not only possible, it's essential to reach across the aisle to find the best solutions."

Granholm may have reached a friendly hand across the aisle with offers of cooperation but she had no illusions about a lasting harmony—she pulled no punches in her 2002 campaign. Her themes: anti on big tobacco and pro on the environment, seniors, education and health care. Even as she recognized the role of a powerful business sector, she took aim at oppressive policies of large corporations and zeroed in on computer crimes, especially identification theft and child pornography.

Perhaps most significantly, Granholm crystallized her thinking that diversifying did not necessarily mean turning away from the automotive industry. To the contrary—she envisioned huge opportunities for restoring financial health by diversifying within the automotive industry. She acted on that premise and she acted aggressively.

"One of the positive things we've done," Granholm commented during her second term, "is we took our tobacco settlement money and securitized about a billion dollars of it into diversifying the economy through startup companies in four specific sectors that we identified. We listened to experts who looked at the landscape and said, 'You have to build on your strength. If you're going to foster growth, look at investing in advanced manufacturing, at the high-end opportunities in research and development of the automobile, not the repetitive motion kinds of jobs.'"

There was low-hanging fruit to be plucked, Granholm reckoned, in fields adjacent to and supportive of the automotive industry. She made alternative energy a high priority, proclaiming, "We are a state that's got so much R&D focused on the next engine as well as the fuel that goes into the next engine—ethanol, bio-fuel, and then the next generation of ethanol. We've got this tremendous position as the Great Lake State—using water and wind—and we have the world's largest producer of polycrystalline silicon, the stuff that goes into solar panels.

"We're the auto capital and some would say the auto industry has contributed significantly to global warming," Granholm openly acknowledged, "Wouldn't it be a great 'man bites dog story' for Michigan to lead the nation in alternate-energy production?"

When I discussed initiatives such as this with Granholm in 2010, she pointed to synergy available in the talent and resources in the state's universities as validating her conviction that alternative energy would be a great strategy for investment for Michigan.

Her economic advisers advised her to look at opportunities in the life-sciences corridor as well as homeland security and defense. So Granholm securitized the state's tobacco settlement money and created a $2 billion, ten-year program to invest in companies that would locate and grow in Michigan in those areas.

"The year 2006 was the first round of funding," Granholm said. "We funded eighty of those companies to take root here." Her plan called for more rounds of funding in future years and she also asked the foundation community to do the same thing with the goal of triaging efforts into creating new sectors.

Granholm asserted that this was the most robust diversification program of any state in the country. But she was well aware that the wisdom of her aggressive program would not be measured until many years after she is out of office.

"It's a long-term strategy," she acknowledged. "You've got to start companies and provide the support, knowing that some will succeed, some will not. You've got to have a long-term view when you're doing that."

Granholm realized that the ultimate success or failure of another of her ambitious initiatives, in education, would not be measurable until long after her second term as governor expired.

In the nearer term, Michigan had a more fundamental and pressing need—jobs—bringing them to Michigan from elsewhere, saving them, growing them. So while she trained one eye on the far horizon with aggressive diversification and education programs that could radically change the economic landscape of Michigan, the other eye was on getting people back to work.

"You've got to go to other places and bring companies back," Granholm said. "That's why our strategy has been to go anywhere and do anything to bring jobs back to Michigan.

"We're the victims of globalization but we're not going to be victimized by it. Instead we're going to take advantage of it. So let's go to countries that are in about the same stage of economic progress that we are, countries like Germany and Japan. If you want to play in the global arena, target mid-sized companies—the big ones can already play. But the mid-sized companies want to know how they can have a foothold in America. We want to make it very easy for them. Since 2003, we've been able to get $6 billion in international investment in Michigan—all in an effort to diversify our economy."

For these efforts, Granholm was criticized and even mocked by Republicans in the state legislature. Many of these legislators were political babes in the woods who had no clue how a state government works—term limits had created a legislature overflowing with represenatives who could barely find their way around the Capitol, let alone cope with the legislative duties. When Rick Snyder, her successor, sang from virtually the same hymn book in 2011-14—using almost the identical language and rationalizations—the same legislators heartily applauded his "bold initiatives" and enthusiastically supported his overseas trips in quest of new business.

But Granholm knew she was trying to lead a massive turnaround of a state that for nearly a hundred years had been the auto capital of the world. "We want to hang onto that automotive footprint, that legacy, that endowment," she said. "But it's going to look different because we're going to be 'high end', so that's where our focus has been, in addition to creating and investing in the talent."

Even as Granholm tried to bring new jobs to Michigan, she had to cope with the lure of cheap labor that siphons jobs to China, Mexico and India. Following the counsel of her advisors to counter that threat, Granholm decided to emphasize investments in the talents of people.

"As a result of our history," Granholm said, "people went from high school to the factory, so we're in the bottom third with respect to the number of adults in our population with college degrees. It's a whole paradigm shift that we've got to create. Our goal from Year One was to double the number of college graduates in Michigan over the next ten years. So our strategy has been to up the high-school standards and require kids to take a college-prep curriculum. In addition, the plan gives every child—not just the ones who were going to go to college anyhow—a scholarship to make them realize that they are college-bound. Those are some of the immediate strategies. Long-term, we focus on early childhood, to have kids prepared. "

In Granholm's second term, as Michigan embarked on that transformation of its education system, the state was in the difficult position of having both a labor surplus and a labor shortage at the same time. There was an over-abundance of basic manufacturing workers, with hundreds of thousands of people out of work, even as there were vacancies in more skilled areas. For Granholm, education was the way out of the quagmire.

"We've got 300,000 people who have had the rug pulled out from under them," Granholm said. "They've been working for twenty to thirty years and now they're on the outside. So how do you give them a job with dignity? What you do is, while they are on unemployment, work the community college in their area to give them free tuition that is specifically relevant to job vacancies in their area, for example in fields like healthcare. We call this, 'No Worker Left Behind.' We're trying to really change how we think about job training—have it employer-driven."

Granholm cited figures that at first seemed paradoxical. She noted that there were 90,000 job vacancies in Michigan at the same time the unemployment rate hovered near 10 percent. "That's because we have a skills gap," she explained. "The system before was focused around the worker. A worker says, I want to be an English teacher, or something like that. But we don't need English teachers, what we need are nurses. So instead, what we say is, we'll provide your education if you go into a field that we know has specific vacancies identified by the employers in your area. If you go through that program, we'll get you certified and placed and we'll pay for your training."

Granholm announced her No Worker Left Behind program in August 2007 as a one-time offer in effect for three years. "Take it or leave it," she said. "If you go into it now—with these community colleges and you stick with it—you'll get placed and you'll have a new career."

One of the obstacles for displaced adults has been that they had to work in any kind of a job they could find just to put food on the table. That meant they had no time to upgrade their skills to get certification. A feature of Granholm's program was to make it effective while people are still on unemployment with some money coming in, or while they were on trade adjustment. In the short term they would not have a gap in income while they underwent intensive training in a new field.

Granholm left no doubt she would have preferred to concentrate on laying foundations for the long-term. But she was a political pragmatist and knew that was not a choice available to her. A governor simply could not minimize Michigan's greater-than-average quota of immediate problems. Taking to heart the old saw that a problem is simply an opportunity in disguise, she said philosophically, "A crisis is a terrible thing to waste."

Granholm sought cooperation from an increasingly polarized legislature, but was stonewalled at every turn. Using a crisis as a cattle prod to get things done was a tactic Granholm employed again and again in her State of the State messages and indeed at every opportunity: "This is the moment, this is exactly the time to make the right strategic investment. This is not the time to withdraw or retreat," she insisted. "This is the time to be bold. We are not going to shrivel; we are going to invest in our people. We're going to invest in diversifying. We're going to invest in the talent that is necessary."

That tactic worked—sometimes.

"This whole effort to rewrite the business tax (in early 2007) was a great result because it flipped the old business tax on its head," she said. "It provided incentives for R&D businesses and small businesses. The tax structure itself focused on diversifying the economy while it helped the businesses that remain because it gave them a personal property tax break that was very significant.

"The whole structure was crafted to further the economic agenda. On the other side of the aisle they wanted to do a $600 million cut. Where would that have come from but from education? The same thing with the whole debate on higher education. This is the time to invest," she said in 2010, "so you can provide access to higher education, a goal that we all have. But if you don't fund it how are you going to get there?"

Granholm was unwavering in her defense of adequate funding

for education, at all levels. A better-educated work force was a prerequisite to a heathy economy. It was a time to invest in education, not starve it.

"Obviously, cost is important. In a world where employers can pay fifty cents a day, cost is not a race that we're going to win in this country. So for us, it's got to be a new strategy and the strategy has to be quality, has to be investing in talent. That's why I think, frankly, there is going to be a slight rebound in manufacturing. Because robotics are going to address the quality issue, the repetitive motion kinds of jobs. But you need people who know how to program the robots. You need to have a new level of skill that you've never had before."

Granholm insisted training and retraining had to be employer-driven. "We're not going to pay tuition for a worker who wants to go back and get a degree in French," she said.

The retraining program envisioned by Granholm was much more than a response to the chronic critical imbalance in skills and needs in Michigan's workforce. She believed such a program had to elevate education to the priority Michigan had to aspire to if it is to be a leader, or even a healthy competitor.

Consistent with her emphasis on long-term strategies, Granholm continued to push for early childhood education despite unrelenting opposition on funding. Her hope was that the business community would support it for pragmatic reasons. "Business leaders will partner on education," she said, "when they see that it's the way to ensure they will have a strong future workforce that will make them successful."

As Granholm entered the final months of her term, she was also looking beyond her own tenure on another important and thorny issue. "This is true with health care also," she said. "I think the business community is going to make sure that universal health care becomes a reality in this country, because they're competing globally and other countries are providing health care for their businesses."

Granholm had strong views on one of the chief reasons for the painfully slow progress on critical legislation. She often cited term limits as a major cause of legislative inaction and the impasse on budget that took the state to the brink of shutdown in September 2007.

"As applied to the executive branch, term limits are a good thing," she continues to assert, now that she is out of office, just as she did while governor. "But they need to be lengthened or eliminated for the Legislature because there is a huge startup cost due to the lack of experience. Government is hugely massive and when you consider there is federal, state and local government, there is layer upon layer of complexity. With term limits, the goal is to get the most inexperienced people and that is one goal we're achieving in the Legislature. There is no sense of history or relationships."

Term limits on her own office meant that Granholm's tenure as governor ended in 2010. A favorite parlor game then among political junkies was what Granholm would do next.

Some speculated that Michigan's first female governor might be in line for an appointment to the U.S. Supreme Court. Others insisted such a dynamic activist would never accept a role too sedate and removed from the public eye.

"She loves public service," former colleague David Katz said. "She's never been motivated by anything else. You can see her leading something like the Red Cross, or, like Liz Dole, taking on world poverty."

Others cited her proven ability to raise funds and insisted she would be a great success as a university president or head of a foundation.

—m—

FOR THE TIME BEING, GRANHOLM HERSELF WAS GIVING NO INDICATION of where she would go, what she might do next, nor sharing any thoughts about her two terms as governor.

In may be that such roles are in Granholm's future. But the first thing she did after walking out of the Governor's office was to head for the sun in California and quiet time with her family.

If the hot buttons Granholm pushed as governor are any guide to her own personal priorities, she would not be reluctant to eventually take on a worldwide cause involved with poverty, education, hunger or the rights of women or children. But some close friends and political colleagues wouldn't be surprised to see her instead devote at least some of her time and energy to more personal and lower-key efforts.

"She does a lot of things for individuals that she doesn't mention and doesn't want publicized for political purposes," says Maxine Berman, who has produced position papers for Granholm for years. "She has always mentored younger people. She is acutely aware of everybody and their feelings. When she speaks at an event, she invariably recognizes people who just don't get noticed—janitors, the kitchen staff, and waitresses. Even though as governor she has to travel in important circles, she is always aware of people not in that circle."

Berman sees mentoring as something that will always be a part of Granholm's life, regardless of other roles or occupations. "Some women make it and then shut the door behind them," Berman says. "Not Jennifer Granholm. There are many women who would never have gotten where they are without her. And she deeply appreciates those who went before her, like Millie Jeffrey, founder of the National Women's Caucus and a driving force in starting Emily's List."

The *Berkeley Daily Planet* had long ago taken note of Granholm's strong sense of loyalty in a July 30, 2004, article:

Two years ago, Jennifer Granholm confounded experts and became the first female governor of Michigan. Tuesday afternoon, she confounded the experts again when she triumphed as the last speaker at the Emily's List gathering (Emily's List is the premier PAC that encourages prochoice, Democratic women to run for elective office).

*Governor Granholm seemed an unlikely choice to follow a power-
house foursome of Ellen Malcolm, the founder of Emily's List, Nancy
Pelosi, the leader of the House Democrats, Barbara Mikulski, the leader
of the Senate Democratic women's caucus, and Ann Richards, former
governor of Texas and notorious political wit. Indeed, each of the speak-
ers seemed to gain energy from her predecessor, so by the time Ann
Richards left the stage to tumultuous applause, many in the audience
wondered how Jennifer Granholm could possibly live up to her billing.
These doubts were quickly dispelled as she delivered a simple but compelling message: If women are to take their own power, they must begin
by honoring the brave women who have gone before them forcing open
the doors of equal opportunity. Governor Granholm mesmerized the audience with her personal story, praising her mentor, the late Michigan
activist Millie Jeffrey.*

While Granholm has a strong sense of history and honors the
advances made by those who came before her, she knows the jury
will likely be out for many years on many of her initiatives during
her eight years as Michigan's chief executive. "I'm not so naïve as
to think you can bring in an entirely new sector in a short amount
of time and have everything done," she acknowledged. "But we
will have set in motion the things that are necessary to transform
Michigan, including the rewriting of the business tax. I know that
through persistence we can get it done."

AS IT DEVELOPED, THERE WAS NOT JUST ONE NEW ROLE for Granholm, there
were several.

She was appointed Distinguished Practitioner of Law and Public Policy at the University of California, Berkeley. In autumn 2011,
she taught a graduate course titled "Governing in Tough Times" in
which clearly she could speak from personal experience. As a senior advisor to The Pew Charitable Trusts" Clean Energy Program,
Granholm led a campaign for a national clean-energy policy that

promotes and funds research and manufacturing for wind, solar and advanced battery industries in the United States.

She became a regular contributor to NBC's *Meet the Press* and co-authored with husband Dan Mulhern, *A Governor's Story: The Fight for Jobs and America's Economic Future*, detailing the lessons that Michigan's experience can offer to America.

Her "hyperactive and sharp-tongued" address at the 2012 Democratic National Convention left no doubt that her political priorities and personal views had not changed a whit since she left the governor's office.

"I don't look in the rearview mirror," she told me when she was wrapping up her service as Michigan's forty-seventh governor. "I like to learn from experiences, and then move forward. There will always be public service in my future, in some way, shape or form. That doesn't necessarily mean elective office. But it does mean giving back in some way."

Carl Oglesby was no naïve, starry-eyed school kid infatuated with playing the rebel. He was a well-read student of history, the author of powerful and highly acclaimed dramas for theatre, and a charismatic, compelling orator. No wonder the Feds considered him at the very least a "person of interest," and—in their nightmare scenarios—potentially a dangerous anarchist fully capable of leading a national uprising.

"It isn't the rebels who cause the troubles of the world, it's the troubles that cause the rebels," Oglesby said.

Oglesby had been very close with several of these new Weathermen, particularly Bernadine Dohrn. But Dorhn and her future husband Bill Ayers were convinced that peaceful efforts were impotent. They were taking control over SDS, on the way to scuttling it and forming the Weather Underground Organization. Yesterday's hero, Carl Oglesby, was now squarely in their bull's-eye.

～✺ 12 ✺～

DOVES, HAWKS, AND THE RAVEN IN THE STORM

Carl Oglesby—
National Insecurity and the Old New Left

PEOPLE TEND TO REMEMBER WHERE THEY WERE AND WHAT THEY WERE DOING when their boss, their spouse, or an FBI agent said, "We need to have a talk."

When Roy Cummings—let's call him—chief of the Ann Arbor bureau of the FBI, said that to me over the phone, it got my full attention. I was in the basement of my home in Ann Arbor, shooting pool with Carl Oglesby. It was 1965 and I was working then at Bendix Aerospace Systems Division. I held a secret clearance, which I had held for nine years. I had been cleared for the first time after my sophomore year in college for a summer job at Rocketdyne, a division of North American Aviation in Canoga Park, California. The clearance stayed in effect through jobs in the defense-space industries at Chrysler Missile Division and Lockheed Aircraft, as well as Bendix.

Oglesby also had worked at Bendix until some months previously. We were both writers and in these go-go days for contractors to NASA and the defense department, both of us had been promoted quickly into supervisory positions while in our mid-twenties.

Carl was head of the editing group in the publications unit; I was manager of specifications and standards for military systems and then configuration manager for space exploration systems.

However, early in 1965, when Oglesby was still working for Bendix, he became interested in the candidacy of Wes Vivian, a liberal running for Michigan's second district seat in the U.S. House of Representatives. Assuming Vivian would be a peace candidate, Oglesby wrote a position paper for him on why the United States should get out of Vietnam. Vivian and his cautious Democrat advisors rejected it, saying in effect, "We're in favor of peace, but first we have to win an election."

So Oglesby published his paper in *Generation*, the student literary magazine of the University of Michigan. The article ran in the same issue in which the script for his Hopwood Award-winning stage play *The Peacemaker* appeared. A student who was a member of a new radical group on campus called Students for a Democratic Society read Oglesby's Vietnam essay and visited Carl to "have a chat about the war and how you can help put an end to it," as Oglesby characterized it to me. Before long, he was the radical theoretician for the Ann Arbor chapter of SDS and quickly emerged as the movement's most articulate and compelling voice.

Reflecting back on it forty years later, Oglesby told me, "One thing that attracted me to SDS, beyond the politics, was the prospect of turning my talents to the creation of an American grass roots theater. I wanted to mount plays with themes I felt strongly about."

Oglesby had been a playwright of considerable promise when he dropped out of Kent State University after two years. He "took a shot" at acting in New York but returned a year later to Kent State, graduated and "bounced around doing this and that for a year." Finally, a friend from Kent State days, Don Thomson, coaxed him to Ann Arbor and helped him get a job as a technical writer at Bendix. There, he hit his stride writing drama, winning a Hopwood Award and seeing production of the last two of his four plays.

His theater project with SDS never got beyond the wish stage.

Soon, his full attention was consumed in helping to build opposition to the rapidly escalating American military involvement in Vietnam. Oglesby's oratorical brilliance drew many new members to the Ann Arbor SDS chapter, where he helped organize a teach-in. He immersed himself in planning the massive SDS peace march on April 17, 1965, in Washington. Very quickly, the magnetic Oglesby became a model and a mentor nationwide for idealistic young people discontented with the establishment.

Just seven months after he left Bendix for SDS, he was elected president of the leftist organization. With Oglesby gone from Bendix, I was one of a few employees there who was not a die-hard enthusiast of Barry Goldwater, the ultra-conservative senator from Arizona who went on to lose by a landslide to President Lyndon Johnson in November 1964.

The campaign slogan for Goldwater was "In Your Heart, You Know He's Right," with the so-obvious double meaning for the word "right." But when Goldwater commented that if elected he would consider using tactical nuclear weapons in Vietnam, Democrats weren't the only ones who saw visions of mushroom clouds. John Descutner, another Bendix employee and friend of Oglesby's and mine, put a big hand-painted banner in his car's rear window, "In Your Guts, You Know He's Nuts."

Goldwater's candidacy rekindled long-smoldering embers and soon right-wingers were once again inflamed. The tendency to assume guilt by association had been diminished but certainly not eradicated with the discrediting of communist witch-hunter Senator Joe McCarthy. Super-patriotism was again on the rise. Any muttered dissent about the carnage in Vietnam quickly labeled the dissenter a pinko or a fellow traveler, if not a fire-engine red Commie. I was an outspoken critic of the war, holding forth with gusto as the token anti-war kook in a conservative residential neighborhood and a very conservative workplace. Oglesby was a close friend, and with hawkish fervor rising in some quarters, I expected to hear from some investigatory official or other about my friendship with a prominent SDS leader.

The only surprise, then, was that my phone didn't ring before that evening.

Was it only coincidental, I wondered as I listened to the voice of FBI man Cummings on my phone, that at that moment I was watching Carl Oglesby chalking his cue stick. Although Cummings gave no indication, I was quite sure it was Oglesby that Cummings wanted to talk to me about. What I didn't know was if the FBI's interest was solely in my friend or in me as well for associating with someone so prominently involved as the "radical theoretician" of the already notorious left-wing SDS.

Oglesby was no naïve, starry-eyed school kid infatuated with playing the rebel. He was a well-read student of history, the author of powerful and highly acclaimed dramas for theater, and a charismatic, compelling orator. No wonder the Feds considered him at the very least a "person of interest," and—in their nightmare scenarios—potentially a dangerous anarchist fully capable of leading a national uprising.

Undoubtedly, a fresh addition to Agent Cummings' dossier on Oglesby was the ringing address he delivered only weeks earlier—his November 27, 1965 address at the SDS-sponsored March on Washington:

> *Revolutions do not take place in velvet boxes. They never have. It is only the poets who make them lovely. What the National Liberation Front is fighting in Vietnam is a complex and vicious war. This war is also a revolution, as honest a revolution as you can find anywhere in history. And this is a fact which all our intricate official denials will never change...*
>
> *Far from helping Americans deal with this truth, the anticommunist ideology merely tries to disguise it so that things may stay the way they are. Thus, it depicts our presence in other lands not as a coercion, but a protection. It allows us even to say that the napalm in Vietnam is only another aspect of our humanitarian love—like those exorcisms in the Middle Ages that so often killed the patient. So we say to the Vietnamese*

peasant, the Cuban intellectual, the Peruvian worker: 'You are better dead than Red. If it hurts or if you don't understand why—sorry about that'.

Author Kirkpatrick Sale said of Oglesby's November 27 address: "It was a devastating performance: skilled, moderate, learned and compassionate, but uncompromising, angry, radical, and above all, persuasive."

Other audiences listening to Oglesby in different settings would have used different words, but the take-away and the impact would have been about the same. That is because Oglesby had an uncanny ability for reading his audience. Then he would hit them where they would resonate.

He would speak to anyone at any time. The stronger the resistance to his point of view, the more he liked it. He already knew what his point of view was—he had no interest in hearing it echoed back to him. Oglesby had been a champion orator in high school and positively salivated over the prospect of going toe-to-toe with the most able and informed opponents he could find. He had also been an actor and knew how to command a stage. If the situation demanded it, he could discourse extemporaneously for hours, citing facts, statistics, historical parallels, recounting anecdotes, quoting from literature and authorities, whether classical, contemporary or obscure. Or he could respond with a single pithy remark that said it all: "It isn't the rebels who cause the troubles of the world, it's the troubles that cause the rebels."

Oglesby was also that rare creature: a careful and patient listener to people with opposing points of view. He often told me that he learned far more by listening to those with whom he at first strongly disagreed than he did from kindred spirits. He also learned from himself, working things out even as he spoke.

He once told me about driving in the country west of Ann Arbor one day, going over something in his head. He was groping for the way to express a knotty concept. Finally he nailed it. But he needed an audience to try it out on. Seeing a herd of cattle in a field near the road, he stopped the car. He got out and addressed them, "Cows, hear me out. I ask that you consider another way of looking at the problem... ."

Had a farmer come up at that moment and asked if there was any hope that the war in Vietnam would end and at last could there be peace, Carl would have taken a beat, pondered. He would stroke his bearded chin and in the voice of a southern farmer say, "Well now, I 'spect that could happen, but only if someday they call a war and ain't nobody shows up."

Oglesby drew from his deep roots in the South. His father was from South Carolina, his mother from Alabama. They met in Akron, Ohio, where Carl's father worked in rubber mills. Carl grew up so immersed in the auras of the South that his first stage play, *The Season of the Beast*, was set there. That play was produced in Dallas, Texas, in 1958 and abruptly shuttered in the face of criticism that it was nothing but "a Communist yankee atheist's attack on down-home religion." Carl shook his head and smiled when he told me "you had to admire the passion of that critique."

His Hopwood Award-winning play, *The Peacemaker*, recreated the bloody Hatfield and McCoy feud of the Great Smoky Mountains. Oglesby used the American classic feud of warring families to make incisive points about the grievances—real or imagined— that drive men to wage war, the bitter consequences of their actions, and the price exacted from those who try to make peace.

But Oglesby was no two-dimensional intellectual artiste. And he was certainly no dilettante. It frustrated him to not excel at whatever he did, so he worked at new interests with passion and diligence. He got better at golf much quicker than any student I had ever taught. He was an accomplished musician on classical guitar and made sweet music on the lute and dulcimer. Before Oglesby left Bendix, Bruce Loughery, an engineer, heard that he played the recorder and invited him to sit in with a group that met there one evening a week. Bruce told me that before they began, he asked

Carl to play something so they could see whether he would fit in. "After fifteen or twenty minutes," Bruce said, "we all just quietly set our instruments aside and spent the next hour listening."

Over the previous few years I had taught Carl the rudiments of the geometry and physics of pocket billiards and introduced him to the exhilarations and frustrations of golf. In return he gave me lessons on the classical guitar, passing along his prized acoustic Goya to me when he got a new one. He got the better of our bartered teaching but more than made up for it in other ways. Though I never got very good on stringed instruments, Carl was relentless in pushing me. When I told him that Jitundra Patel, a friend of ours, was returning to his native city of Baroda, India for a visit, Carl insisted I must have Patel arrange to get a sitar made for me.

The haunting music of sitar virtuoso Ravi Shankar was freshly popular on college campuses and Carl was intrigued with the prospect of learning an exotic instrument. I was barely a novice on the guitar and here Oglesby was goading me into having a complex, foreign instrument hand made in India and shipped to me. The idea of having a sitar custom made seemed bizarre and presumptuous, not to mention expensive. Still, Carl pressed me so earnestly, I gave Patel money and asked him to do it.

As it turned out, the hand-made sitar was not so costly after all and it was indeed a thing of beauty. It had two decks of metal strings and adjustable frets, permitting infinite variation in atonal sounds. A large bulbous gourd was mounted at one end, a smaller one at the other, each polished to a mahogany sheen. The gourds served as resonators for the sounds generated by the nineteen strings. There was a tiny carved ivory elephant to fine-tune the primary melody string and a plectrum to fit over the index finger and that finger alone plucked the wire strings.

Oglesby, of course, borrowed my sitar at once. I didn't see it again for months. By then he had found an Indian student at U of M who taught him the fundamentals and Carl in turn instructed me. For a time I practiced scrupulously, trying to make the sitar weep, growl or sing as it did for the great Shankar. Late at night, after Marcy and the kids were in bed, I would get out the marvelous instrument and turn off all the lights. Then, staring at a tiny red light on the stereo player that glowed like a red giant planet in deep space, I would strum one single note, exploring its every nuance. Hours would pass—how many I had no idea—as I plucked and caressed that note again and again and again. Finally, Marcy would get out of bed to ask if that was the only note the instrument was capable of.

When the day finally came that I had mastered that note, I solemnly placed the sitar on a rack I had mounted for it on the living room wall. I enjoyed looking at it, consoled by the knowledge that Ravi Shankar said he had practiced the sitar under a tutor daylong seven days a week for seven years before he felt deserving of playing in public. Carl could make music on it; I would not be ready for a recital any time soon.

Carl not only played instruments, he composed music and eventually made two psychedelic folk rock albums of his own compositions, released by Vanguard. He sang in his husky baritone and played his acoustic guitar but he told me he was most pleased with "the arranging and mixing, which I drifted into because the song engineer just didn't seem to get what this was about."

Through his writings, his riveting presence as a speaker, and his musical talents, he was able to communicate with people in many ways, on many levels. No wonder then that local FBI chief Roy Cummings took notice of such a person at the helm of SDS.

I knew Cummings casually, but I had never talked with him in his official capacity. I had met him when I was asked to be a candidate to manage a nearby country club where he was a member. At that time, Cummings and I had lunch to discuss the position. We got along well then, but I soon decided that catering to a couple hundred members while trying to upgrade the club on a modest budget was not an appealing prospect. After I withdrew my name from consideration, I saw Cummings a few times at the homes of mutual friends. The last time, however, was several months before. We had no business to discuss of which I was aware. So although the tone of his voice was cordial as always, I knew his agenda was definitely business. I guessed the topic for discussion was Carl Oglesby and SDS.

Thinking about it a while, I realized I also had another slight connection with SDS. Tom Hayden was an author of "The Port Huron Statement," the charter and agenda of the organization, and was therefore its spiritual godfather. It seemed unlikely that Cummings would know that in 1957-58 I was a senior editor at the *Michigan Daily*, the student newspaper at the University of Michigan, and gave a couple article assignments to sophomore Hayden.

I was about to find out, however, what was on Cummings' mind, having agreed on the phone to meet him at his Ann Arbor office. When I went back to the pool table and told Carl what the phone call was about, he laughed. Then he said, "The only surprise is that it took them so long. Sure, talk with them if you want to. I'd rather have them asking you about me than a few other people I can think of. Anyhow, they probably know by now everything there is to know about SDS."

"What makes you think that?" I asked.

"We have to assume the FBI has already infiltrated the movement," he said. "If they haven't, they're not doing the job the taxpayers are paying them for. And that's okay. In fact, it's all to the better, because if they report back honestly what we're about, we won't have any problems. There is nothing going on that I'm aware of that should worry anyone. Unless you find the prospect of people living in peace to be threatening."

Oglesby said that it would do neither of us any good for me to be evasive with the FBI because I knew nothing about the inner workings of SDS. I did know how strongly Carl felt about politics, social issues and U.S. foreign policy. In fact I shared some of his views, although I certainly didn't have the passion that had compelled him—married as he was with three small children—to give up his job and join the movement at a bare subsistence salary. That salary soon became a major issue as the more strident SDS factions strenuously complained that it was hypocritical of Oglesby to insist on being paid. For his part, Carl was adamant. "I have three kids," he said, "and while I can't afford daily orange juice for them on this pay, I damn well at least am going to give them bread and milk."

Two days later, I sat with Cummings in the cluttered, somber FBI office in downtown Ann Arbor. He told me he had finally found a manager for the country club and was glad to have that off his plate. He talked about golf, about family, about the weather—about everything except the one subject I was now certain he wanted to talk about. Obviously he was saving that for lunch.

Only when we got into his car did Cummings mention Carl Oglesby. It was as though he had brought up a mutual friend we both knew well and needed to update each other on.

He asked, "Have you seen your friend Oglesby lately?"

The thought flashed that Cummings might well have known when he telephoned that at that very moment Carl was shooting pool with me in my basement. Carl had a distinctive red Alfa-Romeo he had bought a few years earlier with the money that came along with a Hopwood Award. It would be an easy matter to tail Carl's sports car or spot it around town or campus.

"I have," I said. "We shot pool at my place a couple days ago."

When we got to Weber's Restaurant on the west side of Ann Arbor, Cummings asked where would I like to sit. I motioned to a table by a window. He countered, "Maybe it would be quieter if we took a table in the back." The restaurant was all but empty and any table would have been quiet, but I followed him to the back, far away from the few patrons. I looked around at the nearby light fixtures and wall hangings, wondering where the microphone was hidden.

As we sat down, Cummings told me—apropos of nothing we had been talking about—that his father had voted for Socialist Party candidate Norman Thomas in the 1932 presidential election.

That was obviously by way of establishing Cummings' *bona fides* as an open-minded guy who believed that citizens were entitled to their own personal political views, provided of course that they were not plotting the violent overthrow of the legally established government.

It seemed to take forever for Cummings to get to it, but then, what did I know about FBI interrogation techniques. We finished lunch and were into a second cup of coffee when he finally got to his own main course of the interrogation menu.

"I admire these young people, I really do," he said. "I grant them the sincerity of their convictions. Freedom of speech. Freedom of assembly. Peaceful dissent. Those freedoms are in the best traditions of this nation."

No argument from me on that.

"Your friend, Carl Oglesby, he's clearly a very bright young man. Destined to really make a mark, wouldn't you say?"

I said that Carl was a fine writer, a versatile musician, and a man of many talents. Mediocre at pool and golf, but I expected he would be successful at whatever he did.

"And what is it that Mr. Oglesby wants to do, Bill?"

Whoa, here it comes.

"You'd have to ask him that yourself," I replied.

"You both were involved in communications at Bendix, is that right?"

"Depends on what you mean by communications, Roy. I was responsible for specifications and standards and now I'm involved in what's called configuration management."

"I'm not familiar with that term," he said. "Mind explaining?"

"That means I see to it that the scientific equipment for one of the Apollo missions will fit properly in the spacecraft, can be handled by astronauts in spacesuits, and can be operated from a power supply when it's deployed on the moon. None of what I just told you is classified, by the way."

Roy laughed. "I'm sure it isn't or you wouldn't have told me.

What about Mr. Oglesby? He was in another sort of communications, wasn't he?"

"Carl was supervisor of the technical editors in the publications unit."

Cummings looked puzzled.

"Hmm. I'm not sure I understand," he said. "He wasn't working with sophisticated communications equipment? Then how is it they are able to communicate so swiftly from one part of the country to another."

I didn't know what Cummings was talking about and told him so.

"The SDS folks," he said. "These kids are just amazing, how quickly they get word to each other around the country, and overseas as well. I would have thought your friend Oglesby had brought some advanced technical wizardry with him from Bendix that enabled these people to communicate so rapidly."

Now it was my turn to laugh.

"If there were anything like that at Bendix it would sure be news to me. And even if there were, stuff like that is certainly well out of my friend Carl's area of expertise. He's no technical whiz. He's a word guy, like me. As for quick communication, why wouldn't the SDS people just pick up the telephone, like everyone else does? What's faster than that?"

Cummings seemed seriously deflated to hear that Oglesby was no technical communications genius. He pursed his lips and nodded. "Well, maybe some folks don't like to use the telephone. For whatever reasons."

Later that day I got a call from Carl at my Bendix office. He asked if I wanted to shoot some pool that evening. We could meet at the billiards room of the Michigan Union. While we played pool, I told him about my lunch meeting with FBI agent Roy Cummings.

"Sophisticated communications equipment, huh?" Carl said. "That's a laugh. As clumsy as we are at SDS with technology—especially me—we'd probably be better off with a flock of carrier pigeons."

"What's wrong with just using the telephone?"

"It's a safe assumption that my phone is tapped. And since they know you're a friend, yours probably is too."

—⁓—

Over the coming months, student protests sprouted like spring flowers across the country. At Kent State, the University of Michigan, the University of California–Berkeley, and dozens of other campuses, college kids targeted whatever they weren't happy with. That meant not only the Vietnam War but also university-based research in support of the military-industrial complex or racial or ethnic discrimination in the fraternity system. On some campuses it meant local injustices perceived in course requirements, dress codes, class size or the grading system.

In one Oglesby speech, "Let Us Shape the Future," at an antiwar rally in Washington, D.C., on November 27, 1965, he had inveighed against what he saw as using anti-Communist aid to third-world nations when the real driving force was to protect or promote American economic interests. He called it "corporate liberalism."

In a ringing and oft-cited passage he thundered, "For all our official feeling for the millions who are enslaved to what we so self-righteously call the yoke of Communist tyranny, we make no real effort at all to crack through the much more vicious right-wing tyrannies that our businessmen traffic with and our nation profits from every day."

A boiling point was reached in January 1966 when the Johnson administration abolished automatic student draft deferments. America was now "knee deep in the Big Muddy," as folk singer Pete Seeger called the Vietnam War, with the body count of American soldiers soaring into the thousands. All able-bodied college-age males were now fresh meat for the killing fields. Johnson's decision to expand American involvement in Southeast Asia and flood Vietnam with more troops by ending college deferments proved to be a powerful recruiting opportunity for SDS.

By November 1966 when Oglesby wrapped up his year as president of the organization, more than three hundred new college campus chapters of SDS had been established. Membership had soared under his leadership from 2,000 members to more than 100,000.

By the end of that year, Oglesby was seldom in Ann Arbor. He had spent most of the year on the road, helping launch new SDS chapters, organizing political protests, and attending meetings. His wife Beth remained in Ann Arbor at their house on Sunnyside Street, tending their three small children while Carl was immersed in the movement. He was constantly either traveling or getting ready to, or in meetings with Ann Arbor SDSers. He would speak wherever there was an audience to listen. Sometimes he would wander off the campus to downtown Ann Arbor and strike up a conversation with someone on a bench waiting for a bus.

Somehow, he managed to fit in trips to Cuba and North Vietnam that must have drawn considerable attention from Roy Cummings and his FBI colleagues and likely triggered renewed interest of investigators in anyone who knew him.

Across the United States, temperatures continued to rise as military recruiters were driven off campuses by overwhelming numbers of demonstrators. Whether they were peaceful protest groups, grungy bands, or angry, dangerous mobs depended on your political point of view. SDS leaders had grown increasingly efficient and assertive. Chanting "Make Love, Not War!", SDS chapters disrupted ROTC classes. Shouting "Burn cards, not people," they drew thousands to bonfires where draft cards were set ablaze.

SDS was growing rapidly but the seeds to its own destruction had been planted in it innocently at conception—now they began to germinate. The fundamental theme and message of the "Port

Huron Statement", the exposition of their mission, had been aggressive and action-oriented but in no way did it promote violence:

> We would replace power rooted in possession, privilege or circumstance by power and uniqueness rooted in love, reflectiveness, reason and creativity.... As students for a democratic society, we are committed to stimulating this kind of social movement, this kind of vision and program in campus and community across the country. If we appear to seek the unattainable, as it has been said, then let it be known that we do so to avoid the unimaginable.

Seeking the unattainable may have attracted the vast majority of those who flocked to SDS. But while most were drawn by the values enunciated in the "Port Huron Statement", there were inevitably those who also brought with them a willingness—and for some an eagerness—to achieve peace through, well, violence. At first that took the form of destroying draft records and equipment in buildings they occupied in sit-ins. Then, at Columbia University, SDS members physically removed professors and administrators from their classrooms and offices. When they were criticized for using violence while espousing peace, they insisted they were "only using force, not violence."

The debater in Carl Oglesby must have known the movement had sailed into treacherous waters when it began parsing words to differentiate force from violence.

It didn't take Oglesby long to suspect that some of the most violent acts were being committed by FBI agents planted in the organization. Their assignment, he became convinced, was to perpetrate acts that would outrage the general population and set the stage for a brutal crackdown on dissent against the war and most especially to grant sanction to the decimating of SDS.

Beginning in 1967, I watched these events play out from a new perspective. At Bendix, I had been working for the last three years on only NASA space exploration systems—I had long since advised the management there I would no longer be involved in weapons programs. Much as I liked my job and although I had many good friends at Bendix, it was increasingly intolerable to make my living at a company so prominently a part of the military-industrial complex. So, in early 1967, I left Bendix and went into a totally different environment as director of publishing and managing editor at U of M's Institute for Social Research.

I had not seen or heard from Oglesby in several months when a mutual friend told me Carl was in town and wanted to see me. The friend told me where Carl was staying and added that I shouldn't mention his whereabouts to anyone. It seemed there was now great ferment within SDS. For two years it had been fragmenting into splinter groups and sects with wildly different strategies and tactics.

Carl called and we talked briefly by phone to set a time we could get together. He said our mutual friend would come to my office to bring me up to date on what was going on within SDS and its implications. That was obviously something he couldn't do over the phone.

I learned more about one offshoot sect—the incipient Weathermen—that had been advocating blood and thunder. They proclaimed themselves as communists and as the rightful leaders in the battle against the oppressive U.S. establishment. Peace-based strategies had failed, they insisted; the time for violence was at hand. Included as targets for that violence were not just the American war machine and the capitalist oppressors, but also those factions of SDS that would not sign up for the Weatherman's agenda. Moderates and intellectuals in the movement were on their purge list. The name Carl Oglesby was at the very top.

Oglesby had been very close with several of these new Weathermen, particularly Bernadine Dohrn. But Dorhn and her future husband Bill Ayers were convinced that peaceful efforts were impotent. They were taking control over SDS, on the way to scuttling it and forming the Weather Underground Organization. Yesterday's hero, Carl Oglesby, was now squarely in their bull's-eye.

I picked Carl up at his friend's house in Ann Arbor. He immediately said he wanted to see the farm I had recently moved to, so we headed out on a rainy night on the twenty-mile drive to rural Jackson County.

I didn't know how much time we would have to talk privately so I asked him right away how safe he felt because it seemed obvious to me that SDS had changed greatly since he first got involved. He told me either it had changed considerably or he had been very naïve—and his money was on the former. Yes, he said, there was indeed an aura of violence that had not remotely been there at the beginning. Now there were those that wanted bloodshed and some who wanted that blood to be his. The Weathermen, led by Dohrn, Mark Rudd and David Gilbert were on the way to commandeering the SDS movement. Carl, himself a folksinger, was bemused that the name of the group came from Bob Dylan's *Subterranean Homesick Blues*, with the lyric, "You don't need a weatherman to know which way the wind blows."

As I listened to him talk, I was reminded of my meeting two years earlier with FBI agent Roy Cummings. The FBI had been wrong about the fledgling SDS being a front organization for the Communist Party and about Carl Oglesby being a threat as the leader of a group seeking the violent overthrow of the government. Not only was Oglesby not a communist, he was by most objective standards more of a bleeding-heart anti-war pacifist. He told me he considered himself "a radical centrist." Other times he preferred the term "libertarian."

For me, in the grander sense of the word, he was a political realist in that he was opposed to an unjust, unjustifiable, unwinnable war laden with catastrophic consequences. It didn't take a genius to see that the Vietnam misadventure would cost incalculable billions that could and should be better spent so many other ways. Ironically, within SDS Carl Oglesby had come to be seen by many as an establishment moderate dressed in a radical's garb, despite the lofty rhetoric, guitar and beard. As if being tarred as a liberal or moderate weren't enough, the ultimate condemnation was that he was now and always had been several shades too bourgeois. It was said that he actually played golf and shot pool. That made him an even more noxious presence and insidious threat.

Ironically, the FBI considered Oglesby dangerous for reasons exactly opposite to those of the Weathermen. As wrong as they were about SDS's most visible front man, FBI agents had rightly sensed that such an organization—no matter how well motivated and sincerely committed to peaceful change—could serve as a greenhouse in which poisonous weeds could sprout. As Oglesby reflected back on it, he could see that there long had been militant elements in SDS. A question that likely would never be answered was whether or not some of those shrill voices within SDS clamoring for violent action were planted FBI agents.

I told him I was glad that he had extricated himself from SDS. He asked me to update him on me and my family. I said I had not only changed jobs since the last time I saw him, we had also moved from Ann Arbor to the place he would soon see, a farm in the countryside of Jackson County where Marcy, the kids and I were remodeling a century-old farmhouse.

"We're cleaning up the land to ready it for building a golf course," I said. "It will be an old-fashioned, Scottish-penitential links. It will nestle in the land as if it had been left there by the glacier. Gently rolling fields. Ponds, marshes, woods. Many ways to do penance for your transgressions."

Carl laughed, "Sounds like lines I might write for a character to cap a grand soliloquy in Act I, Scene 3."

Carl fell silent for while, then chuckled.

"Golf. Pool. Those Lebanese western sandwiches you used to cook for me and Beth," he said. "All those proletarian pleasures that disgust the SDS folks. All those simple, fun things that folks do that give the Weathermen evidence they were right all along about me being irretrievably middle class. Golf and pool with Haney. God, those were good times."

At that moment, the car stalled. I pulled off the highway onto the shoulder. I knew what the problem was—the fuel line had a vacuum bubble in it. Typically it would clear in a few minutes. Carl had just lit a marijuana roach and taken a couple hits off it. Just then I looked in the rearview mirror at the flashing red light on the car that pulled up behind us.

"Oh, Christ," Carl said, as he shoved a plastic bag into his sock. "I hope they don't ask for my ID, too. There's a warrant out for me. See, there was this pushy news cameraman and there was a scuffle and his camera got busted and—"

"Sir, please step out of the car," the officer said to me, shining a flashlight through the rain-splattered window, "Your license and registration, please."

I walked behind the officer back to the police car, grateful for the rain that might evoke some sympathy for our plight. Mostly I was relieved to get the policeman away from the distinctive aroma of pot. I explained to the good officer that I had a recurring problem with air in the fuel line and expected it would be cleared up by now. He ran his checks on me and the car, then handed me back my papers. He said he would follow us for a while in case the car stalled again.

After a few minutes that seemed like an hour, the police car veered off on an exit. I took a deep breath. Carl relit his joint. I wondered how it must be for him, looking over his shoulder for a cop with a warrant, wondering whether a room was bugged or a phone tapped. And, not least, searching the face of the next person approaching on the street, wondering it that were someone on a mission from the Weathermen.

So much had changed in those two years while he was almost constantly traveling around the country. That first year, Carl had been a darling of the New Left—in more ways than one. There had been the "very close relationship with Bernadine Dohrn for a while there," he said. He was a magnet for bright young women. One skill he had never really tried all that hard to master was the ability to resist temptation. He had even mesmerized the freshman chairperson of the Young Republicans at Wellesley College, Hillary Rodman, a turning point in her life, as she has commented.

"But now that SDS had transmogrified itself into something alien," he said, "it is no place for a peacenik intellectual."

Carl told me he was planning to move to San Francisco with wife Beth and the kids. Perhaps there he could rebuild a marriage that had been severely shaken over the past two years. Or perhaps not. He really didn't know.

One thing seemed clear as Carl and I talked for what would be the last time for several years: the New Left—or whatever it was now—would have to go on without him.

When we finally turned into the gravel driveway of the old farm I was now calling home, Carl beamed. The rain had swept out and a fresh new front had moved in. The moonless sky was bright with stars. Before going into the house, we walked a hundred yards or so onto the land to get away from the splash of the mercury vapor light, the better to see the stars. The air was perfectly still and off in the distance, as the old literary cliché went, somewhere a dog barked.

Both of us were writers, but I had no words that were worth breaking the silence for. Neither did Carl. It had been a long time since we had been together and somehow we knew it would be longer still until the next time.

—ᵚ—

IN 1972, CARL OGLESBY CO-FOUNDED THE ASSASSINATION INFORMATION BUREAU, a group dedicated to the full exposure of the assassination of President John F. Kennedy. He once again became a prolific writer, producing many essays, articles and speeches for Boston newspapers and magazines, as well as *The Nation, The Washington Post, Life, Saturday Review, Dissent* and *Playboy*. His first book, *The Yankee and Cowboy War: Conspiracies from Dallas to Watergate*, was published in 1976. For a time, he did a little of this, a little of that. Then he went on to teach courses at M.I.T. on the origins, history and principles of radical thought in the United States.

In a phone call in 2004, when he was still in a painfully long recovery from being gravely ill with peritonitis, he told me, "Ironically, now that I can get almost anything I write published, I'm actually afraid I have nothing to say worth putting in the isolation and the agony to write." I told him once he was back to good health, he would feel much differently.

Finally, he regained his health and his intellectual footing. He reached back to those heady days of the '60s to tap in once again to his greatest strength—his ability to tell a story. After years of silence followed by more years of plowing old ground to unearth the story he was uniquely able to tell, in 2007, Carl Oglesby completed writing his magnum opus. That monumental memoir, *Ravens in the Storm: A Personal History of the 1960s Anti-War Movement,* was published in 2008 by Scribners. It would be praised as the most thorough and authoritative account of the rise and fall of SDS and the New Left, of its impact on the catastrophic Vietnam War, and of the changes it wrought in the American political landscape.

Carl sent me the page proofs for the book while it was in progress at Scribners. I had a few comments and suggestions for him and we discussed that by phone. He told me the years of research for the book and writing had taken a great toll. It had dominated his life to the point of near obsession. It had drained him physically and psychically.

"I feel I have spent the final drop of my creative juices," he said.

But he knew that it was something only he could do, something therefore that he had to do.

"I took the title from the Book of Genesis," he told me. "You remember the passage, 'And God said to Noah, I have determined to make an end of all flesh; for the earth is filled with violence...'

"Well, in the '60s, people thought the Vietnam War was only about doves and hawks. Anyone who has read the Bible knows about Noah releasing a dove from the ark to find land. Finally, the dove came back with an olive leaf in its beak.

"But what often isn't noticed is that the dove was not the first bird sent out by Noah. First, he sent off a raven. And the raven flew into the storm and did not return."

In an episode of Mad Men, he would have been cast as the brilliant yet poised iconoclast who quietly led his shop to record profits. It plays out differently in the real world of advertising agencies where beneath the glitz and glamor, uneasy lies the head that wears the crown in a profit-producing office in a privately held company... Ron Monchak had a very tempting target on his back...

There were many more books for Monchak's editorial blue pencil. Each book was different, each was special to an author and a readership and all were special to Monchak, now comfortably in his element, far from client pressures and corporate intrigues.

13

MINING FOR GOLD
IN THE RUST BELT

Ron Monchak Takes the Road Less Traveled Out of Madison Avenue

FUELED BY THE AUTOMOBILE INDUSTRY, and notwithstanding its economic woes, Detroit is one of the nation's most vibrant advertising markets. In the Motor City's advertising industry, the movers and shakers are seldom modest about their accomplishments. But one of the most successful executives and creative geniuses in Detroit's ad world was also its quietest enigma.

Those who knew Ron Monchak as a creator of imaginative advertising and as a brilliant ad agency chief executive rarely knew about his other talents and pursuits. People who had known him for decades seldom knew more than one side of a multi-faceted man; that's exactly the way he wanted it.

Poised and reserved in his spacious Bloomfield Hills agency office, away from it Monchak was an innovator and a bold risk-taker. He was more likely to laugh about his rare failures than accept credit for his many successes. Apart from the world of prime time 30-second TV spots and slick print ads, he was a writer of screenplays, fiction and essays; an underwriter of New York stage plays; and a low-key but highly effective contributor to many communities and causes. Only those very close to Monchak knew that his deepest satisfactions came as a book publisher.

But for all his savvy, Ron Monchak committed the unforgivable sin for a top executive in American business: He was too trusting, too successful and too well liked for his own good. That does happen in corporate America. As if that weren't enough, he also sat precariously on a very large stack of private company stock.

Monchak had built his agency's success the old-fashioned way—he gave his people the resources they needed, and then rewarded them for their performance. Those are admirable virtues when running an independent business, but they aggravate the hell out of overlords of conglomerates. Entrepreneurial spirits are not suffered gladly by holding company top executives with a cookie-cutter mindset. Let a maverick run free to have success doing it his way, those managers fear, the next thing you know other office heads think they can do it their own way too and get away with it. Producing glittering financial results seldom excuses deviating from the ordained path. Not when there is a fat cash cow primed for the slaughter.

The agency presided over by the non-conformist Monchak was the Detroit office of D'Arcy Masius Benton & Bowles. That office annually posted the highest morale in a holding company called The MacManus Group, one of the world's largest advertising and communications conglomerates with nearly a hundred operating units around the globe. No matter that his agency produced the profit that, year after year, mopped up the red ink from dozens of chronically under-performing sister units. No matter that the revenues his agency produced kept the parent company from blowing apart the first few dicey years after a risky merger of diverse cultures. And no matter that the generous compensation packages enjoyed by top corporate officers in New York derived in great part from the revenues he produced in Detroit.

In an episode of *Mad Men*, Monchak would have been cast as the brilliant yet poised iconoclast who quietly led his shop to record profits. It plays out differently in the real world of advertising agencies where beneath the glitz and glamor, uneasy lies the head that wears the crown in a profit-producing office in a privately held company. That was because Monchak had a very tempting target on his back: he was one of the three largest stockholders in the company. While stock in the privately held company had zero face value, it would be worth many tens of millions if the holding company went public or sold itself to an even-larger conglomerate. Monchak held a fortune in non-negotiable stock. Rather than bring him comfort, he predicted that one day his own fortune-on-paper would bring his downfall. For once, his hunch was spot on.

Eventually the MacManus Group conglomerate sold itself for $995 per share in the then-largest deal ever in the advertising industry. By the time that transaction was engineered, Monchak and dozens of other senior officers who had worked for decades to create immense value for the company were gone—and on their way out were required to surrender their stock. Under private company terms, they received not a penny of compensation for that stock and much of it was never re-issued, thereby greatly increasing the value of each remaining share in the hands of the dwindling cadre of top officers.

In an industry that prides itself on originality, one would think that a Ron Monchak would be admired and appreciated. But it is a sad truth in American business that innovative and independent thinking is lauded far more in theory than it is tolerated in practice. Regardless of their lofty rhetoric about fostering a climate in which individuality and creativity can flourish, what most CEOs really want is obedience. They want employees to click their heels, tell the boss what he wants to hear and do it the way he wants it done. That is because what CEOs value most highly and guard most jealously is power. Money is a close second, of course, but in modern corporate America if you have all the power, the money will inevitably follow, one way or another.

To many CEOs, power means a free hand not only to set performance goals but also to reach over the shoulders of managers several tiers down in the organization and tell people exactly how you want them to run their activities. Unquestioning compliance often becomes more important than the goals themselves. That is where Monchak departed radically from his corporate bosses. He had this dangerous notion that what counted was results. Results count, yes. But how a manager achieves those results counts even more.

Monchak's *modus operandi* was simple: Agree with each manager who reported to him on reasonable stretch goals for the coming year. Agree on benchmarks and a schedule to achieve those goals. Give the manager the necessary resources. Make yourself available if something unforeseen comes up. Then—importantly— get the hell out of the way. At the end of the year, review performance with the manager and adjust his compensation according to the results produced against the goals.

In the early 1980s, before I had met Monchak, I was director of communications for the Bendix Corporation. There, one of my responsibilities was corporate advertising. Monchak's agency (which then was a private and independent company called D'Arcy Mac-Manus & Masius, or DMM) handled my advertising account. I saw how he led his organization. His managerial style was familiar because years earlier—when I was publishing books at the Institute for Social Research and the University of Michigan Press—I had published several volumes by authorities on organizational functioning. Monchak's approach perfectly matched the principles and practices of the most successful organizations. I knew that his agency had a motivated work force with high morale. DMM had a reputation as perhaps the best agency to work at in the state. My regard for Monchak as a leader of an organization motivated me in 1982 to leave Bendix to work for him in what was both an exhilarating creative environment and a solid business setting.

But things changed swiftly. In 1984, DMM merged with the New York agency Benton & Bowles to create DMB&B. The new combination of initials also stimulated a creative wag in the agency to coin a new catch phrase: "We're not stupid, but we are dmbb."

B&B was an old-line package goods agency, which had for fifty years been the main marketing partner for Procter & Gamble. Monchak's office was dominated by General Motors and had handled Cadillac and Pontiac since the 1930s. Under the new regime, Monchak's Detroit office was as successful as ever, but he no longer had the freedom to run it as he saw fit. Although the post-merger environment was not what he would have it be, Monchak was a pragmatist who accepted a situation he knew he could not change substantially. He was offered the presidency of the newly combined company. That was a lucrative plum of a gig, but that would have required that he move to New York City. While that was the dream destination for many in the business, Monchak had no desire to do that. Then, when Monchak's long-time colleague and supporter Hal Bay abruptly retired from his new role as vice chairman after a few short months, Monchak found himself with a new boss. He was now ultimately answerable to the chairman and chief executive officer, Jack Bowen.

Bowen could have come directly out of central casting to head up an advertising agency—or a major corporation or a fair-sized country for that matter. He was a brilliant businessman. More than that, he was poised, gracious and congenial. Although he himself was a Yale graduate with genteel sensibilities, he was keenly perceptive about everyday American tastes. He was a man of principle and integrity and that drew him to admire and respect those qualities in Monchak. The suave, silver-haired Bowen shared three other qualities with Monchak: a sense of humor, a sense of balance, and a sense of perspective. Both men were at their coolest when temperatures all around them were the hottest.

There was never any doubting who was in charge. While Monchak did not always agree with Bowen's strategies and decisions, his respect for Bowen was so great that he loyally followed his new leader. Bowen, for his part, knew that Monchak skillfully ran the

star profit-producing office in Bowen's portfolio of marketing services agencies. Although Monchak's hands-off management style
and generous sharing of the proceeds of success down to the low-
est levels of his office was foreign to the Benton & Bowles culture in
which Bowen had grown up, he couldn't dispute that Monchak's
approach worked.

Still, there were strenuous arguments over cause and effect.
Were profits astronomical in Detroit because morale and productivity were high, or was morale great because of that rich stream of
black ink from GM?

Whatever, Bowen and Monchak reached détente—each could
settle for not getting entirely what he would have preferred. Monchak's office continued to send "gold to the mother ship," an ever-
increasing share of revenue handed up to the holding company. In
return, top corporate management cut DMB&B Detroit just a little
extra slack. Still, with typical holding company mentality, headquarters was certain the Detroit office could post even bigger profits if only Monchak would fire a few more old-timers and tighten
down on expenses.

Then Jack Bowen retired and the days of agreeing to disagree
with corporate headquarters ended. When Bowen retired, he made
it clear that a condition of his turning over the reins was a solemn
commitment that in the best interests of clients and employees,
DMB&B would remain a private company, owned by less than two
hundred senior executive shareholders.

In the '90s, as times got ever tougher in the advertising industry, it was obvious that the good old days were gone forever.
For Monchak, that meant the ceasefire with the holding company
headquarters was over. From then on, each quarter brought a
new corporate mandate for more profit from the few successful
offices to offset the predictable-as-clockwork shortfalls from more
than half of the agency's hundred or so operating units. Because
DMB&B Detroit was the most profitable, to that office fell the
most onerous levy.

"What are they bitching about in Detroit," George Simko, one of the conglomerate's top executives said. "Any monkey could produce a twenty-percent profit margin with all that GM business. Just walk down the hall at GM headquarters and hundred-dollar bills stick to you."

That kind of attitude made it clear that, henceforth, Monchak would get scant credit from his corporate overlords for the success of his office. The "any monkey could post big profits in Detroit" attitude became the prevailing view as the holding company failed year after year to create consistently profitable offices in other important markets such as London, Paris, Sydney, Los Angeles and Chicago.

At the same time, General Motors continued to steadily reduce its compensation to agencies. When the first cuts in agency commissions were instituted in the early 1980s, they came with an explanation that agencies would receive less money for the same amount of work but would be given more work to compensate for the revenue reduction.

"They did a better job delivering on the first half of that equation," Monchak said, "than they did on the second part."

So even as General Motors was steadily cutting his profit margin, Monchak's New York bosses were passing the hat to him because the offices in St. Louis or Frankfurt or Mexico City had again come up far short.

Despite all that, for several years after Bowen retired, Monchak's Detroit agency continued to outpace every other operating unit in the company. He was proud of his people and their performance but increasingly distressed that the profits his agency produced had to be used to fund up sister agencies that year after year promised healthy profits only to post millions of dollars of losses. Profit earned by the efforts of several hundred employees of Detroit's DMB&B agency was gold being mined in the Rust Belt only to be stashed in the corporate vault, never to be seen again in Detroit. At year's end, Monchak routinely found himself thanking his employees for yet another terrific year while apologizing for being unable to reward them fairly in bonuses or salary increases—as in years gone by—for the wealth they had created.

That the morale of the office remained the highest of any unit in the holding company was due in great part to the faith, respect and trust that DMB&B Detroit employees had for their leader. But Monchak was concerned about more than the welfare of his employees. He resented seeing the parent company make capital investments to benefit clients of other offices while doing nothing to enhance capabilities to serve his clients. New offices would be opened in third world countries because Procter & Gamble—the 800-pound gorilla client of the New York office—wanted an agency presence there, even though the new shop was certain to operate in the red for years. Or money would be poured into a small domestic office awash in red ink and with no realistic hope of surviving. And always, if Anheuser-Busch wanted DMB&B St. Louis to add creative firepower, and have the agency absorb the cost, Presto! they got it.

"Where is something I can take to Cadillac or Pontiac," Monchak asked at a meeting of the Board of Directors in New York. "What can I show General Motors we have invested in that's on the leading edge with resources to help them? Since 1934 we have been Pontiac's exclusive agency. We've been doing advertising for Cadillac since 1912, and have been their sole agency since 1935. For decades our Detroit agency was out there on the frontier for them, developing capabilities and resources to keep them ahead of their competition. Now, that has changed. The funds we previously applied to those purposes have in effect been confiscated. DMB&B Detroit sends the revenue to corporate headquarters where it is poured into Asia or Australia or South America to keep a chronically under-performing agency afloat. Or to open a new office where P&G or Mars wants you to establish a beachhead for them."

I was the recording secretary at those Board meetings. The feeling in the room was electric. Every executive there knew that without the revenue produced by DMB&B Detroit, the holding company would simply not be solvent. Many of them appreciated that fact. The top corporate officers were rankled by it.

"I would just like to know," Monchak continued, "where is it written that only DMB&B Detroit can make its numbers? I would just like to be able to go back to my clients and my people and say, 'Good news. Here's what we're going to do for you.'"

For all his polish and poise, Monchak liked telling a folksy story to make a point. It was quite a juxtaposition, him doing a backwoods voice while looking as if he just stepped out of an Armani ad—an expertly tailored suit or sport coat with a pocket square tucked in the breast pocket, all topped by his full head of hair perfectly coiffed.

"Guy goes into a store and asks for a box of salt," he would say. "Clerk tell him, 'That'll be 80 cents.' Guy says, 'Store down the street sells the same box for 70 cents.' Clerk goes, 'Well, why don't you buy it there?' Guy answers, 'They're out of it.' Clerk says, 'Big deal, when I'm out of it I sell it for 60 cents.'"

Ron's little stories at first seemed apropos of nothing. But finally, at one Board meeting, he had had enough of polite listening and no action. Emboldened by the strong urgings of his key executives back in Bloomfield Hills, he tried another tack.

"Farmer has two chickens," he said, and around the table, fellow directors smiled or shook heads, wondering where this one was going.

"One chicken is healthy and lays nutritious eggs. The other chicken is sickly, lays no eggs at all. So the farmer does the obvious thing." And there Monchak pauses, until everybody looks up at him, awaiting the punch line. "He kills the healthy one to make broth for the sick one."

A ripple of laughter, quickly subsiding as they get the point.

Long silence. People shuffle their feet. Someone coughs. Corporate execs look at each other and frown.

But Monchak is not through. He stands there, nodding his head slightly, looking at each of his fellow directors in turn. Some of them preside over the failing operations that have drained the company. Agency heads from Latin America and Eastern Europe, many have gone years without once showing a profit. They have been the beneficiaries of the labors of men and women they have never met; their benefactors are several hundred people in Detroit working on advertising for General Motors, Whirlpool, FTD and Dow. They've never met Mr. Goodwrench but he's been paying their salaries.

"Traveling salesman is driving down a country road," Monchak says, startling a couple directors who thought he had made his point.

"Salesman has a load of new mailboxes in the back of his pickup truck. Does a double take when he sees a strange sight in a field, something he's never seen before. Turns into the driveway and stops in front of the farmhouse. Farmer comes out, shaking his head. 'Don't need a mailbox,' farmer says. Salesman gets out anyhow. 'I know. I see you have a fairly new one. But there's something I noticed in your field. Never saw anything like that, wanted to ask you about it.'"

I stop taking notes, having heard this one before. Everyone in the room is apprehensive about what's coming next.

"Farmer waits for the salesman to go on. 'That pig in the field. Never saw a pig with a wooden leg before.' Farmer gives him a look. 'That there's a special pig. Saved my life, that pig. Me and my whole family. Owe that pig a lot.' Salesman asks how that could be, a pig saving lives. 'Way it happened, we're all sound asleep when the heat stove goes on the fritz, puts out fumes and now we're all unconscious. Then it catches fire and the place is about to burn down. Pig there sees this, knocks down the fence, comes crashing against the door 'til he breaks it down. Squealing so loud I come to, wake the family. We get the fire out. That pig saved our lives, this house, everything.'

"The salesman says, 'What a story. That's incredible. So the pig hurt his leg, crashing through the door, and you fixed him up with that wooden leg.'"

Again Monchak pauses.

"The farmer shakes his head, 'Oh no, that didn't hurt him none. But a pig does something like that for you, you don't eat it all at once.'"

And he sat down.

A bigger laugh this time, but just for an instant, then silence. A silence total and ominous.

A gauntlet had been thrown down. From that moment it was clear that corporate management had to know just how serious Monchak was about redressing inequity. He was determined to treat fairly the employees who year after year produced the corporation's largest pool of profit. He was on a mission to bring something to the table for clients that had supported his agency for decades. And he was not in this alone. Or so he thought. He had been goaded by several of his senior staff back in Detroit to tell corporate they were tired of earning strong profits only to get bonuses that were a fraction of what they deserved.

Monchak's folksy fables were the final nails. Corporate management concluded that it was simply too disruptive, too dangerous to have a maverick running a major business unit, albeit the most successful, most profitable in the company. No more Mr. Nice Guy. They wanted their subordinate managers to run their businesses the way they were told and stop bitching about it. They wanted it done their way, even if that meant hurting morale, which would lead to lower productivity and smaller profits.

So they did what corporate chieftains often do in such situations. They took the temperature of a few key people at DMB&B Detroit and its client companies to see if they would revolt if a change were made.

As for clients, when their advertising agency considers a change in staff, their response typically depends on how pleased they are at the moment with the TV spots the agency has been producing. If they are high on the recent ads, they let you know that you damn well better not change the creative director. But changing the head of the local office, well, unless it happens to be an old college room-mate or a golfing buddy, very often a client decides it really doesn't make that much difference. The client will tell the agency, "Your company, your decision. Just be sure that we get the service we need from you going forward."

Soon after Monchak's in-your-face Board meeting performance, a top corporate officer, Clayton Wilhite, the company's president, came to Detroit. As president, Wilhite was in the role that Mon-chak himself had turned down in 1985, the year of the merger that created DMB&B. He sounded out the office's key managers who worked with clients. These were the very people who for years had prodded Monchak to "get tough with those bozos at corporate and let them know we're fed up with sending a dollar east and getting less than a dime back." They now had an opportunity to staunchly back up the man to whom they owed so much and to whom they had promised "we're behind you all the way."

Monchak knew how it was played. He knew that if several of them spoke up and guarded his back, corporate wouldn't dare move against him. But he also knew that some might think a change was inevitable and they would want to be seen as loyal not to Monchak but instead to the top corporate hierarchy

A week after Wilhite's visit, he summoned Monchak to New York. Before he went to the airport, Monchak asked me what I thought about his being ordered into a star chamber session to talk about "succession planning for DMB&B Bloomfield Hills." That was an interesting choice of terms because for years senior office heads had complained that there was no succession planning at the top management tier of the holding company. Monchak told me he found it particularly ironic that this succession planning issue should be raised in regard to his DMB&B Detroit agency. He had contended for years that there were several people who could take over his position in the event that something happened to him.

Then he went to New York and met with Wilhite. He called me

as soon as the short and not-so-sweet meeting was over.

"Unless I agree to just become their puppet, they want me out," he told me over the phone. "They said they don't think I'd have the stomach for the draconian slashes they're going to insist on for this office. That's one thing they're right about. If I can't go along, they'll replace me with a guy who'll do it their way and keep his mouth shut. They've already identified someone who has assured them he'll give them what they want. But they want it to appear as a completely voluntary retirement. For everybody's sake, they say."

He paused for a long moment, then laughed. "Gee, you don't suppose the fact that I'll have to turn in my stock and not get a penny for it has ever occurred to them?"

This was the moment Monchak had expected since the first day the deal was struck to merge DM&M with Benton & Bowles to create DMB&B. He had said then that although it was proclaimed as a merger of equals it was in reality a takeover by B&B. What followed was an all-too-familiar scenario. First, there had been "rightsizing," which was nothing less than forced retirements, firing people and doubling workloads on already over-worked employees. At the same time, further tightening down the expense side of the budget to milk out every last dime of cost. Slash the bonus pool. Then came a freeze on hiring, raises and promotions.

But as losses continued to mount at sister agencies, headquarters demanded whatever additional dollars could be squeezed out of DMB&B Detroit. Next was a mandate to eliminate the little morale touches that Monchak authorized that cost peanuts, comparatively, but had for decades created a family atmosphere. The agency overlords saved pennies and bought many dollars of ill will when they dispensed with giving turkeys to employees on Christmas and hams on Easter. Next they canceled the Christmas party and the summer picnic. Finally, they eliminated the small awards for exceptional performance and milestones of service and stopped reimbursements for continuing education expenses.

The expense line was being prettied up to make the holding

company more attractive to potential suitors. But in terms of employee morale, loyalty and quality performance at the cash-cow office, it was death by a thousand cuts.

Corporate management had decimated a managerial style that had made DMB&B Detroit not only the jewel of the holding company, but also perhaps the most desirable, successful agency to work at in Michigan, if not the Midwest.

When Monchak returned to Detroit, we sat in his office and talked about it. He explained it as if it were something from which he was personally detached.

"It's simple, the way it's done," he said, "almost elegant in its simplicity. They wouldn't phrase it this way, of course, but it's at the core of the first and last things they teach you in MBA school. It's what they salivate for, a situation like this, a cash-rich private company. It's the holy grail for a zealous MBA type."

He paused and smiled. "It also helps if you're more than a little ruthless.

"First you dole out lavish stock allotments to a dozen or two of your top executives and key creatives. It will eventually be to your advantage to be almost obscenely generous. You let them sit on that stock for a while. Two years. Five. As long as it takes. The stock has no face value—they can't redeem it for anything—but you give them a few dollars per share every year. A guy has, say, ten thousand shares, it adds up.

"Then one day when the economic climate is just right, you strike. One option is to take the thing public. Problem there is you're into a lot of red tape and disclosure requirements and more headaches than you want.

"Better is if you're in an era of consolidation, of mindless acquisition. Then you do a really big deal and sell it for far more than it's worth. Since you know you're going to do that some day, you start culling the herd, rounding up those shares. To do that you knock off those boys you gave the big stock allotments to a few years back. It may cost you a little, say a year's salary, some other goodies, for doing nothing but sitting there with a phony emeritus title. But that's chump change compared to what you're getting."

I asked him, "Okay, what *are* you getting?"

"Wealth," he said. "You're getting very, very rich. You've just liquidated a private company that has taken thousands of people decades to build all that equity. They're gone now, at least the guys holding the biggest chunks of stock. A few retired, the rest got forced out one way or another and on the way out the door, they turned in stock that had zero par value. So when you knocked them off and they turned in their shares, they didn't get a dime. And of course you didn't re-issue that stock, so it made each share you owned worth just that much more. In this case, a whole lot more."

He looked out the window to the west, toward the Bloomfield Hills Country Club, just over the rise and beyond the small woods. That proximity—yet another way to entertain clients—was a major reason that the agency had sited its headquarters here decades ago.

"You don't go after the fawns and does. And you'll need the bambis to serve as foot soldiers. You have to retain a handful of execs to keep the place going until you're well out of it. No, what you do, you target the big stags. That's where you make your killing—whacking the big bucks, you might say.'

He laughed. Neither of us said anything for a while.

"Stockholder value, that's what you preach. That's the mantra. That's the chant droning behind everything they teach you in the eastern MBA schools. Of course it has nothing to do with increasing value for the real stakeholders—the people who actually built the company and created the worth. They don't get a cent out of that mountain of equity—the employees, the retirees, the suppliers, or even the people who provide the income that made it all possible, the clients. It's all about kiting that perceived value of the entity so you can unload it at a ridiculously top dollar to someone who likely in a few years will work their own version of the gambit on somebody else with even deeper pockets."

I asked him if he was going to fight it. What was he going

to do now?

"Remember that old cigaret slogan, 'I'd rather fight than switch'? Not me. I'd rather switch than fight. So I'm going to switch to what I always wanted to do. I'm going to put my time and energy into being more of what I am. I'm a writer. I'm going to write. And if you will take me in as a partner and teach me the ropes, I'm going to publish what other people write. I'm going to publish books that are, as you've been saying, worth cutting down a tree to get the paper to print it on. That's what I'm going to do."

I was getting up to leave when Ron said, "You wouldn't believe it."

"Believe what?"

"How quiet it's going to get in this room over the next year. You've read your *Julius Caesar*. You know what's going to happen with the guys who've been pushing me to get tougher with New York, prodding me to let corporate know Bloomfield Hills has had enough of mining gold to ship back to the corporate vault. Those same guys will be stroking my successor before this body is cold. They've got families. They've got house payments. Life goes on."

MONCHAK HAD KNOWN HE HAD A CHOICE before he gave what amounted to an ultimatum at the last Board meeting in New York. He could have kept his mouth shut and gone along. That would mean surrendering the way he believed a business should be run decently as well as profitably. It would mean acquiescing to the enforcing of a managerial style and business culture he felt was flawed and self-defeating.

The other choice? Leave.

Fortunately, he was financially able to retire, albeit quite prematurely. The psychological transition would also be easy because there was always far more to him than his role as an advertising agency head. There was now something more meaningful to him, he told me, the prospect of book publishing, into which he could pour his time, energy and creative talents. He knew that what he would do in the future would be far more fun and fulfilling than running an agency under conditions that had changed so drastically in recent years. He was right—what he was at heart was a writer, and a fine one. He was also a damned fine editor. He loved books and working with other writers. He had long been interested in the book publishing I had done.

For years, Monchak and I had been going to lunch together, usually trying out the next new Asian restaurant opening somewhere in the suburbs. We seldom talked at lunch about the advertising or public relations businesses—there was so much more to learn from one another. He didn't play golf or follow sports, but for some reason he wanted to know more about them.

One incident was typical of how blasé he was about sports and celebrities. Jack Nicklaus had been signed to do commercials for Monchak's client, the Pontiac Motor Car Division. A location shoot was scheduled at Bloomfield Hills Country Club. The ninth fairway of the golf course was barely a quarter mile over the hill to the west of the agency's parking lot. Monchak wandered over to join his creative team and production crew on the golf course, waiting for Nicklaus to show up.

"Here he comes!" someone finally shouted.

There across the fairway strode the Golden Bear, his blond hair gleaming in the sun, one of the world's most recognizable sports figures. Alongside him was a nondescript man, his agent.

Monchak watched them approach, then said, "Okay, so which one is Nicklaus?"

At our lunches, Ron would ask me about raising vegetables, about sports he had never understood, about the NASA space programs I had worked on many years earlier. I had been to some places he was interested in and we would talk about New Zealand, Japan, Thailand, Casablanca. But he taught me much more than I ever taught him—about writing for film, underwriting theatrical productions, his philosophies of building and running an effective organization. He had an encyclopedic knowledge of cars and introduced me to designers, engineers and car magazine editors he had known for years. But of all the subjects we discussed, the one Monchak kept coming back to was book publishing.

He had known for some time that once he retired he would need a place to go and something challenging and stimulating to do. With his unusual combination of interests and talents, book publishing seemed the perfect place. We talked about a book I had teamed with our mutual friend Stan Stein and others to publish in 1987, *Spartan Seasons: The Trials and Triumphs of Michigan State Sports*. The author was Lynn Henning, sports writer for *The Detroit News*. When MSU won the Rose Bowl that season, book sales spiked. Ron wanted to hear more. I told him about two other pending projects with *Detroit News* reporters and columnists. One book was *Detroit's Powers & Personalities* by Tim Kiska. The other was *A Guide to Detroit & Michigan Restaurants* by *News* restaurant critic Sandra Silfven.

To Ron, those seemed like books that could be fun and maybe even successful. So he asked me if he could come in as my partner in Momentum Books Ltd., the successor to the company I had cofounded earlier to publish *Spartan Seasons*.

One of the terms of Monchak's departure from DMB&B was that he would remain in the figurehead position of chairman of the Detroit office for a year. When Wilhite came to Detroit to announce the management changes, he lauded Monchak for his great contributions to building and managing the most successful agency in the company. Ron had characteristically kept his own counsel and almost no one else at the agency realized that retiring on that timetable was a corporate management decision, not his.

Ron Monchak was now officially a lame duck.

As we walked back to his office after the announcement, Monchak said again, "Watch how quiet it becomes very quickly in my corner."

He was very aware that—no matter how respected, admired and loved a boss may be—in American business it is the position that confers power, not the person in that position. And that was fine with him because he had a new career he was eager to segue into.

He had phone calls to make so I went back down the hall where a knot of managers were clustered about Robin Smith, the man who had been elevated to Monchak's role as managing director. Ron himself had endorsed that move, knowing that Smith had long been spending time socially with the holding company top execs. It was clear they had come to consider Smith their kind of fellow. He was on the same wavelength with holding company top management in terms of rigidly managing the expense side of a budget, terminating people as corporate management dictated. He also represented a distinct departure from Monchak's hands-off managerial style that encouraged individual responsibility and fostered an entrepreneurial spirit.

Standing in the hallway, flanking new agency head Smith, were the two managers who had for years been the most fervent in urging Monchak to "be tough with those greedy bastards in New York." Now, due in part to their having prodded Monchak into a hard-line approach, the man who had more than once saved their jobs was out. There they stood, patting the new boss on the back.

Monchak, a student of Shakespeare, would not have been surprised. He might have said, "The king is dead. Long live the king."

What would have cut him more deeply than the impersonal corporate knife in the back, however, were the small personal betrayals. One of the men who had been the most forceful in urging Ron to play hard ball turned to me and said, "Maybe we'll have a better relationship with corporate now that our managing director isn't going to New York and poking them in the eye with a stick."

I looked at these two fellows and thought how easy it is for some men to rationalize when they betray a trust. Monchak was more stoic. He knew that some of his key managers might decide that to get along they had to go along. Despite all he had done for them, despite the fact that they themselves had urged him to draw a line in the sand with corporate management, he knew some of these men would turn, would choose to curry favor with the over-lords at his expense. And yet, throughout that awkward "chairman emeritus" year, Ron Monchak continued to be accessible, cordial and helpful to everyone.

Now what remained was to see if his rueful prophecy would come true. "I know when they'll finally do the big deal," Monchak had joked many times, alluding to the company going public or selling itself to the highest bidder. "The day after I turn in my stock."

He was wrong on the timing but dead right on the facts. The stock that Monchak had accumulated for years, that he personally had helped to grow so substantially through his effective leader-ship, eventually made a few top people at the holding company very, very wealthy and also created a few dozen other millionaires. Monchak had turned in tens of thousands of shares for which he received absolutely nothing. When the deal was done, each of those shares was valued at $995.

"I gained a lot more than I lost," Monchak told me. "Getting into book publishing was the best thing that ever happened to me. A few weeks after I was out of advertising people would ask me, Do you miss it? Miss it, I'd say? I don't even think about it."

I had told Ron countless times that book publishing is an ex-hilarating vocation, a noble calling and a consuming obsession. It is also an absolutely lousy business.

"So?" he said. "I'm not in this to make money. If I don't do this, what am I going to do? I need a place to go to in the morning. To work at into the evening if I want to. I've seen it happen time and again with people used to operating in a stimulating environment. They retire, thinking they will play golf, go boating, do whatever. And what happens? Their brain atrophies. They no longer have challenges, problems to solve. No creative tension. I have no illu-sions about book publishing being even a break-even venture. But this is what I want to do.

"Look, every investment I have ever made has gone south. You want to see a play fail, just let me invest a hundred thousand in it. You want to see an odds-on favorite stumble in the stretch, just have me bet on it. I am the patron saint of lost causes. Who was that character in the cartoon L'il Abner? The one who walked around with a black cloud and lightning bolts flashing over his head?"

"His first name was Joe," I said, "and his last name, I believe, was spelled B...t...f...s...p...l...k. I never knew how to pronounce it." Whatever, he was Mr. Black Cloud. A magnet for financial disaster."

There was ample evidence for the prosecution that Monchak was not exaggerating his skein of bad luck and lost gambles. Because of his enthusiasm for a play being developed to open on Broadway, my wife and I invested for the first—and last—time in a theatrical production. It was an award-winning drama that had first been mounted to rave reviews and big box office in New Zealand and Australia. The play was called *Shimada,* an engrossing tale of a soldier who suffered torture in World War II at the hands of a cruel Japanese officer and later came to confront his tormentor as well as all his other demons. Ben Gazarra was the lead with Ellen Burstyn heading a strong cast led by an accomplished director. Monchak had his own theatrical underwriting company called Archangel and was in for $125,000; that made my $15,000 seem paltry but it was a bit of a plunge for us.

We went to New York for the sold-out premiere and sat anxiously through the production. My brother Bob, who himself had been a prisoner of war in Japan in World War II, flew in from California for opening night. Together, we anxiously bided time at the after-glow party while awaiting the make-or-break reviews. As backers, we chatted with the playwright, the cast and their friends, including Anthony Quinn, there as moral support for his friend Ben Gazarra.

The atmosphere was the typical mixture of hope and dread.

When we finally opened the *New York Times* and read Frank Rich's review, all hope disappeared. Critic Rich savaged the play as xenophobic. That should have been no surprise, as there was indeed fear in America of Japanese economic aggression—Japanese conglomerates and investors had recently gobbled up one American icon after another. We had thought the play rose far above blind nationalism, dealing with timeless issues of morality—that is how it had been received and reviewed in its run in award-winning run in Australia. Not so in America.

The next morning we got a call from the producer informing us that by itself the Rich review was the kiss of death. The opening night performance we had seen had also brought down the Broadway curtain for the last time on *Shimada*. Advance ticket buyers would have their money refunded. The play was shuttered and in one night our investment, Ron's and everyone else's was worthless.

Monchak could recount other examples, but there was no disputing that as a rider of dead horses, he had an impeccable record.

I followed Ron into retirement from the advertising business—albeit only briefly—and we did more and more books. When a manuscript intrigued Ron or when he got an idea for a book, he was free to decide personally whether to proceed on it. He took on several titles that he knew stood little chance of recovering their investment but that he believed were worth seeing print. When I told him I was tapped out and couldn't continue to match his investments, he insisted that the worth of my earlier investment in launching the place and teaching him the business more than equaled the money he was putting in. He wanted to do books he deemed worthwhile and if they lost money, well, so be it.

"Looks like I brought my black cloud with me into Momentum," Monchak would say when a book got rave reviews but struggled to break even. But it didn't deter him.

In 1995, an elderly woman from New York sent Ron an unsolicited manuscript on a topic that was far removed from anything we could hope to do successfully. Victoria Hertig's working title was something like, "The Girl in the Woods." Her manuscript purported to be a factual account of her terrifying experiences as a Polish survivor of a Nazi concentration camp. The writing was awkward and unpolished, but the tale was compelling to Monchak, perhaps in part because of his own Eastern European heritage. So instead of returning the manuscript with a form rejection slip, he did something publishers know they shouldn't do. He sent a friendly note to Hertig expressing regrets and wishing her success with another publishing house.

Hertig did what any aspiring author would do. She immediately telephoned to hear more of Monchak's thoughts. At the end of their long conversation, Ron came into my office shaking his head. He admitted sheepishly that the author had talked him into rewriting a few pages to show her what he had in mind. "I'll do that and then she's on her own," he said.

Two weeks later he sent her several completely rewritten chapters. That brought another call from the appreciative author and before Monchak knew it, he was in deep. He found himself totally overhauling Hertig's entire text, under the *nom de plume* "Franklin Fox."

It took months for him to get the manuscript into publishable shape. Finally, he and the author agreed on a title, *Flowers of Hope: A Haunting True Story of Passion and Betrayal.* Ron ordered up a press run in hard cover with a jacket design aimed directly at any reader's heart strings. The copy for the back cover of the jacket proclaimed:

> ...the heartbreaking true story of a young girl who yearned to find love and beauty in the enchanting Carpathian Mountains of Poland before World War II. While barely fifteen, her bliss was shattered by the brutal realities of carnal lust, and national and ethnic pride. Forced by her father to marry a man she didn't love to protect the family's honor, she watched with horror as invading armies and vengeful groups bloodied the sacred soil of her homeland.

Well, that ought to raise the eyebrows of talk show hosts and book reviewers.

And it did.

But after our promotions person lined up author interviews, Hertig called Monchak to tell him about an unexpected problem.

"I couldn't believe what I was hearing," Ron told me. "The book is finished. We're shipping copies, lining up interviews and promotions. Now she tells me that her son, a prominent doctor, has major objections. Seems he was unaware of any of this sordid family history until he read his mother's book. He never knew that when his mother was a fifteen-year-old girl she was raped in her bed by a drunken friend of her father. And that his mother was then forced by her family to marry the man who raped her. Now that the son knows his father raped his mother, he feels the book will disgrace the family."

It was a dilemma. We had a lot of money invested in the book but if it were to go on the market, it would destroy the author's family, so said the author.

"She says maybe we can still publish it if we change it from rape to consensual sex," Ron said.

"We can't do that," I said. "We've billed this as a true story, even using the word 'true' in the subtitle. She can't rewrite history. It was either rape or it wasn't. And remember, she wrote that the guy not only raped her when she was fifteen, he did it again after they were married when they met up by accident in a Nazi concentration camp. If it wasn't rape, the whole story falls apart. She's got a huge credibility deficit when she says she would be willing to change such a crucial point just to get the book out. Besides, the book is printed and copies have been shipped."

The next day Hertig called to say she wanted to reimburse us for our expenses already incurred. Characteristically, Monchak declined her offer. In a few days, she called again. This time she told Monchak the story was true, after all, exactly as she had told it the first time. Now she would agree to our selling the book but she promised her family she would not make appearances to promote it.

We knew from previous experience how important active participation of the author is to a book's success. At one end of the spectrum, we had Ernie Harwell, author of our recent *Diamond Gems*. Ernie had a built-in media platform and a sterling reputation and was terrific about doing signings, giving talks, sitting for interviews, doing whatever he could to give visibility to his books. At the other end, we had published *The Oxford Gourmet Cookbook*, a fine book by restaurateur Ted Richman, who had owned The Fox & Hounds. Only when the book was coming off the presses did Ted confide that he couldn't handle speaking in public and wouldn't do appearances, signings or interviews.

Our very successful book, *The Simply Great Cookbook*, by restaurateur Chuck Muer sold briskly through several printings because Muer loved glad-handing at book-signing events at his chain of seafood restaurants. But then, Muer steered his yacht "Charlie's Crab," out of port in the Bahamas, heading to Jupiter Beach to do a book signing. Unknowingly he headed directly into the "Storm of the Century." The Muers and their two best friends were lost at sea and never seen again.

So several experiences told us that without an active author, there was no hope for *Flowers of Hope*.

Ron was disappointed—and undeterred. He chalked that one off and went on.

A Hollywood friend pitched him a book on the actor Nick Nolte. It was a celebrity bio with thin national appeal. Reader tastes were in a cycle in which biographies and celebrity books were moribund categories and this project therefore came with a double kiss of death. It would be of interest to only a slim and shallow market of film buffs, potential buyers reachable only with a national promotional campaign or by high-priced ads in film publications. It was exactly the kind of book a small regional Michigan publisher could not hope to do successfully.

Still and all, it was a highly authoritative and well-written Hollywood insider manuscript. Stories based on behind-the-scenes doings in the film industry were a special interest of Monchak's. Moreover, he knew he could enhance the book as its editor. The author, Mel Weiser, was a friend of Ron's and a very persistent fellow. Ron just couldn't say no and so he decided to fund it fully. A few months later, we published *Nick Nolte: Caught in the Act.*

For a time, it appeared Ron had at last gotten lucky. Weiser's manuscript was a compelling account of what often happens off camera in Hollywood. His text focused on the quixotic Nolte as he alternated brilliant screen performances with bizarre off-screen behavior that made him both a darling of the tabloids and a ripe target of them. The book chronicled Nolte's exploits on the set of the feature film *Jefferson in Paris* where he indulged in enough fine French cuisine that the costume that made him look svelte in early shots was bulging at the seams as shooting went on.

Late in filming, Nolte was in agony as he tried to get out his skin-tight trousers, finally yelling for help. A cast photographer snapped off several pictures of him lying on the floor, legs jutting up in the air as co-star Gwyneth Paltrow tugged and wrestled to get his pants off. *National Enquirer* wrote a hefty check for rights to the photos and an article about the book. It was the kind of publicity a publisher dreams about.

Buoyed by the news of the forthcoming *Enquirer* spread, Monchak ordered an increase in the press run to 10,000 copies. That is a trivial number for a national publisher, but a bold move for a small one in Troy, Michigan.

The painfully candid book got rave reviews and was praised as "the finest inside-Hollywood book ever." Nolte came off looking very good on some pages and frankly repulsive in others. Weiser was a longtime friend of Nolte's and had worked with him on several films, but Nolte felt betrayed by the warts-and-all treatment and would have nothing to do with promoting the book. After the initial flurry triggered by the *Enquirer* spread, sales slowed, then plummeted. Most of the press run remained on skids in the warehouse.

Ron finally discovered what it is that keeps small publishers hooked—the occasional hit that dims the memory of the misses. He worked with author Michael Ranville on a book any serious publisher would be proud to have brought out. It was the story of how Edward R. Murrow used the story of Lt. Milo Radulovich to bring down Senator Joseph McCarthy in his tyrannical witch-hunt for Communists under every bed, a sordid chapter in American history when lives and careers were destroyed by mere guilt through association. Monchak took personal charge of Ranville's book and conceived the title: *To Strike at a King: The Turning Point in the McCarthy Witch-Hunts.* Radulovich visited our offices to thank us for doing the book and to tell us that George Clooney told him the book inspired and informed his Academy Award-winning film, *Good Night and Good Luck.*

A surprise success came in the form of a book Ron signed up, *Gansta in the House.* The author, Mike Knox, was a 15-year veteran policeman in Houston who tapped into a hot topic at just the right time. Not only that, Knox and his resourceful wife also promoted the book aggressively and it went through several printings. It also helped communities understand and presumably cope better with the growing wave of gang violence.

In keeping with of our mission to publish books we deemed worthwhile without expecting them to post big numbers nationally, we did Michael Betzold's controversial and definitive treatment of assisted suicide and Jack Kevorkian in *Appointment with Dr. Death.* The book contributed to thoughtful television productions by the BBC and PBS, the latter winning an Emmy for Betzold.

We developed edgy works like Maxine Berman's provocative opus on women in politics, *The Only Boobs in the House Are Men* with the cover tagline: "A veteran woman legislator lifts the lid on politics macho style." Berman had been in the Michigan State Legislature for more than ten years and was one of the toughest and most effective legislators of any gender. She also was that rare author who came up with a title for her book that actually nailed it.

We added to our line of definitive books on Detroit and Michigan subjects by bringing out the authoritative *Deer Hunter's Field Guide* and followed that with the *Deer Watcher's Field Guide*, both by John H. Williams. Along the way, we continued to publish books on food, restaurants and dining—ten in all—on categories from chicken and seafood to wild game, from soup to Thai cuisine, from tailgating recipes to English gourmet cuisine.

Monchak captured the essence of the irrepressible David E. Davis in a book he developed and titled *Thus Spake David E.* Author Davis was a world-class procrastinator and after his long and distinguished career as editor of several automotive magazines, it appeared he would never take time to do the book he had always wanted to. Monchak personally sifted through hundreds of Davis's columns and essays and wove them into a coherent fabric that was a fitting tribute to one of the automotive world's greatest journalists.

We did several books meant to elevate the understanding if not the image of Detroit as a place with a rich history and with special people. *Rockin' Down the Dial* was the definitive book on Detroit radio as a beacon of popular music over the decades. Aided by Tom Ferguson's deft editorial touch, Detroit health guru and television personality Peter Nielsen told his story in *Will of Iron* about overcoming a childhood illness that nearly killed him. Turning to bodybuilding to heal his emaciated body, Nielsen became Mr. International Universe and did it without "buying his muscles from a pharmacist" as Ferguson put it, in contrast to so many champion bodybuilders.

There were many more books for Monchak's editorial blue pencil. Each book was different, each was special to an author and a readership and all were special to Monchak, now comfortably in his element, far from client pressures and corporate intrigues.

We poured much more time and money than we originally planned to into doing books we believed in. We teamed with our authors to get attention paid to their works. Neither Monchak nor

I would waste the time of busy people by asking them to review a manuscript or provide a blurb for a book jacket when there was only a remote chance they would be interested. But conversely, if the two of us believed that a book was important, funny or relevant, there was a good chance other people would feel that way too. As a result, we rarely got turned down by a celebrity or national figure from whom we sought an endorsement. So, M. Scott Peck (author of the Number 1 best-selling *The Road Less Traveled* and many others big sellers) wrote a glowing foreword for our *Bankrupt: A Society Living in the Future* by James V. McTevia. So did then-Chrysler president Bob Lutz and award-winning author P.J. O'Rourke for the David E. Davis book. Authors Elmore Leonard and Jim Harrison gave us jacket blurbs for *The Ultimate Lark* by restaurateur Jim Lark, proprietor of one of America's finest restaurants. Senators John McCain and Carl Levin and many others took time to write forewords for us.

Book publishing in the Midwest is no easily tapped vein of precious ore. On the financial balance sheet, what we were mining was often more like fool's gold, but we also brought to the surface some 24-karat nuggets. This was not big-time, New York publishing. This was not whack the ones that don't have legs after four weeks, and hope that a few out of every hundred titles hit big to mop up the ocean of red ink from the failures. This was small-time, collegial publishing where author, editor and publisher team up to create a book that is worth having cut down a tree to get the paper to print it.

"Every day, I wake up looking forward to coming into this place," Ron often said. "What we're doing here might make a small difference we'll never know about. But even a small difference is worth making. Regardless, there's nothing I'd rather be doing."

I felt much the same way, having founded the company. But with Monchak as my partner it had become something more and something different. I was grateful that it had become such a satisfying part of the life of a friend and business colleague who had done so much for me and for thousands of people fortunate to have worked under his leadership. But it bothered me that while book publishing fulfilled needs for him, it was a draining proposition financially for both us, particularly for Ron.

We talked about this often at lunch. One day Ron looked up at me abruptly from his bowl of sizzling rice soup. He surprised me with an uncharacteristically serious question.

"Assuming you had a choice—which notwithstanding Jack Kevorkian, people don't often have—how would you want to die?" he asked.

I had to think about that a bit. I had run a couple of marathons and was still running ten to twelve miles a couple days a week, so that affected my preferences.

"I guess I'd like to be finishing my last training run before a marathon. I'd be at the crest of a hill and out of a clear sky Wham!, I get hit with a bolt of lightning."

Ron was a notorious non-athlete who recoiled at the thought of working up a sweat. He smiled as he decided what he would choose.

"I'll have what you're having," he said. "Except for the running."

When we got back to the office, Tom Ferguson, whom we had installed as managing editor, gave his typically dismal forecast of yet another year of red ink. "We're doing good books. Maybe some important books. But face it, we live in the post-literate age. Nobody reads anymore. You want my advice from a business perspective, I say fold it."

"Well," Monchak said. "We're not folding it."

A few months later, Monchak showed up at the office looking like he had applied a too-orange suntan treatment out of a bottle. He hadn't wanted to miss our morning meeting with author Donald Haas about his prospective book, *Money Forever: How to make your money last as long as you do.* When I asked Ron if he were ill, he said that almost overnight he had gotten jaundiced. He sat in on part of the meeting, then left at 11 a.m. to see his doctor.

At 2 p.m. he phoned me from Crittenton Hospital in Rochester.

"I've got good news and I've got bad news," Ron said. "First, the good news is that the doctor says I can last another twenty-five years, once they get the treatment protocol in gear. The bad news is that I've got leukemia."

He called me again the next day from his hospital bed. He was in good spirits but actually giggled—the only time I ever heard that sound from him—when he said his medication made him dopier than usual. He asked about a couple book projects he had been considering, but then quickly said, "That can wait. I'm having trouble concentrating."

The next day his family told us he had been transferred to the Barbara Ann Karmanos Cancer Research Institute in Detroit. He had arrived there in a coma. He rallied and slumped on and off for three days. Major organ failure, we were told. Then, unbelievably, scarcely a week after he came into the office looking jaundiced, on June 26, 2001, the great and generous heart of Ron Monchak was stilled.

Jack Bowen and Ron Monchak had admired and respected each other since Ron reported to Jack in the early days of the merged advertising agencies. Bowen was working in his garden in the Maine countryside when he heard of Monchak's passing. It took him fourteen hours and a maze of transportation connections to get to Rochester, Michigan, for the funeral. At the memorial service he said, "There is no way I would have missed paying my respects to such a dear and wonderful man." Bowen's reaction and his sentiments were typical of the overflow crowd gathered in final tribute to a person who had done so much for so long for so many.

Ron Monchak's legacy is in the thousands of careers he nurtured and the many he saved in the advertising world. It is in the health and vibrancy of the upgraded Cranbrook Institute where his efforts as treasurer contributed so much. Perhaps most dear to him and permanently it is in the books he edited and published that very probably would not have seen print otherwise. It was enough for him that his books brought readers a kernel of knowledge, an insight or a smile.

He felt that his challenge as a mentor, editor or collaborator was to help an author find and fine-tune the voice to tell the story. Then, as a publisher, to create a book that did justice to that voice and projected it clearly to the intended reader. He left his stamp on copy by gracefully helping the author say his piece or often just by leaving no trace that an editor's hand had been there.

But to all the people who knew and worked with him, the impression left by Ron Monchak was indelible.

"The Tigers organization has made a decision
to go in another direction."

It was like a Shakespearean tragedy in which two parties
are manipulated by an outside force and are powerless to
stop events. Forever after they remain silent because the
greatest shame of all is that the world see that they have
been duped. Then how did it happen?

~⚬ 14 ⚬~

THE INFERNO AT
MICHIGAN & TRUMBULL

Ernie Harwell Writes Two Swan Songs

For, lo, the winter is past,
The rain is over and gone;
The flowers appear on the earth;
The time of the singing of birds is come,
And the voice of the turtle is heard in our land

From the Song of Solomon

ON A COLD WINTER EVENING IN DECEMBER 1990, I answered the phone and felt a warm summer breeze. It was the mellifluous baritone of Ernie Harwell. We talked a few moments, then Ernie said he had a favor to ask: could I be with him at Tiger Stadium in the morning. There was going to be a press conference and it was important to him for me to be there.

My wife Marcy and I had been with Ernie and Lulu Harwell at Meadow Brook Hall a week before for a special dinner. As people of a certain age do, we talked about health and knew they both were feeling well. But something Lulu said to Marcy now seemed ominous.

"I think they might be trying to get rid of Ernie," Lulu had said.

"They wouldn't dare do that," Marcy replied.

"Oh yes, they would," Lulu said.

I couldn't believe it either. Still, my first thought when Ernie called me to ask me to be with him at the Stadium was that he was going to announce his retirement, for whatever reason. But if he wanted me to know the purpose of the press conference, he would already have told me, so I wasn't about to ask him.

As I started the drive to the Stadium, I thought about the many good times Ernie and I had shared. Most of those times were far away from the ballpark and had nothing to do with baseball. Marcy and I had enjoyed regular lunches, dinners and quiet talks with Ernie and Lulu. The two ladies would talk mostly about family while the insatiable reader Ernie and I talked about books, among other things. We both remembered well that it was the subject of books that had begun our friendship on a sunny day in May 1984. That was when I had urged Ernie to write his first book, *Tuned to Baseball*. On the flyleaf of the first copy off the presses of that book Ernie wrote, "Best to Bill, who made it all possible—thanks for your direction, support & friendship."

I remembered a day just a year before when Ernie called me in my New York office to ask if I had an extra pair of tuxedo pants. He had invited me to be his guest at his induction that evening into the Hall of Fame of the National Sportscasters and Sports Writers Association. But after Ernie flew in from Detroit and had gotten to his hotel, he discovered he had forgotten to pack the bottom half of his tux. I didn't have an extra pair of tuxedo trousers so he decided he would just wear a pair of regular dark blue pants. "With the dim lighting," he said, "I'll bet nobody will ever know the difference."

He was right.

Approaching Tiger Stadium, I thought about the documentary film I had done recapping Ernie's career, *The Great Voice of the Grand Old Game*. We had premiered the film at an event at Meadow Brook Hall honoring Ernie. Then at the request of the National Baseball Hall of Fame we sent it to Cooperstown for permanent inclusion in the Harwell collection along with the baseball books he authored. I was grateful that I had been able to open a door to a rewarding book-writing career for Ernie.

Since the moment the night before that I heard the tone of his voice on the telephone, I was concerned about this short-notice Tiger Stadium press conference,

As I pulled into the parking lot at the Stadium, I felt more and more uneasy. Had Ernie and Lulu actually seen this coming? If Ernie was stepping down I knew it was not by his own choice. The baseball club's management was inept, no disputing that, but they couldn't be so out of touch that they didn't realize that Ernie Harwell was the one shining, sustaining symbol of the Detroit Tigers. Could they?

Short of a meat locker at the South Pole, there must be few indoor places that feel more bitingly cold than the cavernous concrete and steel tunnels beneath Tiger Stadium in midwinter. All along the hallway, reporters and television announcers clustered in threes and fours, asking each other what was going on, their frozen breath floating in the air like thought balloons. Some acted as if they had inside knowledge and weren't about it share it, but it was clear to me that nobody—except Ernie and Tiger management—had a clue. The most frequent speculation I heard was that Ernie was going to say he was hanging it up for health reasons. That was ironic, coming as it did from a few sports writers thirty years younger than Ernie and in nowhere near as fit of condition.

Down the hall there was a splash of light from the room where the conference was being set up. Lighting men from several television stations adjusted their equipment. Piercing squeals of feedback echoed as sound crews tweaked their dials. There were perhaps fifty people packed into the small room, where at one end there was a table, two chairs and a microphone.

Over the next ten minutes, several newspaper columnists and television reporters came up to me to see what I knew. Just about every prominent sports journalist in Detroit was there. I noticed that Joe Falls wasn't. A week later he called to tell me he had been away on vacation, something he would grumble about ever after and irrationally blame Ernie for making a major announcement without him present.

George Cantor, *Detroit News* columnist, asked me what Ernie was going to announce. Several years earlier, when Cantor was a travel writer, I had published the first volume of his set of guidebooks on the Great Lakes shoreline. George, who had covered the 1968 World Series-winning Tigers earlier in his career, was probably the only reporter who believed me when I told him I really didn't know and only hoped it had nothing to do with health. Other reporters were aware I had worked with Ernie on his books and that we were friends. Being skeptical is a journalistic prerequisite and I could tell they didn't believe me when I pled ignorance.

The Tigers vice president for marketing, Jeff Odenwald, saw me and came over. Odenwald was one of the dozen or so key people on a committee I headed to raise funds for Oakland University, through the Gehringer-Kaline Meadow Brook Golf Classic. Odenwald seemed to be the senior management official in the room. Tigers President Bo Schembechler was nowhere around.

Odenwald looked grim. He looked around the room and shook his head.

"This is more than I bargained for," he said. "But it's time."

That left no doubt what was going to happen.

I could tell by the look on Odenwald's face that he assumed I already knew what the announcement would be. At that instant, I knew the reporters had guessed wrong. Ernie would be stepping down, all right, but it wasn't by his own choice.

A TV sports anchor took Jeff by the arm and said he wanted to get a one-on-one with him after the announcement. I turned away to say hello to a reporter who waved to me, then stopped when I heard an unmistakable voice behind me and felt a hand on my shoulder. It was Ernie, thanking me for coming out on a winter day to be with him. He said the proceedings would get underway in a few minutes. Then he moved to the table and sat alongside his attorney, Gary Spicer.

Dan Ewald, of the baseball club's staff, opened the proceedings with one brief comment that Ernie had a statement he wanted to make. Ewald quickly stepped aside.

Ernie thanked everyone for coming out, then got right to it. He said the words Tigers fans thought they never would hear, "The Tigers organization has made a decision to go in another direction."

The room had already grown quiet the moment Ernie stepped up. Now, except for the cameras, it was perfectly still.

"They have decided to install a new radio play-by-play man," Ernie said.

It was as though an electric current surged through the room. Reporters stopped taking down notes, shook their heads and looked around at the stunned reactions of their colleagues. Cameramen with gaping mouths zoomed in on Ernie. He was clearly the most composed person there.

He said he respected the right of management to make this change, though he did not agree with their reasons for it. Ernie expressed his appreciation for all that the organization had done for him over the years. He stressed that it was the right of a company's management to make personnel changes for whatever reason. Ernie explained that the Tigers had wanted him to say that this was his decision, but he could not do that because that was not true. He felt his abilities had not diminished, that he was capable of calling the play-by-play well into the future. But now he would stay on only through the 1991 season.

When Ernie finished his remarks, it was obvious that most of the journalists had checked their professional detachment at the door.

One after another, reporters lobbed soft pitches to Ernie, giving him every opportunity to criticize management, to say he felt betrayed and unappreciated. He would have none of it. He held to the high ground. He said he had been fortunate to have been behind the Tigers' microphone for thirty-one years.

Reporters saved their hardball questions for Odenwald. Their questions left no doubt that Tigers management had made a monumental blunder. Didn't they know that any fair-minded person who had heard Harwell over the years knew that he was as sharp as ever? What was this "new direction" that seemed the sole justification for forcing him out? Moreover, to millions of fans, Ernie Harwell was the franchise, the one constant star in a galaxy of mediocrity. His voice alone brought warmth and light in a run of cold, dark seasons. In other words, even for the Tigers front office— league-leaders in bungled business decisions and P.R. gaffes—this was a really stupid move.

Odenwald was determined to stay on message. He reiterated the party line: the Tigers and WJR had jointly concluded it was "time to go in another direction." It was clear from what wasn't said and from Odenwald's demeanor that the baseball club's management counted on the loyal Ernie to acquiesce and go quietly. They wanted him to say the decision was entirely his, but Ernie refused to do that. So, realizing Harwell's enormous popularity, Odenwald had convinced Schembechler to allow Ernie a press conference in which he could express himself in his own words. The alternative was for the club to announce the change and they knew that would undoubtedly trigger an explosion of outrage.

One had only to look around the room at the set jaws and furrowed brows to write the next day's headlines.

Mitch Albom's reaction in the next edition of the *Detroit Free Press* lauded Harwell for his classiness and lambasted the Tigers for their total lack of it:

> *He refused to whine. He refused to grovel. Because he is a gentleman, he refused to slam his bosses for the lousy thing they had done.*
>   *Allow me.*
>   *Oh, you bet I'll slam them. And behind me is a line from here to Alpena waiting to do the same. What the Tigers did Wednesday was one*

*of the most shameful acts I have ever witnessed from a sports franchise,
and, considering the company, that's sinking pretty low. They took a
man who is a national treasure and told him to start packing. They took
a man who literally taught baseball to hundreds of thousands of fans,
summer after summer, and they told him he's too old, his time is up.*

They fired Ernie Harwell? Is that allowed?...

*They have killed the voice of baseball. Even worse, they have robbed
a gentleman of his dignity. And in doing so, they have lost all of theirs.*

Shame on them.

The room emptied quickly, most of the reporters hurrying to
phones or back to their offices. While a TV reporter interviewed
Ernie, Odenwald came up to me and said, "We felt it was time to
make a change. We knew going in it would be a tough transition.
After all, he was a Hall of Fame announcer, so the public reaction is
bound to be negative."

Jeff had not been with Tigers very long, having spent most of
his baseball career in other major league cities, most recently in
Chicago. Clearly, he did not comprehend the enormity of what had
just happened. Underlying the reporters' question was their belief
that Tigers management had just liquidated its prime asset. Behind
every question was the conviction that the baseball club was capriciously discarding a Hall of Famer, the most beloved public figure in Michigan, a man revered throughout the baseball world. To
these journalists as well as to fans nationwide, Ernie Harwell was
the embodiment of the very best of the Grand Old Game and now
he had been cast aside for no discernible reason other than management wanted "to go in another direction."

If the reactions in that room were shared by readers and viewers of the coverage of the press conference, the new direction would
be downhill and the speed would be breakneck.

"Yeah," Odenwald said again, "there'll be some heat all right."

"You bet there will, Jeff," I said. "It's going to be an inferno and
a lot of Tiger front office asses are going to get scorched."

—ⲟⲟ—

YOU DIDN'T HAVE TO GO FAR NOR WAIT LONG TO SEE FANS' REACTIONS to the sacking of a legend. Producers of bumper stickers, T-shirts, and billboards were working overtime with messages like, "Say It Ain't So, Bo" and "We Want Ernie!" Fans threatened to boycott the team as well as to quit ordering pizza from owner Tom Monaghan's Domino's Pizza chain. At Joe Louis Arena, Red Wings fans interrupted a hockey game with chants for Ernie.

In a national column, baseball historian Curt Smith wrote, "Bo Schembechler and Tom Monaghan should be ashamed of themselves. You cannot overestimate the damage this has done to the Tigers. If you are a businessman, you don't fire your best asset."

Efforts at damage control by the Tigers' front office failed miserably. Bill Haase, senior vice president, said Ernie's skills had started to diminish, but was unable to cite a single mistake Harwell had made. To every party line comment, columnists and fans responded with guffaws.

Schembechler took the initial blasts of heat, saying he had made the final call on the move. For months he remained tight-lipped about what led him to that decision. The press and others continued to heap blame on him. He had earned some of it, but not all.

Much later, WJR boss Jim Long told me and others that he himself had made the decision to fire Ernie. "I want to set the record straight. It was me, not Bo, who wanted to make the change."

Wrong again.

Fans didn't know whom to believe so many of them decided to blame everybody. Many articles were written and TV commentaries aired. Countless conjectures and supposed inside stories were put forth. But none of the journalists got the whole story and none of them got it completely right.

It took a while before I put all the pieces together. I talked with Jeff Odenwald about his version of how the decision was reached. Long after the furor died down, I discussed that December 1990 day with Jim Long, general manager of WJR, the Tigers radio broadcast flagship station. A few years later, I invited Tigers President Bo Schembechler to be featured speaker at the Gehringer-Kaline fundraiser and at the event we talked about what had happened and why.

When the dots were connected, it was not a pretty story. Many people continued to lay the blame entirely on Schembechler. That was understandable because as president of the ball club he certainly had to approve any decision of this magnitude. Plausible, yes, but not entirely correct. Bo personally took much of responsibility for a decision he reluctantly endorsed only after he was told the initiation came from the management of WJR. Jim Long of WJR likewise took blame, but he went on to say it was a decision he concurred in only because he had been told that the Tigers initiated the process on the pretext that "Ernie was slipping a little bit." So, each party thought the pressure was coming from the other and each was merely cooperating in a move they really were not enthusiastic about.

It was like a Shakespearean tragedy in which two parties are manipulated by an outside force and are powerless to stop events. Forever after they remain silent because the greatest shame of all is that the world see that they have been duped.

Then how did it happen?

My opinion: If Schembechler and Long had talked directly and candidly at the outset instead of through meddlesome middlemen, they would have seen quickly that the top management of neither side—not the Tigers, not WJR—wanted this. Go-betweens misled both parties. Each thought the other was initiating the idea of making a change. Neither Schembechler nor Long wanted to roadblock a move the other partner considered necessary. Both felt like they were going along with what the other side wanted.

It was not the first really boneheaded idea that took on a life of its own. As is the way with ill-conceived blunders, from there things really got out of hand. Even more bizarrely, the startling recent success of another Detroit sports franchise was innocently a contributing factor.

The Pistons had captivated the town in 1989 and were on their way to a repeat in the 1990-91 season, knocking off the Boston Celtics, the Los Angeles Lakers, and every other NBA team to claim back-to-back championships. Saddled for years with the dreadful Lions, the often-woeful Wings, and the toothless Tigers, area sports fans were starving for a winner. Out at The Palace of Auburn Hills, Chuck Daly and his Pistons had produced a blue-collar team that came to play every day and took pride in their performance. Hungry for a winner, area sports fans passionately embraced a lunch bucket team that produced all-out effort, victories and championships. George Blaha, the voice of the Pistons, was as outstanding in calling the fast-paced professional basketball game as Ernie Harwell was in the more leisurely game of baseball.

The Pistons success at the gate gave the Tigers' marketing "brain trust" an idea. The baseball club had put only a mediocre team on the diamond. Attendance had stagnated. They searched for ways to energize fans to come out to the park. Inept promotions and gimmicks hadn't done the trick. A new paint job could cover up only so much. Gee, you think maybe a more hip, glib radio voice would stir fans up? The fatal flaw in that reasoning, of course, would have been obvious to the most casual fan. Baseball and basketball have only two things in common. One, both are played with a ball. Two—and this is what drove the decision— they are both businesses and sports businesses are, to a great extent, marketing driven. You've got a dull product? Tart it up with lipstick, bangles and neon, maybe people will take notice.

Anyone who thought about it for half a minute would realize that trying to stimulate interest in baseball by having a breezy pair of announcers was a dopey idea. But yes, baseball was certainly a business and even the bizarre and desperate notion that a new announcing team might somehow spur ticket sales seemed worth a try.

The 1991 season was the last for Harwell in the Tigers booth with long-time partner Paul Carey who announced his own retirement, something he said he had planned to do. For 1992, in his typical gracious fashion, Ernie Harwell did everything he could to ease the way for the newly anointed announcers, Seattle Mariners play-by-play man Rick Rizzs and Bob Rathbun, an East Coast sports announcer. Harwell had long been the most sought-after speaker for fund-raisers and events throughout Michigan. That winter and spring, he continued his legendary speaking schedule and gave interviews. He made appearances to help worthy charities, delivered inspirational talks to large organizations, and met with small church groups. At every opportunity, he praised the incoming broadcast team and asked Tiger fans to show them the same loyalty they had shown him. He was sure fans would like the new on-air radio team.

Ernie Harwell did not often make the wrong call—this was the rare exception.

Other people also tried to let the new pair know they would be welcomed warmly. Reporters and TV announcers gave them prominent, positive treatment. Regular fans pitched in. After the appointment of Rizzs was announced, I called him at his home in Seattle. I told him I was one of many Tiger fans who had heard good things about him and wanted to welcome him to Detroit. I said he would find Tiger fans enthusiastic and loyal to their ball club despite its difficulties. Rizzs asked if I knew Ernie Harwell; I said I did and I told him I would send him a copy of *Tuned to Baseball* on which I had worked with Ernie. I told Rizzs he would find Ernie very gracious and that he would do everything he could to help him get established with Detroit Tiger fans.

The new Tigers radio broadcast team went on the air with Detroit Tigers baseball for spring training in 1992. Ernie Harwell spent that season broadcasting the CBS game of the week and fourteen games for the California Angels. "I didn't bring the Angels a whole lot of luck," Ernie told me later. "They lost thirteen straight before finally winning a squeaker."

It didn't take long for the Tigers front office to see what a mess they had made. Having shot itself in the foot by moving out a highly popular figure, management began to realize early in the 1992 season that their choice of a new radio team was another self-inflicted wound. This one was mortal. The style of the new pairing struck a jarring note with fans. While Rizzs was capable enough calling the game, fans did not take to what they deemed a contrived and phony style of color commentary by Rathbun.

For decades Tiger fans had been accustomed to announcers they trusted to stay on top of the action and to pick the right spots to provide insights and anecdotes. They were used to the pace and the chemistry of Ernie and partner Paul Carey. Fans wanted announcers who gave them credit for knowledge of the game. They grew weary of the new broadcast team's ceaseless chatter, a stark difference from the days when Ernie and Paul would let the sounds of the ballpark feed through the microphone. The new announcing duo was quickly dubbed the "plastic pair" by fans who felt they were being talked down to by announcers who didn't have enough respect for the game they were calling or for their listeners.

In 1992, the first season for Rizzs-Rathbun, the Tigers slumped well below .500. For thousands of fans who had never heard a Tiger ballgame called by other than the Harwell-Carey duo, it was a difficult adjustment—many long-time Tigers followers opted not to make it. But there was one bright note. Ownership of the ball club passed from one pizza baron to another—Tom Monaghan to Mike Ilitch. With that change came a ray of hope for a more enlightened era at Michigan and Trumbull.

Fans did not have to wait long. In 1993 the Ilitch ownership delivered a much hoped-for stroke of public relations genius: Ernie Harwell was brought back to an enthusiastic reception by baseball fans everywhere. It was not exactly like the good old days, but he was at least now part of a three-man radio broadcast team with Rizzs and Rathbun.

The 1993 edition of the Tigers improved but fell out of contention in another disappointing season for everyone connected to the ball club. I was prepared for a bittersweet ending when, on

October 4, I met with Ernie in New York to spend the day with him on what was to be his final baseball broadcast.

The morning started with breakfast at the Grand Hyatt Hotel with *Detroit News* reporter Tom Gage who was covering Harwell's last game. After that interview, Ernie and I then left early for Yankee Stadium so he would have time before the game to make the rounds and say his good-byes. Good thing that he allowed plenty of time.

We went first to the private stadium club where officials and guests were having lunch. Everything stopped when Ernie walked in. One person after another embraced him.

Then we began our walk around the cavernous park. We couldn't walk more than a few steps without someone coming up to Ernie. Media people, Yankee officials, ushers, stadium personnel, broadcast crews, dignitaries of all kinds. He seemed to know them all by name.

Could it possibly be like this for Ernie in every American League park? I imagined it could. I knew I had a relationship with him that was special to me, but clearly I had a lot of company. So did all these people at Yankee Stadium as well as countless thousands more in baseball dugouts and front offices and umpiring crews and stadium ticker takers and ground crews and security workers and hotel clerks and custodians around the country.

Finally it was game time. We went up to the broadcast booth where Rizzs and Rathbun were readying their notes. Compared with Ernie's cozy, perfectly positioned booth in Tiger Stadium, the Yankee Stadium setup was cold, impersonal and distant from the field below. Ernie took his place at the front row of the visiting announcers booth between Rizzs and Rathbun. I took a seat a few rows up the sloped tier of seats behind the broadcasters' table. I sat next to *Detroit Free Press* reporter Michelle Kaufman who had been assigned to do a special article about Ernie's final game. Soon a couple more reporters and then a steady stream of V.I.P.s and Ernie's friends came through the booth.

Opera singer Robert Merrill came to ask Ernie to do a duet

with him on *Take Me Out to the Ballgame* during the seventh-inning stretch. Ernie laughed and said, "Bob, I think the fans would appreciate a solo by you much more." The Spanish language broadcast team invited Ernie to do a half-inning for their fans. Yankees radio announcer Tony Kubek invited Ernie to his booth to talk and do some play-by-play. Yankee general manager Gene "Stick" Michael came in to thank Ernie for his enormous contributions to the game.

When it was time for the seventh-inning inning stretch, Merrill did his solo and the public address announcer informed the crowd that this was the final game of a legendary baseball announcer. The crowd stood and applauded as Ernie waved.

In the eighth inning, I heard a knock at the booth door. The security man must have taken a break, I guessed, because there was the knocking again, insistent. So I went up the stairs and opened the door. I had not met the man but I recognized him at once. It was The Boss of the New York Yankees.

"Ernie," he said. One word. Ernie.

I went down the steps and told Ernie that someone wanted to see him.

Ernie went up the steps, smiling, and put out his hands. George Steinbrenner, his eyes misting up, hugged Ernie, said something softly in his ear. Whatever this powerful figure in baseball said I didn't hear, but the look on his face told how greatly he respected and admired Ernie Harwell. How much he—and baseball—would miss him.

—m—

THOSE CEREMONIES ON THE HISTORIC GROUNDS OF YANKEE STADIUM were fitting tributes to baseball's classic announcer. At the time we did not know it, but before long Ernie Harwell's legendary career would go into extra innings.

—W—

WHEN WINTER RELEASES ITS ICY GRIP AND CROCUSES SPROUT, it is that time of year for baseball fans: hope springs eternal. That was never more so than for the opening of the 1994 season for faithful followers of the Detroit Tigers. There behind the microphone, calling the play-by-play on PASS Television was Ernie Harwell.

Ernie told me this was one of the most memorable moments in a career that then spanned fifty years. He said that for memorability, it was right up there with an historic moment for him forty-three years earlier.

In 1951 Harwell had called the play-by-play of one of baseball's most famous moments. It is perhaps the single most talked-about moment in baseball history. He was calling the action live on NBC-TV of the final game of a three-game playoff between the Brooklyn Dodgers and the New York Giants. This game would break a first-place tie and send the winner into the World Series. Harwell's announcing sidekick, Russ Hodges, was calling the game on radio.

Ernie told me that at dinner the night before the game Hodges had pressured him to switch assignments. Hodges was eager to do the coast-to-coast television coverage, considered the glamorous assignment in those early TV days. Ernie laughed him off and told Hodges, "No, Russ, I'll stick with TV on this one. It's your turn on radio."

When Bobby Thomson hit his game-winning three-run home run in the bottom of the ninth inning, Harwell's call of the "Shot heard 'round the world" was lost to posterity because there was then no recording of televised games. Not so with the radio broadcast where Russ Hodges shouted five times, "The Giants win the pennant!" Hodges call was recorded, has been played countless times, and will always have a special place in baseball lore.

"My call on the television audio is drifting somewhere out there in the ether," Ernie said. "I don't even remember how I called the most dramatic homer ever hit. Even Miz Lulu doesn't remember what I said. That memory is long gone."

From 1994 through 1998, Harwell called Tigers games on PASS television. In 1999, he returned to a familiar spot behind the radio microphone to do the play-by-play. After his forced "non-renewal of contract" in 1991, Harwell had tacked on another ten years broadcasting Detroit Tigers baseball, a total of forty-two years in all covering one baseball team.

Several times in those years, Ernie invited me to the ballpark to spend the day with him. We would arrive at the park hours before game time so he could get me credentialed to go out onto the field to talk with players, coaches, umpires and his friends on the grounds crew. Then we would go the press box reception area where we could talk leisurely with the other teams' announcers and officials and whatever former Tiger players and greats from other teams happened by. Kirk Gibson, Lance Parrish, Milt Wilcox, Alan Trammell, Dave Bergman, Bill Freehan, Mickey Stanley, Darrell Evans, Willie Horton—they all beamed when they spotted Ernie. We'd go to the broadcast booth and get updated by Ernie's broadcast partner, Jim Price, and hear the latest joke from engineer Howard Stitzel, who also had an uncanny knack for predicting a late-inning Tiger home run.

One year Ernie invited me for a game with the Seattle Mariners. We were talking with Seattle manager Lou Piniella outside the Mariners clubhouse when I noticed a slightly built Mariners player coming down the corridor toward us. The player was accompanied by a man Piniella said was an interpreter. They came directly up to us.

"Excuse me, please," the interpreter said. "Ichiro Suzuki asks me to request for him the honor of meeting the great Ernie Harwell."

Here stood Japan's greatest ballplayer, a certainty for Cooperstown. He was a deceptively small man who played the game in the style and with the passion it was played in the days of Ty Cobb, slapping hits to the opposite field, beating out bunts, stealing bases, and fielding his position with grace. High on his agenda coming to Detroit was to meet the man who was the voice of baseball in America. Ichiro shook Ernie's hand, bowed and smiled like a raw rookie meeting his idol.

My next annual Comerica Park outing with Ernie was set for a September afternoon in 2001. The plan was that I would pick up Elmore "Dutch" Leonard, then swing by Ernie's house and the three of us would spend the day together at the park as we had a couple of times in the past. Dutch was a long-time Tigers fan, even though his nickname came from the much-traveled Emil "Dutch" Leonard who pitched in the majors for twenty years, but never for the Tigers. At a few minutes after 9 a.m., I called Dutch to confirm what time I would pick him up.

"Bill, have you got your TV on?"

"No, why?"

"Turn it on. Any channel."

I did. I watched in disbelief. It couldn't be real.

"Dutch, what's happening?"

"A large airplane just flew into one of the twin towers at the World Trade Center. And... oh my God, one just hit the other tower. What the hell is going on?"

I had no more idea than anyone else. Dutch and I stayed on the line, staring at the television coverage, saying nothing for what seemed a very long time.

I called Ernie. He was unaware of what was happening.

"Looks like I'll have to give you boys a rain check," he said.

THE NEXT YEAR WOULD BE ERNIE'S LAST AS A BASEBALL BROADCASTER. This time it would be entirely his choice and this time everyone understood it really would be final. For Tiger fans, it was hard to imagine springtime coming to Michigan without Ernie Harwell opening the broadcast of the first pre-season game from Lakeland with his annual recitation from the Song of Solomon, "For lo, the winter is past, the rain is over and gone..."

September 15, 2002 was Ernie Harwell Day at Comerica Park. In addition to the ceremonies, honors and salutes to Ernie on the field, the Tigers management arranged for a private suite for the Harwell family and friends. There Marcy and I sat with Lulu, their family and closest friends as the curtain came down with appropriate dignity and class on a remarkable career.

There was a good reason that people were so moved by the end of this era. As George Cantor had written years earlier of Ernie and his sidekick Paul Carey: "People welcomed them into their homes because they sensed that they were genuine, honest, more worthy of emulation than most of the heroes whose feats they described."

At that ceremony—and at every opportunity—Ernie delivered his familiar paean to baseball:

> Baseball is the President tossing out the first ball of the season. And a scrubby schoolboy playing catch with his dad on a Mississippi farm.
>
> A tall, thin old man waving a scorecard from the corner of the dugout—that's baseball. So is the big, fat guy with a bulbous nose running home one of his 714 home runs.
>
> There's a man in Mobile who remembers that Honus Wagner hit a triple in Pittsburgh forty-six years ago—that's baseball. And so is the scout reporting that a sixteen-year-old sandlot pitcher in Cheyenne is the coming Walter Johnson.
>
> Baseball is a spirited race of man against man, reflex against reflex. A game of inches. Every skill is measured. Every heroic, every failing is seen and cheered—or booed. And then becomes a statistic.
>
> In baseball, democracy shines its clearest. The only race that matters is the race to the bag. The creed is the rule book. And color, merely something to distinguish one team's uniform from another's.
>
> Baseball is a rookie (his experience no bigger than the lump in his throat) as he begins fulfillment of his dream. It's a veteran

too—a tired old man of thirty-five hoping those aching muscles can pull him through another sweltering August and September.

Nicknames are baseball. Names like Zeke and Pie and Kiki, and Home Run and Cracker and Dizzy and Dazzy.

Baseball is the clear, cool eyes of Rogers Hornsby, the flashing spikes of a Ty Cobb; and an over-aged pixie named Rabbit Maranville.

Baseball? Just a game—as simple as a ball and bat. And yet, as complex as the American spirit it symbolizes. A sport, business and sometimes almost even a religion.

Why, the fairy tale of Willie Mays making a brilliant World Series catch and then dashing off to play stickball in the streets with his teenage pals—that's baseball. So is the husky voice of a doomed Lou Gehrig saying: "I consider myself the luckiest man of the face of this Earth."

Baseball is cigar smoke, hot-roasted peanuts, *The Sporting News*, Ladies Day, Down in Front, *Take Me Out to the Ball Game*, and *The Star-Spangled Banner*.

Baseball is a tongue-tied kid from Georgia growing up to be an announcer and praising the Lord for showing him the way to Cooperstown. Still a game for America—this baseball.

Then Ernie added a final tribute: "Tigers fans, I had the greatest job in the world—a job I loved to do. But most of all, I appreciate you fans. I appreciate your loyalty, your support and your love that you've shown me, especially the love."

Ernie Harwell's last broadcast would come two weeks later, a road game with the Toronto Bluejays. I had been with Ernie for his previous swan song game, in 1993 at Yankee Stadium. Now I wanted Marcy and me to be near him for when the curtain came down September 29, 2002 in Toronto's Skydome. The evening before Ernie's last game, we called him in his Toronto hotel. He asked where we were.

"We're in a hotel in Toronto, not far from you," I said. "We

© Michelle Andonian

Perhaps no one saw more views in more major league ball parks than Ernie Harwell. When asked what was his favorite photograph of a baseball field, he said it was a shot taken in Tiger Stadium by Michelle Andonian, one of Michigan's most outstanding photographers. Harwell felt it conveyed in an instant the essence of a game for all ages.

know you'll be tied up every minute and don't expect to see you. Marcy and I just want you to know we'll be in the Skydome for the game tomorrow, not far away from you."

As we sat in the stands at the Skydome, we looked up to the visitor's broadcast booth to spot Ernie. I remembered how he often said that it was the game that was important, not the guy behind the microphone talking about it. Still, after forty-two years, Tigers fans felt such a close relationship with their announcer that even a graceful departure on Ernie's own terms was difficult.

Fortunately, two years earlier, Dave Dombrowski wisely chose Dan Dickerson to join Ernie and Jim Price to be third man in the radio booth in 2000. Dickerson was cast in the Harwell mode. He conveyed a style that most Detroit baseball fans had grown up with.

Dickerson knew that no one could ever really replace such a legend, and he had no intention of trying to take Tiger radio play-by-play "in a different direction." Instead he was learning at Ernie's elbow during the transitional years of 2000-2002 and he subscribed totally to the Harwell advice that as long as he gave his very best and was comfortable with himself, Tiger fans would give him their loyalty. The successor was already being well groomed by the master.

"One thing to put at the top of your list of things to remember," Ernie said. "There's no way you can give the score too often. Someone just tuning in, that's what they want to know. I used to keep a little two-minute hourglass right in front of me. After a while I didn't have to turn it over to remind myself it was time for the score."

This time, as Ernie bowed out for good, Tiger fans had reason to hope management would choose someone in the Harwell tradition. When it came time for Tigers management to name a successor to Harwell for the 2003 season, Tiger loyalists did not expect that Dave Dombrowski would repeat the blunders of his predecessors. Instead, Dombrowski listened to the fans. He generously took an hour from his busy schedule to talk baseball with me and to listen to my hopes that he would name Dickerson to succeed Ernie. Undoubtedly he heard the same from many Tigers fans because there was great relief and praise when he named Dan Dickerson to be Ernie Harwell's successor.

Marcy and I didn't get to hear Ernie's last broadcast live because we were in the Toronto stadium, out of reach of his radio signal. But we knew what Tiger fans back in Michigan and the Midwest would be hearing. Old geezers and young kids and fans of every size, age, gender and color would be tuned to Ernie Harwell and Tiger baseball. They would listen to the still strong voice of a trusted announcer with a hint of Georgia in his baritone describe a batter who "stood there like the house by the side of the road and watched that one go by." Or that a hitter was "out for excessive window-shopping."

But next year, they would never know if a foul ball was caught by a lady from Ypsilanti or a gentleman from Dexter. Because, like a towering drive headed for the second deck, Ernie Harwell knew that just like that disappearing baseball, the next spring when the voice of the turtle was heard in the land, he too would be l...o...n...g gone.

But never forgotten.

Acknowledgments

There is no way to thank adequately those who lived out the stories told of in these pages. For some of them, the final chapter of their life has already been written. But what they did, who they were, the impact they made—that lives on. Each left footprints and memories of an exciting, robust, productive life well worthy of being captured for posterity.

Others featured in this book remain very active on the current scene. They continue to make a difference in their communities and often far beyond Michigan's borders.

I talked with each of them about their life and their work. With some, we talked many times over the years about getting their story down. For several of them, we managed to do just that. For a few others we were at work on a manuscript when fate intervened. The world is the lesser for being bereft of an autobiography of J.P. McCarthy, Dutch Leonard, Ed Cole, George Pierrot, Jack Kevorkian and the others touched on here. In these pages we at least have glints of insight into what they were thinking as they imagined, created and innovated. Or as they challenged society, flouted convention, or simply did their chosen work so well they changed the world around them. The accounts in these pages of the stories of these men and women, past and present, will, I hope, serve as my thanks to them.

Many generous and able folks lent a hand over the eight years that this manuscript competed with other books and the busy-ness of life for an existence of its own. Brian Dickerson's broad and deep understanding of things Michigan emboldened me to prevail upon him for the foreword that capsulizes so well what this book tries to do.

I will always be grateful for the encouragement, support,

criticism, suggestions, or editorial and substantive contributions of Jack Lessenberry, Rebecca Powers, Laura Berman, Phil Cousineau, Larry Parrott, John Delzell, Stan Stein, Peggy Daitch, Gretchen Snow-Ruff, Joe Colucci, Peter Eckstein, David Katz, Dan Mulhern, Jerome Marks, A.J. "Tony" Procassini, and Dale Jurcisin. And, certainly the list goes on: Maxine Berman, Michael Betzold, David Cole, Berl Falbaum, Eli Zaret, Michael Ranville, A.J. O'Neil, Chris Cook, Char DeWolf, Christina Lovio-George, Lynn Henning, Paul Stawski, Suze Tooroian, Michelle Andonian, Tom Wilson, Joe Dumars, Lisa Murray Ilitch, Larry Deitch, Zaid Elia, Danialle Karmanos, Dennis Archer Jr., Jim Scalici, Ray Serafin, Bruce Felton, Suze Farbman, John Cortez, Marilyn Anne Smiatacz, and Mike Ryan.

Marcy Haney helped in ways beyond count, not least in providing a fresh, objective viewpoint and candid advice about what worked, what didn't.

Special thanks to Jacinta and Ken Calcut of Image Graphics & Design for yet another super effort on design and composition to add to the lengthening list of books on which we've worked together. Bill Wearne and the top-notch staff of Thomson-Shore printed and bound these volumes well more than four decades after my first book with them. Randy Kuckuck and his Seattle Book Company team are valued partners in promoting and marketing the book.

To others not called out here by name, I gratefully acknowledge my debt to you.

Everyone mentioned above did their best to see that I did justice to the facts as well as to the men and women written about in these pages—any failure to get it right rests with me alone.

Bill Haney
July 2014